FARM AND WORKSHOP
WELDING

WITHDRAWN

FARM AND WORKSHOP
WELDING

ANDREW PEARCE

Everything You Need to Know to Weld, Cut, and Shape Metal

Fox Chapel
PUBLISHING

Frontispiece illustration: *Hardfacing with MIG*
Photographs by Andrew Pearce unless otherwise credited
Book layout by Liz Whatling
North American technical editor Brian T. Yarrison CWE, CWI

Marked photographs on pages 18, 19, and 98 courtesy of ESAB North America.

First published in Great Britain by Old Pond Publishing Ltd., in 1992 as *Farm Welding* and then in 2007 as *Farm and Workshop Welding*. First published in North America in 2012 by Fox Chapel Publishing, 1970 Broad St., East Petersburg, PA 17520.

ISBN 978-1-56523-741-4

Library of Congress Cataloging-in-Publication Data

Pearce, Andrew, 1948-
Farm and workshop welding / by Andrew Pearce.
    p. cm.
Rev. ed. of Farm welding / Andrew Pearce. 2007.
Includes index.
ISBN 978-1-56523-741-4
1. Welding. 2. Farm equipment--Maintenance and repair. I. Pearce, Andrew, 1948- Farm welding II Title
TS227.P3935 2012
671.5'2--dc23
                    2012004024

To learn more about the other great books from Fox Chapel Publishing, or to find a retailer near you, call toll-free 800-457-9112 or visit us at *www.FoxChapelPublishing.com*.

Note to Authors: We are always looking for talented authors to write new books. Please send a brief letter describing your idea to Acquisition Editor, 1970 Broad Street, East Petersburg, PA 17520.

Printed in China

First printing

Contents

Introduction

Almost anyone can weld. All that's needed are basic hand/eye co-ordination, an idea of what's going on and a little guided practice. So far nobody has come up with a book that grabs the reader's hands and says 'do it like this!', and until someone does, pictures are worth a lot of words. So pictures are the heart of this book, forming a visual guide for beginners and a fault-finding service for anyone who wants to improve.

Although far from the last word on welding (plenty of other sources have much better claim to that), the advice here is practical and aimed at the farm welder. Use this book for reference, dipping in and out to find snippets of info, the occasional hint or maybe a way to get yourself out of a problem. It's not for sitting down and reading in one hit … unless you have a particularly high boredom threshold.

So what's coming? Ten sections. Arc welding mild steel is first, covering equipment, rod selection, plant set-up and work in various positions. And, as most people trip up on the same problems, there's a look at common faults and ways to fix them.

Section 2 deals with GMAW welding, a process increasingly favored in workshops. Then it's the turn of the farmer's most flexible friends, gas welding and cutting.

With the basics sorted we can move on to trickier stuff. First is TIG work – material-wise the most versatile of all techniques, yet also the one that takes most manual skill – then the increasingly affordable process of plasma cutting. Next come welding pipe and cast iron (both useful weapons in anyone's armory) followed by hardfacing, which is handy to extend the service life of soil-engaging parts. The 'joining' section of the book finishes with two simpler techniques, soldering and welding plastics. These are surprisingly useful for saving money and keeping equipment in work, with welding plastics little known outside the vehicle repair and specialist fabrication industries.

Rounding everything off are sections on common workshop skills – drill sharpening, the use of taps and dies and basic blacksmithing.

Of course, a book can take you only so far. A good practical course is the best way to improve; check out local colleges and training groups.

Farm and Workshop Welding is based on articles which first appeared in Power Farming and Farmers Weekly magazines. Weld examples were produced by the author, by the Welding Institute's ex-chief instructor Max Rughoobeer, by ESAB's Welding Process Superintendent Mick Andrews and by plastics specialist Dave Tucker. The Welding Institute provided sectioned weld pictures. Blacksmithing techniques were demonstrated by Sussex smith Frank Dean, who sadly passed away in 2004. The advice and help of all is much appreciated!

ANDREW PEARCE
January 2007

Don't take Risks

Here's the line taken on safety throughout this book. Today's duty of care requires that businesses and individuals both do, and are seen to do, the right thing regarding safe working practices.

I don't intend to witter on at every turn about staying safe. Adults must pack a sufficiently well-developed sense of responsibility to look after the well-being of others, of children and of livestock.

If a risk or hazard exists that might not be obvious, I'll try to point it out. Nevertheless, the responsibility to use good, sensible and legal working practices rests entirely with the reader.

When welding, cutting or grinding use protective equipment – eye shields, fireproof clothing, footwear and respiratory protection – as specified by Occupational Safety and Health (OSHA) guidelines, or the equivalent in your country. Advice on safe working is readily available: ask your welding equipment supplier, the equipment manufacturer or contact the OSHA directly. Be aware of the presence of children and livestock, and the possible risk to them from hot material, flying grit and ultra-violet radiation. Assess whether your skills are up to the fabrication or repair that you're about to undertake, and think through the safety implications if it fails in service.

The bottom line is this. **If you're not 100% sure about how to do something and/or not 100% confident about the outcome, don't do it.**

First things first

Just what is welding?

It's the process of joining materials using heat. In fusion welding, joint components are heated until they melt together or are positively fused by pressure. Blacksmiths use heat and hammer blows, but here we're more concerned with getting heat alone to do the work.

This heat will come from either an electric arc, a gas flame, or in the case of plastics, from a hot air gun. Filler is usually added to the joint from an electrode or separate rod. Non-fusion welding techniques like braze (or bronze) welding and soldering use heat too, but not enough to melt the metals that form the joint.

Metal Identification

This book deals mainly with welding mild steels. Yet, as not all bits found under the bench or prised from the scrapheap will be mild steel, it might be good to start with a run through of materials and their weldability. Although accurate identification of steel is a complex business, the main classes can be sorted out with a file, a grinder and some basic ground rules.

Wrought iron is no longer very common, but in the past has been used extensively for chains and hooks. It's very low in carbon, and malleable.

Mild steel is the common user-friendly stuff. It doesn't usually harden when heated and cooled, and is easy to bend and weld. Black mild steel is what you'd normally buy: as strip it comes with rounded edges and retains its coating of mill scale from hot-rolling.

Bright mild steel in its flat form has square edges, is shiny and is more accurately sized than mild steel. It's made by cleaning and cold-rolling black mild steel, leaving the metal stronger but less ductile.

Silver steel looks like bright steel but is much harder. It contains chromium but, oddly, no silver and is usually sold in short lengths.

Black and bright mild steels are easily filed and give off long, light yellow sparks under an angle grinder. Both are readily weldable. Silver steel is not.

Adding more carbon to steel makes it harder, and logically enough, produces **carbon steels** (Table 1). As the carbon level climbs, so does the end product's hardness, brittleness and difficulty of welding.

After being formed to shape, carbon steels are often heat-treated (tempered) to boost their resilience. Welding heat can destroy the tempering effect, leaving the joint zone hard and brittle until it's re-treated. Springs are a classic example.

The more carbon in steel, the harder it is to file – and files themselves have a very high carbon content.

So here's a quick test. If an unknown material can't be filed, it's probably not weldable.

The exception can be cast iron; see below. The grinding spark pattern also changes with carbon level. As it rises, the sparks get shorter, bush out closer to the grinding wheel and may be darker yellow in color. If in doubt, compare sparks from the unknown metal with those from a chunk of mild steel.

Alloy steels. Although heat treatment will improve the resilience of carbon steel, really spectacular gains come from adding small quantities of exotic elements to produce alloy steels. All sorts of metals – nickel, tungsten, manganese, molybdenum, cobalt, vanadium – can spice up the mix, and the end result is usually heat-treated to maximize its properties.

Alloy steels turn up wherever toughness, resilience and corrosion resistance is needed. Typical applications are springs, gears and transmission half-shafts. Stainless steel is a variant using chromium to beat corrosion, which for the metalworker is both good and bad news. Although stainless is slow to tarnish, that reluctance to oxidize means it can't be gas-cut. While many stainless steels are

Two jobs using a dissimilar steels electrode: a sash cramp's cast iron endplate welded to the central mild steel beam for more rigidity (left), and a slurry pump's cast steel shear plate resurfaced to near-original dimensions (right).

Table 1. **Materials and their weldability**

Material	Percentage carbon	Weldability	Typical use
Wrought iron	0.01- 0.03	Good	Hooks, chains
Dead mild steel	0.10- 0.125	Good	Wire, pressings
Mild steel	0.15- 0.3	Good	General engineering
Medium carbon steel	0.3 - 0.5	May be made brittle	Structural steels, forgings, high tensile tube, some tools
High carbon steel	0.5 - 0.7	Will be made hard and brittle	Chisels, springs, hammers, railway track
Very high carbon steel	0.9 - 1.5	Not weldable on the farm	Files, razor blades, axes
Grey cast iron	2.0 - 4.0	Needs right method	Casting not subject to shock. Housings, pulleys, manifolds, etc
White cast iron	2.0 - 4.0	Not weldable	Hard layer in wearing parts, camshafts
Malleable cast iron	2.0 - 4.0	Good with the right method	Cutter bar fingers, colter brackets, vise parts, clamps, etc

non-magnetic and weldable, if a magnet sticks to the bit you want to use don't try welding it – cracking is very likely.

Sorting an alloy from a carbon steel is largely a matter of application, though stainless stands out readily enough thanks to its satiny bright finish. Think about cost too: a cheap hand tool is more likely to get its hardness from a tempered carbon steel than an expensive alloy one.

Castings can be recognized by their complex shapes, generally rough surface finish and any raised surface lettering. But is the bit in your hand cast iron or cast steel? Application and a grinding test usually supply the answer.

Grey cast iron breaks very easily if bent or shocked to leave a grainy surface. Yet it stands compression loads very well, so turns up in machine beds, bearing housings, electric motor bodies, belt pulleys, engine blocks, manifolds

and such. Heat treating grey cast iron produces the much tougher **malleable cast iron**, which is close to mild steel in strength and ductility. Malleable cast is used where shock loads are high; in vise bodies, clamps and pto shaft yokes. **White cast iron** is very hard and brittle, properties which are used when a cast part must resist wear. So, for some soil-engaging parts, the molten iron may still be chilled in specific areas while in the mold, forming an outer layer of hard white cast.

Cast steels stand much harder service, being tougher than cast irons and capable of being heat treated to boost their resilience. Cast steels turn up where a durable complex shape is called for.

Telling the two apart is pretty simple. The quickest way is to grind them: cast irons give off unmistakable dull red/orange sparks which don't sparkle, and fade very close to the wheel, while cast steel sparkles clear yellow like mild steel – though the sparks are closer to the wheel and bushier.

Iron and Steels – Carbon Contents and Uses

Blast furnaces make pig iron, which is high in carbon and impurities. Refining produces the series of materials in the table above, with hardness and brittleness increasing as carbon content goes up.

Steels in the lower reaches of the carbon league are weldable on the farm. So are those in the middle, though they need greater care over rod selection, joint preparation and subsequent cooling. High carbon steels are unweldable by normal methods. Adding dashes of other elements to carbon steels gives a wide range of tougher alloy steels.

The hammer test is another decider. Tap cast steel and it rings, while cast iron just makes a dull clunk. Other differences? Cast iron fractures to leave a very characteristic coarse grainy grey surface – break a bit to see – and if you drill or file it, the swarf is powdery. Cast steel produces silvery filings.

When you start to file or machine some cast iron it may seem very tough. This is down to a hard skin of white cast iron, formed on the surface where molten iron contacted cold sand in the mold. Break through this skin and the grey cast underneath files, drills and machines very easily. Cast steels don't have this hard shell.

What should you weld?

Everything depends on the material and its application. Making 100% reliable joints in anything other than mild steel needs the right electrode and technique, and may call for specific procedures before and after welding to retain the metal's properties.

There is only one rule. *Don't weld any safety-related component unless you're completely sure about its makeup and any heat treatment it may have had.* If the part must be repaired rather than replaced, take it to a specialist.

What are the options when safety is not at stake, or 100% reliability is not essential? Here a 'dissimilar steels' electrode may be the answer. Although metallurgists rightly stress the importance of matching rod and material, these jack-of-all-trades rods often get round material mismatches. If you're faced with joining carbon or alloy steel:

• Choose a rod which matches the most awkward of the metals to be joined.

• Preheat. A gas flame heats moderate-sized parts. Move it around to keep heat input even.

• Use the minimum current needed for fusion, and keep run number low.

After welding, let the work cool very slowly. Lay it on warmed firebricks or on dry sand and cover it to keep off draughts. Don't put just-welded work on cold surfaces and never, ever, quench-cool. Even mild steel can harden a little if its carbon content is toward the upper limit, so where strength really matters, don't quench a mild steel repair in water.

Medium carbon steels can be stress-relieved after welding by heating the joint area to very dull red and then cooling slowly. (See Distortion Control, page 71.)

Welding cast iron is covered in Section 6. Preheating grey castings helps a great deal, and low welding heat input followed by slow post-weld cooling is always necessary. Even then, success with cast iron is never completely certain thanks to the material's tendency to crack as it cools. It's important to know which cast iron you're dealing with: malleable cast will cool to brittleness if arc welded, so lower-temperature bronze welding is better. Grey cast will turn to the brittle white form if cooled too quickly.

Section 1

Shielded Metal Arc Welding (SMAW)

Shielded Metal Arc Welding (SMAW, or 'stick') is still probably the most common welding technique on the farm. Best suited to materials thicker than ⅛" (3mm), it scores through equipment portability, a relative insensitivity to wind when working outside and a relatively high tolerance of contamination. These relativities will become clear later on. Stick welding is not the fastest technique, but done properly it produces strong joints in a range of thick materials.

What makes a good fusion weld? Pictures 1.1-1.3 show the basics. Achieving fusion and penetration are the key to sound work in any process: fall down on either and joint strength will be lacking. Four runs (or passes) went into picture 1.2. See how weld metal smoothly fuses into the original (or parent) plates, how it penetrates through them and how the individual runs blend together? The result is plenty of strength in the joint. Where the weld metal and parent plate fuse is a heat-affected zone (1.2, D). Here coarse metal crystals form as the area cools, leaving a relatively brittle band where a weld will often fail. Heat treatment and slow cooling after welding can encourage

these coarse grains to reform into finer, stronger ones.

This can be seen in 1.2, where the joint is actually made from four weld runs or passes. See how only the top one keeps its coarse grain structure? Grain in the one below has been refined (normalized) by the heat of the following weld pass. That's why making a joint with several smaller welds often produces a stronger result than just one big run.

Picture 1.3 shows what's happening during a good SMAW weld. An arc spans the gap between the electrode and the work, generating temperatures of about 9,032°F (5,000°C). Which is one reason why you can't SMAW-weld metals with a low melting point, like lead or zinc; they can't stand the heat. During the weld the rod coating burns, producing gas to shield the liquid weld pool from atmospheric

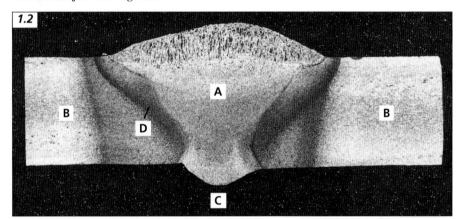

*1.2. Sectioning the joint in (1) shows how weld metal (A) has **fused** with the two parent plates (B) and **penetrated** through them (C). Good fusion and penetration underpin every strong, durable weld. Notice how metal is built up slightly at the top and bottom of the joint to give a convex profile — a smooth blend at the surface where weld and parent metals join avoids stress concentration, reducing the chance of failure. Where weld and parent plate fuse is a heat-affected zone (D). Here coarser metal crystals grow as the weld cools, leaving a relatively brittle area where a weld will often fail.*

1.1 A solid weld – what you're aiming for. Spot the even U-shaped ripples, full fusion at the edges and the lack of spatter? Good welds come from getting right the four variables (page 20).

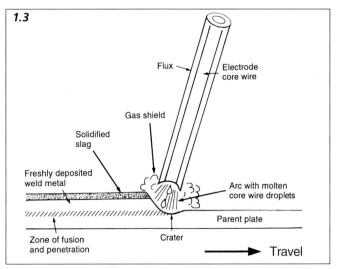

1.3. This is what was going on at the rod tip as weld 1.1 was made.

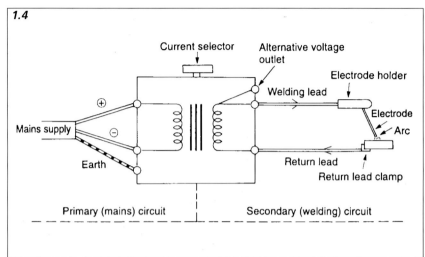

1.4

1.4. The conventional SMAW set is a transformer. High voltages and low currents go in (left); low voltage(s) and high currents come out (right). Welding current flows out of the transformer to the electrode holder, down the electrode, across the arc to produce welding heat, and back via the return lead (arrows). While it's tempting to call the return lead an 'earth', the term applies only to the incoming supply's green-yellow ground wire. Keeping this in good order should keep the user safe in case of a short-circuit (see 1.5).

1.5

1.5. Mains supply plugs get warm in use, and the repeated heating and cooling tends to loosen the terminal screws. What happens if the earth wire pulls out? At best, the plant stops working. At worst you're dead through an unearthed set. Use an earth-trip protected power supply and check for screw tightness every few weeks.

1.6

1.6. To be certain of UV eye protection, check welding filters for proof of compliance with ANSI standards (as of 2012 the latest version is Z87.1) before buying.

contamination and ionized particles to keep the arc running smoothly. At the same time, flux from the coating floats weld impurities to the surface, where it solidifies as a crust of slag. Molten droplets of core wire are pulled across the arc by magnetic force and surface tension, adding extra metal to the joint. Which is just as well or you couldn't weld uphill, downhill or overhead.

General points on equipment and procedures are in pictures 1.4-1.19. Do take a very good look through these, as keeping yourself (and others) in one piece is not unimportant. See also the next section which covers safe working.

SMAW welding heat usually comes from a simple transformer (1.4). AC output models are the cheapest to make as they run straight from an AC power source, like the mains or a generator, and are easily the most common – though DC (direct current) versions are rapidly gaining ground. What's the difference? AC welding current cycles 60 times every second in a continuous wave, from positive to negative and back again. In DC operation the current doesn't go through zero, with the result that a DC

arc tends to be more stable. But as DC sets need a rectifier to change AC into DC, they usually cost more.

In both cases single- or three-phase mains power is transformed down to about 50V. Most sets offer at least one higher output alternative, with 80V common. In simple sets, welding current is adjusted by a selector which alters the relationship of windings inside the transformer. Increasingly seen these days is the welding inverter – a clever box of tricks that uses electronics and a small transformer to deliver current. Lightweight and portable, SMAW inverters are usually DC sets which, given the necessary torch and gas adapters, can be used for TIG too.

Pain in various forms

Burns apart, **arc eye** is the nastiest short-term hazard in any electric welding process. It's caused by high-energy ultraviolet radiation from the arc burning the retina, and will happen if the arc is viewed either directly or indirectly. Short doses of radiation produce a very painful 'gritty' feeling in the eyes after exposure, with the effects lasting a few hours. Bigger doses can

end in blindness. Either way, it is not to be risked.

Bystanders can suffer arc eye too, from either reflected light or by looking sideways (as well as directly) at the arc. UV light will also burn exposed skin, so it's good practice to make a dedicated welding bay. Paint the walls a dark matte color to cut reflections and curtain it from outside view. When working outside the bay, warn helpers and children about arc eye danger and keep curious livestock away.

If you have a heart monitor or pacemaker fitted, don't weld. The strong magnetic fields around leads and equipment may cause the unit to malfunction.

A good welding filter is the only protection from UV light (1.6). 'EW' on a filter glass means it's designed for electric welding. The higher the code number is, the denser the filter on a scale of 8 to 14. Use EW 10 or 11 for most work; lower numbers only protect up to currents of 100A, while the highest numbers cut too much light from farm-size welding currents. Keep arc filters scratch-free with a plastic or glass screen, wiping it often during work (1.7) – you can't see much through fog. Be very sure there's no gaps around the mask's filter housing where arc light can creep in. And whatever you do, NEVER use gas welding goggles for arc work: they don't filter UV light at all.

Which mask to use? The lolly-on-a-stick sort that usually comes with a cheap welding set doesn't last and often isn't big enough for full protection. A flip-down welding helmet lets the operator use both hands when welding or tacking, though these don't suit everyone. If you're planning a lot of work, an automatic self-darkening welding mask is a fine investment: go for one with adjustable shade density and ideally, a manual mode. Various makes are on offer from welding suppliers. See picture 2.28, page 50.

Electric-shock 'tingles' can come from the rod while changing an electrode. These are unpleasant and reflect the relatively high voltages present. The problem is usually worse in damp weather, when current conduction to earth is better. Wearing gloves is the answer.

This takes us to **clothing** (1.8). Go for leather boots on the feet, as sneakers or rubber boots offer no resistance to white-hot metal spatter. Back these with cotton trousers minus spark-catching turn-ups, then cover everything with non-synthetic overalls or a stockman's jacket, done up at the collar to stop flying sparks and slag.

1.7. Fume can soon fog up a mask — keep it clean.

1.8. What the well-dressed welder is wearing this autumn.

1.9. Fixed or mobile extractors pull away fume, making them the ideal (if expensive) solution for a welding bench.

1.10

1.10. A ventilation pack supplying filtered air to the welding mask is an option if fume can't be removed at the source.

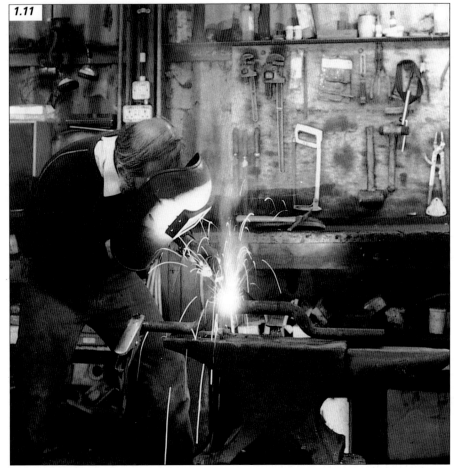

1.11

1.11. Whether you're using fume extraction or not, work out of the rising column of smoke.

Leather gauntlets protect against ultraviolet light and stop hot metal disappearing up your sleeves when welding vertically or overhead. Clear goggles look after the eyes during slag chipping or grinding, while a cap hides any bald patch from showering sparks.

Electrode fume is not the best of stuff to breathe, so OSHA legislation sensibly insists on operator protection. Ideally, remove fume at source with a fixed or mobile purpose-made extractor (1.9). Where fume concentrations are relatively low, a ventilated welding mask (1.10) supplies clean air from a filter pack and simultaneously streams a cooling breeze across the face. Otherwise, a disposable respirator designed to fit under a welding helmet may be enough. Be sure to check for minimum safety specs.

Where work is intermittent and good air movement can be achieved by opening doors or windows, fume will be moved on and extra protection may not be needed. If in doubt, the local OSHA office will advise. Whichever arrangement is used, work out of the rising fume column (1.11).

Grind away paint and plating to either side of the weld line to minimize fume problems and maximize the chance of a good job. Be sure to grind off yellow cadmium plating, for its fume can be a killer. The blue-white smoke from overheated zinc galvanizing is nasty stuff too, at best making you feel ill if breathed for long. Drinking milk may help if you are caught out, but check with your doctor. Watch for hidden plating on the inside of pipes. Sundry paints and degreasants give off poisonous vapors when they get hot, so there's plenty to think about. Take no chances with fume: ventilate, filter and/ or extract.

So that's a fine list of dos and don'ts. But most of it is common sense – try picture 1.15 (page 17) as a test.

Self tune-up

In welding (as in life) it's bad to be tense. Relaxation is central to good control. There are two schools of thought on how to achieve it – either support yourself so only your welding arm needs to move, or develop freestanding control in a legs-spread position (1.12). The first is easier, the second helps you work when there's nothing to rest on.

Occasional welders prefer the first option. Lean on the bench or machine. Take the welding lead's drag off your welding arm by pinching the cable between hip and bench or draping it round something handy – but before you do, make sure the cable's insulation is 100%. A flip-down visor leaves your second hand free to steady the welding arm. Whichever strategy you choose, don't grip the electrode holder tightly; it's a sure way to produce wobbles at the rod tip. Try relaxing that iron grip during work and see how control improves!

1.12. A wide stance helps electrode control.

Don't convert - invert

Traditional power supplies need big, heavy transformers to handle the substantial welding current flows. Inverters stand this notion on its head.

An inverter takes a 60Hz, 230/240V AC supply, rectifies it to DC, and then uses a transistor bank to produce square-wave AC at 8,000-40,000Hz. At these very high frequencies a small transformer can handle the conversion to low voltage/high current welding power, so the physical size and weight of the set can drop dramatically. After transforming, welding-level AC power is rectified back to DC for output, or modified and used as AC. Electronics carry out and control the processes on either side of the transformer, allowing waveforms to be tailored closely to different welding requirements and the set to react very rapidly to changes.

Which rod?

There's no shortage of electrodes to choose from, varying in core wire make-up, diameter and flux type.

Core wire must match (or be compatible with) the metals to be joined. If you're not sure on this, ask a welding supplier: your local agricultural dealer may or may not know the real answer.

Mild steel needs a mild steel electrode, fancier stuff needs fancier rods. Be aware that it's a waste of money using a tough, expensive alloy steel electrode to join mild steel in the hope of getting a stronger result. If the rod is matched to the material and your welds are still failing, then your technique is at fault.

Wire diameter. The narrower the rod, the smaller the arc and the smaller the heating footprint it makes on the metal. Thus thin section steels need skinny rods if arc heat isn't to burn straight through them. Fusing thick sections needs more heat – a bigger arc from a thicker rod.

While you're learning, practice with ³⁄₃₂" (2.5mm) diameter rods. Their short length and small weld pool are relatively easy to control. They'll do for one-pass welding up to ⅛" (3mm) and can be used for preliminary runs in heavier stuff. As joints get bigger, move up to rod sizes ⅛"

and ⁵⁄₃₂" (3.25mm and 4mm). These three diameters cover the majority of farm work.

Note: when talking about the capability of a rod or set, thickness refers to the weld's throat depth – not the thickness of plate that can be joined! (See 1.31).

Flux covering is decided by electrode type and application. Most general-purpose mild steel rods have a flux based on the mineral rutile, with other ingredients to improve arc stability, reduce moisture pick-up in storage and generally make them more sociable to use.

Cellulosic coverings enhance penetration, and are on rods designed for specific purposes like vertical down work and pipe welding.

Low-hydrogen coatings appear on rods intended for high-strength alloy steels, possibly also for service at low temperatures. Very sensitive to moisture content, rods with low-hydrogen coating must be baked before use.

Other electrodes add iron powder to their flux, which bulks the volume of weld metal laid down when compared with normal rods.

So which of this lot do you go for? In practice, rod selection for general farm use is pretty straightforward.

Buying a SMAW Set

Most farm jobs can be handled with 180-200A maximum welding current, which is achievable from a single-phase set. Such units allow mobility around the holding and can be powered by a generator, though some inverters may not like a generator's potentially spiky output – see below. Higher-output welding sets are more bulky, harder to move and usually need a three-phase supply, though work well within themselves at normal currents.

Oil-cooled, copper-wound units are designed for continuous use, running as long as needed on full blast. A typical AC model has 50V and 80V output lines, allowing most types of electrode to be used (a, left and right terminals). These open circuit voltages (OCVs) are explained on pages 19-20.

Some SMAW sets are fan cooled (b). When the windings get too hot a thermal trip shuts the set down, then after a while it comes back to life. The Murex example shown produces DC output which makes for a consistent and very controllable arc, but it's more expensive than the many AC alternatives.

The simplest air-cooled sets (c), have no fan, which means a shorter operating period before automatic shut-down and a longer wait before restarting. Consequently, they tend to be DIY items. Although these basic sets can produce acceptable work, the arc is generally not particularly consistent or smooth-running.

A set's **duty cycle** should be checked before buying. It's the length of time within a ten-minute period that the unit can operate at the current quoted. So a duty cycle of 60% at 150A means the set will run for six minutes in ten at 150A. At lower currents it'll run for longer. The higher the duty cycle, the longer work can go on without the set shutting itself off – important where a lot has to be done.

Three alternative sets, each giving different periods of operation. The oil-cooled, copper-wound set (a) is designed for continuous use: it'll run as long as needed on full blast. The AC output model shown has both 50V and 80V output lines (bottom, left and right) giving flexibility over electrode type usable; these are open circuit voltages or OCVs.
The fan-cooled set (b) has vents for forced-air passage. It'll run until its windings get hot, then a thermal trip operates. After a short cool-down period it comes back on stream. This Murex example produces DC output which makes for a smoother-running arc, but it's more expensive than the AC alternative.
Very common on farms is the simple air-cooled set (c), which is quite capable of producing acceptable work. There's no forced-air cooling, which means a shorter operating period before automatic shut-down and a longer wait before restarting.

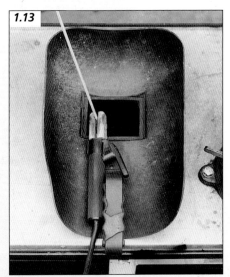

1.13. A good habit to cultivate. Laying the electrode holder in your mask or on something insulating (wood is good) means you know where it is (!) and lowers the chance of accidental arcing. Give gas cylinders a wide berth with the electrode, as accidental contact and the resulting arc could be terminal. It follows that chaining gas cylinders to a metal welding bench is not a bright idea.

Inverter sets (d) use electronics to do away with heavy transformer windings, so can be very light for their output current. This makes them ideal for site work or machinery field repair. But the circuits in some designs are easily fried by sustained over-voltage or sharp voltage spikes, both of which mobile generators can produce. As a rule of thumb, an inverter should only be paired with a generator whose capacity is at least 1.5 times the set's power requirement. For example, a set drawing 5kVA when delivering maximum welding current should only be used with a generator able to deliver at least 7.5kVA. If in doubt, check this with the set's supplier – better safe than sorry.

An inverter's electronic control lets the designer add sundry operator-friendly features. These can include:

• **Hot starting.** To help the arc to start and to boost initial fusion, the welding current is increased automatically for a short while as the arc is struck.

• **Anti-stick.** If the rod sticks to the work, the set senses the sudden sustained rise in current draw and cuts off after two or three seconds. Saves a lot of agitated hopping about.

• **Arc force.** The less experienced (or more knackered) the operator, the more arc length varies during a run. The power supply spots the rise and fall in current, and within limits compensates for them. Input current is thus steadier, minimising changes in fusion and penetration and boosting weld quality. This 'active' compensation goes beyond what's provided by a normal, non-electronic SMAW power supply – see pages 37-38.

1.14. Small things can turn out expensive. Clipping the return lead to a bearing housing (A) forces current through ball or roller contact patches (B) on its journey round the circuit. If these burn and/or develop flat spots, the bearing turns to junk. The thoughtful operator also works out how far gas or weld heat is likely to travel: bearing seals are easily cooked.

1.15. Early alternators could be damaged by welding's relatively high voltages, though modern versions have inbuilt protection. If in doubt, disconnect the battery and alternator before welding on a machine or anything attached to it. Where there are electronic control systems (modern tractors, combines, self-propelled foragers and so on) disconnect the battery and ideally take out any plug-in modules. Alternatively connect a spike catcher (inset) across the battery to damp out surges. Automotive factors stock them.

1.16. How many potential nasties can you spot here? Answer at the foot of page 19.

1.17. Rods from major makers carry full information on the packet and/or product listing. Be sure to check the materials the electrode can weld and the required OCV.
Photo courtesy of ESAB North America.

BUILD
Good Technique 1: Getting Started

Until you get the knack, striking and holding an arc can have you tearing out hair. But there's a simple way – scratch, tap and lift.

With the right current dialled in on the set, SCRATCH the rod tip near the joint to get it hot. Current flows easier from a warm tip. Be positive with the scratching; use a wide sweep that generates showers of sparks.

Bring the rod quickly into position over the weld area, and in one smooth movement TAP it down and LIFT it just a little (1.18 and 1.19). The arc will establish during the lift and you can weld on.

Beginners are often understandably tentative, touching (rather than tapping) the rod on the plate at too-shallow an angle. Come down firmly at a near-vertical angle to get the arc up and running. If the rod sticks to the work, break contact quickly by circling your hand and pulling up.

Sometimes the rod wants to stick even though you're doing all the right things. Check its tip (pictures 1.20 A, B and C). If this is healthy, look next at the return lead and clamp (1.21). The contact patch between clamp and work must be clean for easy current flow, so grind a bright area on the work and attach

Find a good specialist supplier and buy mild steel rods from a major maker like ESAB, Murex, Oerlikon or Eutectic. Minor brands can be good (and are usually produced by one of the big makers anyway), but starting with a big-name brand is always a sound idea. The rod packet should list all the info needed to work with the rod (1.17).

Stock up on sizes ³⁄₃₂, ⅛ and ⁵⁄₃₂" (2.5, 3.25 and 4.00mm), adding a pack of ¹⁄₁₆" (1.6mm) 'sparklers' if sheet steel work is intended and you don't have gas or MIG – though these very small rods can be unexpectedly expensive. If vertical down welding is to be done, make sure that the rod flux produces fast freezing slag – see page 31.

For welding anything other than mild steel, check your set's OCV capability before discussing rod choice with a welding supplier. Firms usually give advice freely, along with lists of electrodes and their applications. As mentioned earlier, 'dissimilar steels' rods cover most agricultural eventualities. For instance, some will weld steels of varying carbon content, low alloy and spring steels, ferritic and austentitic stainless steels to themselves...and to each other. And as dissimilar steels rods are relatively hard, most can be used as a 'buffer' layer between mild steel and a hard-facing layer, reducing the risk of dilution which can cause the expensive top coat to crack and flake away.

Buy specialist rods only when required, as they're expensive. Low hydrogen electrodes are a hassle. In non-critical work, dissimilar steels rods will probably cope anyway and are far less trouble to store and use. Cast iron is a law unto itself and needs dedicated rods and technique – see page 103. Building up worn parts or laying hard metal on new soil-engaging bits calls for specialized hard-facing consumables. Tell your rod supplier the application and he'll recommend something appropriate.

Watch Out

Time to say it again: the cardinal rule is 'Be cautious'. If in doubt over rod selection or technique, let a specialist do the work. It may be more expensive...but then DIY can sometimes end up very costly in unexpected and unpleasant ways.

Finally, a word on rod storage. Keeping rods in their original packet means you hang on to the information. Although good-quality mild steel rods can survive all year round in the workshop if they must, eventually the damp will get to the coating so it's best to keep them dry. An old fridge, modified so the bulb always burns, is good. And at least you'll know the answer to the old question: what happens to the light when you shut the fridge door?

1.18. Getting the arc started is easier if you warm the tip by scratching it on a plate. A generous sweep (arrow) produces the best effect.

1.21. Free current flow is choked by a return lead clamp that's past its sell-by date. Typical trouble spots are the thinned or frayed cable (A) and corrosion where cable and clamp come together (B). Even when the clamp is healthy, big trouble comes from poor contact between the clamp and the job (C). All affect arc striking and potentially the subsequent weld.

1.19. To start an arc cleanly and quickly, tap and lift the rod in one positive movement.

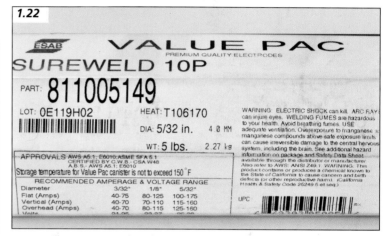

1.22. Still no arc? See that there's enough current coming from the set. Here the pack suggests 80-125A for flat-welding with a ⅛" (3.25mm) rod, so 100A should give easy starting.

Photo courtesy of ESAB North America.

1.20. If sticking is a problem, look at the rod tip first. Is it like (a) or (b)? Condition a comes from heavy-handedness with a sticking rod or damp flux. To rectify, scratch the rod hard until the bare core wire is melted away. Condition (b) comes from a carelessly broken arc at the end of a previous weld; the slag has sealed over the core wire. Scratch and/or tap it hard to break the seal. Condition (c) is good; bare core wire waits inside a cup of flux, ready to establish an arc.

your clamp there. If the return lead can't attach directly to the bits being welded and the current has to go via a welding bench, vise or anvil, make certain there's good contact between the work and whatever it's resting on. A small arc and burn spot often appears at this contact point, so think about that if the job's surface finish or appearance matters.

For maximum current flow, all cables must be in good order with no current-blocking 'bird's nest' of frayed connections (1.21 a & b). New return leads and clamps are cheap, so throw out anything that's substandard. Please don't use the return clamp as a striking-up area; a piece of scrap is a much better bet.

Answer to 1.16. Think about sparks from welding or cutting to see the hazards. A battery on charge gives off hydrogen and oxygen gases, which can explode on contact with hot spatter. The rubber gloves and cloth at the back are likely to catch fire; the electrode holder is not in the mask and its rod tip lies perilously close to the work, risking an accidental arc. Cans of petrol, penetrating fluid and engine oil sit alongside the welding area, while the upended chainsaw will leak fuel vapor or petrol. At floor level the open waste container, cleaning rag box and open grease bucket don't bode well; neither do the inflammable degreasant and oil-soaked sawdust.

If the arc still won't start, check that there's enough current dialled in on the set. But how much is enough? The rod pack gives a suggested range – aim toward the top of it for easy starting (1.22). The pack should also show the minimum open circuit voltage (OCV) needed. If the set can't deliver this voltage, striking will be much more difficult.

BUILD
Good Technique 2:
The Four Variables

Understanding the four variables is the key to a good job. And what are they? Rod angle, speed of travel, arc length and current.

Get each one right and a strong job results. Get one or more wrong and faults appear: lack of fusion, poor penetration, slag traps and undercut – all things that make welds weak.

Current

Current has the edge in importance. If you're short here, the terrible twins – penetration and fusion – will be lacking. Both are vital for a sound weld. Low current also makes it harder to establish an arc.

The first rule of current selection is not to believe the graduations on the welding set! You'll soon learn to see, hear and feel how the rod is running; to monitor what's happening at the rod tip and to alter current accordingly. Changes in welding position usually call for current adjustment too, which will be covered later.

Use the rod pack's information to set the current initially, choosing a setting toward the upper end of the recommended range. More current means more heat, and more heat generally means easier striking, better fusion and more penetration. If the rod packet information is missing, allow 40A per ¹⁄₃₂" (1mm) rod diameter. On all but the highest quality work, a little too much

1.23. Fusion and penetration change as welding current goes up from too low (A) to too high (C). Setting (B) was just right. Undercut and trapped slag are results of too much heat (C, 1 and 2).

current is better than not enough.

To get a feel for current setting, experiment on some scrap. Make short welds, starting from below the packet-recommended minimum and ending above the maximum. See how striking, maintaining the arc and fusion all improve as current goes up?

This is summed up in picture 1.23. If there's not enough current (heat), weld metal just heaps on top of the underlying plate (A), leaving poor fusion and penetration. Where current is too high (C) the weld bead is wide and flat, the final crater is deep, excessive heat melts a wide track and beads of spatter go everywhere. The bead surface is also

often Vee-shaped, thanks to the operator speeding up to keep fusion or burn-though under control. Where current is too high (C, 1) undercut may turn up where the bead and plate meet. This happens because as the arc passes, it melts a crater too wide for the rod to fill; and if the arc is simultaneously too long, some of the rod's precious filler metal will also be lost as spatter. Watch out for substantial undercut, as it provides a notch from which breakage begins. Working too hot also traps slag at the weld edge and in the coarse weld bead's surface, making it hard to chip off.

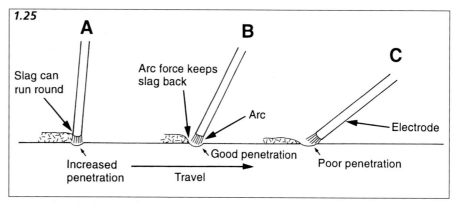

1.25 Rod angle during work has a big effect on fusion, penetration and slag trap production. A and C lead to problems, whereas, like Goldilocks's porridge, B is just right.

1.24. Variable number 2 is arc length. When it's too long, filler metal will skip out as spatter (A). When it's too short, slag can run round the tip to form traps (C). When it's spot-on (B) your eyes and ears will tell you.

Where current is about right (1.23 B) weld metal fuses and penetrates into the parent plate – exactly what's needed for a good weld. The bead is consistent in width and the surface ripples are U-shaped; there's no undercut and little spatter.

For most jobs a little too much current is better than not enough. But don't go overboard or you'll waste rod, create undercut, risk burn-through and porosity, cover the job in spatter and increase distortion by feeding in excess heat. And as an encore the rod's flux coating will break down, and the heat affected zone will be wider than it need be.

Arc length

Variable 2 is arc length. A rough guide keeps the arc just shorter than the core wire diameter, i.e. about 0.08" (2mm) for a ³⁄₃₂" (2.5mm) rod. But this is not a fixed relationship.

Keep your ears and eyes open during work. A good arc has a clear, bright area under the rod tip, and is bordered by a semi-circular curtain of molten slag behind (1.24 B). You'll know when arc length is right, for its noise hardens from a soft, fluttery sound (arc too long) to a crisp crackle as the right length is found. A good-length arc sounds much like the sizzle of breakfast frying in the pan. When the arc's too short the rod dips in the molten slag and everything goes quiet, arc light dims and slag wants to run round in front of the tip. This is a perfect scenario for producing slag traps (page 30).

As your confidence grows, arc length can be used to control slag. If you see a violent swirl starting to develop in the slag just behind the rod tip, a trap is imminent: lengthening the arc a little can save the day. But be careful, for an arc that's too long can itself produce a trap: filler metal lost as spatter means the weld pool isn't properly filled, so slag gets in instead. This is a common problem in fillet joints, where filler metal can take a shorter path to the vertical and horizontal parent plates. Experimenting with arc length (while keeping the other three variables right) is the best way to get a handle on what's happening.

Rod angle

Variable number 3 is rod angle, which affects both fusion and penetration (1.25 A-C). Too shallow an angle (C) lets the arc push weld metal along the work's surface, so there's not much chance of good fusion or penetration. But too steep an angle risks molten slag running round the rod tip to interfere with the arc, causing slag traps (A). The right rod angle (B) steers between these possibilities.

For work on the flat, an angle of about 70° is right. Some electrode holders come with angled grooves in the jaws. If you put the rod in these and keep the holder's handle parallel with the work, then the electrode angle won't be far out for downhand jobs – flat on a bench.

It's usually best to keep the electrode centered laterally over the joint. Angling the rod toward one plate or the other puts more heat into that plate, which is generally bad for balanced fusion. But deliberately aiming the rod to control heat input can be useful, as when welding thin sections to thick ones - see page 26.

Some rods tolerate operation outside normal limits better than others. So experiment with the rods you use, looking and listening as the angle is changed.

1.26

C

A

B

1.26. Going too fast (A) gives no time for fusion or penetration. Travelling too slowly (B) lays down too much metal and the extra heat adds to distortion. Travelling at the right speed leaves a bead that's about twice as wide as the rod's core wire (C).

Speed of travel

The final variable is speed of travel. How fast is fast enough? 1.26 shows the differences. Hacking along the joint at a rate of knots (A) leaves no time for weld metal to be deposited and so the bead is stringy and very weak. Travelling too slowly (B) takes longer, wastes rod, increases distortion by increasing heat input and leaves a large humped deposit. But moving along at the right speed (C) leaves a neat, even bead roughly twice as wide as the electrode core wire, i.e. a ⁵⁄₃₂-0.2" (4-5mm) deposit from a ³⁄₃₂" (2.5mm) rod.

Varying your welding speed during a run is bad. Look closely at 1.26 A and you'll see that even in this acceptable weld, the bead necks down in places along its length. This shows that the speed of travel was not constant. In the fast sections the weld thins out, varying joint strength; surface ripples pulled into Vee-shapes are a giveaway. When welding try to imaging you're a machine, geared always to travel at a set speed down the joint.

Generally, first-time welders use too little current, work too fast with

too long an arc and tend to let rod angle drop during a run until it's too shallow.

MAKING THE WELD 1

Keep it clean

Now to join some metal. Step one is *clean before you weld*. Never mind the italics: that should be written in letters of fire. Agriculture produces a fine range of contaminants, ranging from rust and paint to oil and dung. None of these need actually kill the arc to compromise ultimate joint strength: the inclusions or weakening pinholes they leave behind are enough. So sort out contamination before you begin... no matter what the electrode salesman says.

And if preparation isn't thorough? Rust on the weld area will turn into brittle, weak iron oxide particles in the joint. Grind off (or flame clean/wire brush away) all rust, over and around the weld area.

Paint, oil and animal outfall all vaporize under the arc, leaving blowholes in the weld varying in size from the invisible to the substantial. Normally a run round with the angle grinder is enough

to clear crud. But on jobs where oil or other stuff has really penetrated (like an old oil-containing casting) it's often necessary to make a first run to draw out contamination, then grind that away and weld again.

Whatever the contamination, clean an area about 2" (50mm) wide on either side of the joint. That seems a lot, but it's the best way to minimize fuming from paint or plating. Grind galvanized steel until it sparks bright, showing that all the plating has gone. Joints should get a lick of paint afterwards, so all this generous preparation won't be wasted.

We've already mentioned metal platings, but they're serious enough to re-run the subject. Look out for the dull yellow finish of cadmium plating and grind all traces of it away, as heavy metal fumes are really nasty. The zinc in galvanizing makes a mess of a weld, and the dense blue-white smoke produced does you no good at all. Where there's a risk of fuming, invoke nature's free ventilation by working in moving air. Indoors, use a fume extractor or the appropriate respirator.

MAKING THE WELD 2

Get set up

Now look to preparing the joint metal itself. Overstating the importance of this stage is hard, but still it's often skimped on. Think on the following for a moment:

Any joint must be welded to full depth to duplicate the original material's strength.

So if you're talking butt joints (i.e. two plates laid side by side to be joined by their edges), welding to full depth almost always involves some sort of edge preparation. That is, cutting or grinding away the edges to let the weld get to the bottom edge of both plates.

Material thickness is the trigger. Butts in mild steel up to ⅛" (3mm) thick can be welded without preparation, but thicker stuff (which means most farm jobs, whether fabrications from scratch or simple repairs) needs edge preparation.

Just leaving a gap between otherwise-unprepared edges does help penetration, but not much. Despite all the noise and fury, an arc does not dig very deep. Check this for yourself by welding a series of butt joints in ¼" (6mm) plate, leaving an increasingly large gap between the plates each time. Weld one side of the joint only, and then break it open in the vise and look for penetration. You'll probably conclude that the arc needs help to penetrate. The best way forward is to bevel the plate edges with a grinder or gas cutter.

Lower Limit

As material drops to ⅛" (3mm) or below, blowing holes in the work gets increasingly likely. For most mortals, ⅛" (3mm) sheet is SMAW's lower working limit.

1.27 lays out the general idea. A total angle of 60° (that is, 30° on each plate) is the best compromise between accessibility and gap size, but in practice grind a little more to allow yourself plenty of elbow room. A wider Vee makes the first (or 'root') run easier: if the angle is too tight it can be a slag trap generator. Dodgy technique (insufficient current, travelling too fast, wrong rod angle or too short or too long an arc) is magnified when welding in a Vee.

MAKING THE WELD 3

Different joint types

Here's a run-through of things to think about when SMAW-welding various joints.

First, the basic butt weld of prepared-edge plate (1.27, 1.28 and 1.29). Try really hard to get good fusion and penetration in the first (or root) run (1.27). If the Vee is tighter than 60°, open it out before you start welding. If this can't be done, dial in a little more current than usual to minimize the chance of slag traps. Where the job allows, boost penetration by leaving a gap between the plates' bottom edges, though don't go wider than electrode thickness.

Whack in the first run with a small electrode; ³⁄₃₂" (2.5mm) is usually fine. Using a thick rod at this stage can be counter-productive as it can't reach into a Vee bottom as well as a slimmer one. Having said that, a thicker rod's extra metal and current can help stop slag traps. Try it and see, but watch for lack of penetration.

With a good root run in place, fill the Vee using the basic overlap technique in 1.30. Place each weld so it either

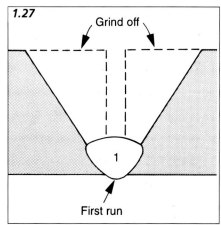

1.27. To get to the bottom of a butt joint in material over ⅛" (3mm) thick, first get rid of the edges with a grinder or gas cutter (dotted lines). Then fire in the first run with good penetration (1).

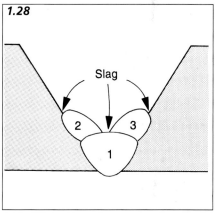

1.28. Fill the Vee using overlapping runs – 1.30 shows the technique.

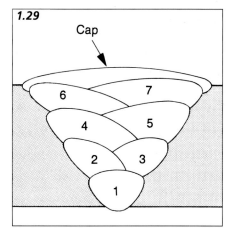

1.29. Finish a wide Vee with a weaved capping run – 1.37 shows ways to weave.

1.30. Overlap technique. Start with a single run, then build a pad by adding more runs so each half-overlaps its predecessor. Angle the rod at 45° and fire the arc at the spot where weld and plate meet. This basic method is brilliant for building up worn parts or re-surfacing.

1.31. In T-joints or fillets, weld throat depth (1) needs to at least equal the thinnest plate. Equal leg lengths (2) give balanced strength, and come from a 45° rod angle.

1.32. Often you'll need more than one run to achieve enough throat depth. Sequence these as shown, using a shallower rod angle for the final pass (3) to keep it pushed well up.

overlaps or stays well clear of its neighbour, as the last thing you want is a narrow, slag-trapping gap between adjacent runs (1.28). Chip off all slag and exercise the wire brush after each pass — good 'weld hygiene' leaves no bits of slag behind to form weakening inclusions in the next run.

Joint width grows as you fill it, allowing the use of thicker rods. Switch to a bigger diameter rather than going more slowly with a small rod, or slag traps will result where there's not enough filler metal. If appropriate, finish off the joint with a weaved capping run (page 27). This will blend the weld's edges into the original plates and 'normalize' the preceding passes (page 11). If you didn't manage to achieve full penetration from the first run, shame on you — but you won't be the first or the last. In such cases, turn the work over, grind the joint line into a U-shape then seal it with a single pass.

To form **a strong T-joint or fillet**, the weld's throat depth needs to be equal to the thinnest plate (1.31). So, when joining 0.2 to ⅜" (5 to 10mm) plate, the throat should be at least 0.2" (5mm) deep. Equal leg lengths give balanced strength: achieve them by angling the rod so it splits the joint in two, i.e. forms a 45° angle. See also page 109.

Good fillet root fusion comes from a mix of careful plate alignment and steady work with a small diameter rod. If plates aren't parallel, one inevitably takes more heat than the other, the gap between them varies and it's easy to make a slag trap at the start. The best way around this is to let weld metal fully fill the joint before moving off, keeping speed down if necessary to be sure it does. Once fusion spreads across the joint, move off. Keep travel speed steady and arc length relatively short to make certain the joint is filled and free from slag traps.

Thick plates will need more than one pass to get the required throat depth.

1.33. *The theory of 1.32 turned into metal. Starting off slowly let the three overlapping runs fuse full-width at the beginning of the joint (far right). See how they then blend into each other and the parent plates?*

In a three-run joint, sequence the passes as shown in 1.32: see how number 2 gives number 3 a 'shelf' to sit on? Keep fresh weld metal well up on the vertical plate during pass 3 by using a shallower rod angle. And where necessary, go up one rod diameter for runs 2 and 3 to fill the space.

Run Number Alert

Don't go overboard when making a multi-pass fillet. Use the minimum number of runs needed to build the right throat depth. Why? Over-heavy weld build-up often makes a joint weaker rather than stronger, as the extra heat can affect material properties. Stress is also concentrated at the edges of the weld.

If slag traps are a problem in fillet welds, check the four variables. Look at current first, as low setting is a prime cause of traps. Welding with limited amps (=limited heat) is always dodgy,

as the bottom plate in a T-joint acts like a big sink, draining heat from the weld. On fillets, use 10-15% more current than for the equivalent butt joint, but don't overdo it: check the vertical plate for undercut at the bead edge, as significant notching produces a weak area.

Where current setting looks good but pesky traps are still appearing, think about your speed of travel. Going too fast doesn't give time for the joint to fill, inviting slag traps and undercut. Arc length also matters. If it's too long, metal takes the short cut and goes to the joint walls rather than the root. If it's too short, slag can run round the rod tip and interfere with the arc.

After this, **lap joints** are relatively easy (1.34). Tack plates together on the non-welded side where possible, and truck along at a speed such that the upper plate's top edge just melts into the weld pool (arrow). If the joint looks 'hollow' or won't fill properly, try the next-fatter rod. As with T-joints, slag traps come

from too little current, travelling too fast or the wrong arc length.

Open corner joints — ones where plates meet to make a 'roof' and are welded on the outside — are just as straightforward as laps. Take great care over set-up; this is half the battle. Tack the joint halves so their edges are parallel, leaving a small penetration gap in material over ⅛" (3mm) thick. Travel along the joint at a speed that sees both outer plate edges melting into the weld pool. Use multi-runs to fill the Vee in thick material, sequencing passes as in 1.29.

Turning over an open corner joint leaves a trough. For practice weld this just as you would fill a prepared butt, using overlapping runs to build thickness as required. Deep Vees attract slag traps like a dead rabbit attracts flies, so use a little more current than normal to cut the risk.

1.34

1.34. Start a lap joint by tacking it so the plates are in good contact. Any gap risks the top plate's exposed edge burning back. Travel at a speed that just melts-in the upper plate edge (arrow).

Horizontal–vertical joints are those that run horizontally between vertical plates, as 1.35 shows. Welds in this position can end up with globs of weld metal to rival Babylon's Hanging Gardens. Too much heat – from high current or travelling too slowly – is the usual cause, made worse where a long arc lets weld metal drop out of the joint. Dial in only enough current to give penetration and a smooth-running arc. Angle the rod to keep the bead pushed up into the joint, keep a constant and shortish arc. Don't travel too slowly.

1.35

5°–10°

1.35. To keep a horizontal–vertical joint tidy, use a short arc, minimum current and don't hang about. Angle the rod as shown to keep the bead pushed up into the joint.

Last but never least, welding **thin sheet to thick plate** is not as hard as it might seem if the two are kept in close contact. Pic 1.36 shows ¹⁄₁₆" (1.6mm) sheet lap-jointed to ¼" (6mm) plate. The corners were tacked to hold the plates tight together then each side was welded.

1.36. Welding thin sheet to thick plate is easy as long as the pair stay in close contact. Fire the arc mainly into the bottom plate, letting arc heat just melt the sheet metal into the bead.

1.36

The arc was aimed so that most of its heat went into the thick plate, leaving just enough warmth to fuse in the thin sheet's edge (arrow). Watch the sheet during operations; if it starts to buckle, it'll burn back quickly and you'll end up in a pickle. Stop, dress the sheet back down and continue.

MAKING THE WELD 5

Stops, starts and other business

Here are several techniques which will make the finished job stronger and neater...or get you out of trouble. The principles apply to GMAW work too.

Weaving is a useful trick used to spread heat and metal. You'll need to weave in all sorts of places: making a 'capping' run on a substantial multi-pass joint; when putting down a layer of hard-facing metal; when welding uphill or downhill and when bridging gaps between plates. Whatever the job, the important thing is to follow a definite pattern and work very deliberately. Pics 1.37 and 1.38 show some patterns.

Whatever the purpose, weaving is best kept simple. Firstly, because that's easier (never a bad thing) and secondly, to lessen the chance of trapping slag in the weld. Either a crescent weave or Z-shaped zig-zag serves most purposes other than vertical work.

How wide should you go? A rough rule of thumb allows up to three times electrode diameter, otherwise the weld's edges may cool too much and you'll get slag traps and/or 'cold shuts'. In a cold shut, fresh metal lies over (rather than fuses with) the stuff you've just laid down, forming a weak point. The motto is 'Take care of the edges and the middle looks after itself', which means making a deliberate pause at each side to let metal flow, fuse and build before moving smartly across the weld face.

1.37. Either the crescent weave (as here) or a zigzag pattern is fine for capping runs. Be very sure to pause significantly at each edge (white dots), letting weld metal fill and fuse. Slag traps are likely if you rush or wave the rod tip about recklessly.

1.38. Where a simple weave would be overstretched, filling between two beads is the answer.

When you're weaving make very deliberate rod tip movements. Waving the rod about pushes heat and metal around, inviting slag traps. Keep those at bay by weaving tight into the face of the weld, i.e. not travelling too far forward for each traverse. On jobs where a conventional weave would be overstretched, infill weaving between two beads can help (1.38).

First cousin to weaving is **building up a thickness** of weld metal. You'll do it while filling a deep prepared-edge joint, when remaking worn bits or when hardfacing soil-engaging parts. Pic 1.30 (page 24) has the basics. First lay down a single bead, using a chalked guide line if it helps. Then add successive runs so

that each overlaps the one before. Use a 45° rod angle, and fire the arc right into the place where the last run meets the plate. Adjust speed of travel so the new metal half-covers the old. Chip off, wire brush and inspect after each run. Repeat until the thickness needed is achieved, watching out for distortion through heat build-up.

A small snag with SMAW is that you have to keep changing rods. How you manage **stops, starts and restarts** has a big impact on weld strength and appearance.

Let's start with **stops**. As a rod burns back keep an eye on the flux coating, particularly when using high currents. If flux starts to fly away from the

1.39. *To set things up for a clean re-start, break the arc cleanly as the old rod burns back to 2" (50mm) length. This will leave a hollow pad (arrow).*

tip in droplets, stop the weld right there; protection from the coating is disappearing. Plan on finishing all runs anyway when the rod burns to a 2" (50mm) stub. It's never worth trying to get to the end of a joint before the rod expires: somehow you never make it and end up leaving a poor stretch of weld.

As the old rod expires, set things up for a good restart by breaking the arc cleanly. Whisk the tip away to one side, leaving a shallow crater (1.39). Wire-brush the area clean.

To **restart** with a fresh rod, warm the tip by scratching it or make a short run on some scrap – not on the return clamp. Quickly position the tip about $^{15}/_{32}$" (12mm) forward of the waiting crater (point X in 1.40), tap it to start the arc and immediately lift the rod. Lifting does two things: gives enough light to see where you're going and minimizes the metal laid down. Keeping the arc relatively long, smartly move the rod tip back to the crater's forward edge (1.40, dotted line). Close the arc down to welding length, then make a very deliberate 'wall of death' passage around the crater to fuse old and new metal (1.40, solid line). Don't rush! Move slowly forward out of the crater, picking

1.40. *To restart, tap the warmed rod tip at point X. Keeping a long arc, move it to the crater's front edge (dotted line), then close the arc to welding length and make a very deliberate pass round the crater. As you come back to the entry point, move on down the joint line.*

1.41. *Waving the rod tip around or rushing during a restart produces a mess (arrow)…*

1.42. *…But if you're slow and deliberate, the restart will be hard to see and will not snag a fingernail run over the area (arrow).*

up normal welding speed as you leave. Done well, you won't be able to feel the restart with a fingertip and will have trouble seeing it (1.42).

Starts at the beginning of a joint can be pesky. Common is a 'snail trail' of weld and a slag trap before a decent weld establishes (1.43). Initially the rod and plates are relatively cold, so metal is slow

to fuse. Moving off too briskly (or with a long arc) produces the fault. The trick is to start the arc just off, rather than directly on, the joint edge. Pause for a while before moving off, watching to see that molten metal fuses with both plates. A small sideways weave usually helps: try it and see.

1.43. Recognize this? A slag trap at the beginning of a weld (arrow) springs from two things; cold plates and an arc that's too long. Pause before moving off or use a run-on plate.

1.44. This nasty finish comes from a combination of bad technique and too much current. The hollow crater (arrow) will be a launch pad for cracks.

Travel 1   Travel 2

1.45. Two in one here. While a flat finish is needed for clean restarts (2), the crater must be filled when a joint is closed (1).

Where an ultra-solid start is important, use a run-on plate. That is, establish the arc on a piece of scrap alongside the joint then move into the work.

End-of-joint **finishes** matter too. An untidy, hollow finale is a launch pad for cracks (1.44). While a flat stop pad paves the way for a clean restart (1.45, 2), the crater at the end of a joint must be filled to maintain strength (1.45, 1). Producing a good finish takes slow, deliberate action. Rush and you'll spoil it. Weld up to the end of the joint as normal. Then move back a little from the edge and pause, keeping arc length constant to pile metal into the crater. Circle the rod tip slightly, but not too wide or weld metal spreads too much. Finish the job by travelling forward a touch and breaking the arc with a quick sideways flick of the rod. Concentrate on keeping arc length steady throughout. Don't pull the rod upwards to break the arc, as this may leave a crack-propagating hole in the finish area.

Tacks are the daily bread of welding. But if a tack weld is to lock plates into the right position (and hold them there under contraction stress, or while things are re-aligned with a big hammer), it needs to be a quality mini-weld rather than a quick blob. Worthwhile tacks in thick material are ⅜"-¹⁵⁄₃₂" (10-12mm) long and fused properly into the joint material (1.46). Where you can, tack on the reverse side of a joint to leave the weld area uncluttered. If this can't be done and you're after a clean surface appearance, grind away the tack's bulk before welding the joint.

On long work, tack as often as you need to hold parts in alignment. Don't skimp on tack numbers, as it takes less time to weld them than to put things right after joint components have bowed or shifted through lack of anchoring.

Here are two hints for quality tacking:

• Save part-used ³⁄₃₂" (2.5mm) rods for the job. A short rod is easier to control, and its small diameter means good penetration in a Vee.

• Use more current than normal to give an easy start and quick fusion. Either shift down one rod size (e.g. from ⅛" to ³⁄₃₂" [3.25 to 2.5mm]) while leaving current setting unchanged, or use a ³⁄₃₂" (2.5mm) rod on ⅛" (3.25mm) settings.

Slag traps are a fact of life. Good preparation, sound basic technique and lots of practice keeps the little burglars at bay — but what can you do when they show up? There are two options. Either grind out the joint and re-weld it (which won't be possible if you can't get a grinder into the area), or use arc heat to melt out the slag and re-fuse the trap area (which is not always 100% successful).

Where possible go for option one. But the second approach will do in a crisis. First winkle out all the slag you can, using anything pointy. Re-welding aims to float the remaining slag to the surface and fuse fresh metal into the joint, so violent measures are called for. Put mega-heat into a limited area by using a lot of current on a small electrode – say 130A on a ³⁄₃₂" (2.5mm) rod. Then strike up just short of the trap, get the arc running nicely and move slowly over the dodgy area, holding a short arc so it digs out all the crud and the void is filled with fresh metal. Picture 1.47 has details.

1.46. Tacks need to be good-quality 'mini-welds', not blobs.

1.47. If you can't grind out slag traps, use a small diameter rod and high current to re-fuse them. Here, A has been given the treatment while horrors B and C wait their turn.

MAKING THE WELD 6
Up, down and overhead

Now for the bit that brings some operators out in a cold sweat – working straight up, straight down or overhead. If there's no chance of taking the chicken's option – which is rotating a vertical job so it's flat – you'll have to decide whether to weld uphill or down.

Vertical down work is usually favorite as most people find this easiest. *But penetration, and hence joint strength, will be poor in all but thin sheet.* Welding vertically down is only good for sheet, for cheering up surface appearance, or for filling awkward gaps where burn-through would otherwise be a problem. Never rely on it where strength matters.

1.48. When welding vertically down, center the rod over the joint to put heat equally into both plates. Angle it just below the horizontal and keep arc length shortish, then travel at a speed that keeps the rod tip just below the descending slag curtain.

Success hangs on having the right rod and enough current. Fast-freezing slag is called for, which will stay above the arc rather than running down under it and getting in the weld pool. ESAB's OK 46.00 is a good choice, and is equally at home welding on the flat or vertically upwards.

Vertical down welds need more current than the same weld on the flat, as the extra force in the arc helps keep the molten pool clear of slag. Start with a setting close to the top of the rod's recommended range. Center the rod over the joint line (1.48) and keep it just below horizontal. Travel fast enough to stay ahead of the descending slag curtain. Don't let the arc get too long or weld metal won't find its way to the pool.

Welding **vertically up** produces deep penetration and apprehension in equal measures. But with the plant set right and the technique sorted, worry will go away.

Electrode choice isn't as critical as it is with vertical down. Most general-purpose mild steel rods will work happily upwards, as gravity carries off the slag.

Heat control is everything. Keep the current down, dialling in 10-15% less than on the flat. But don't go too low or the rod will stick and slag traps form in cool areas. It's a balancing act: experiment at the lower end of the rod's recommended range, settling on the lowest current compatible with trap-free, easy-running work.

While welding you'll see the arc digging a crater and molten metal draining away under gravity. This is where vertical up's fine penetration comes from. But if the area overheats, the end result is a series of dangling blobs like melted candle wax (1.52).

The first pass in a multi-run joint is made without weaving, unless you need to control burn-though. Subsequent runs rely on a weave to support the molten metal (1.49). Each lateral weave creates a horizontal ledge, which is

1.49. A two-pass vertical up joint showing different weave patterns. The first run used a triangular weave, pushing the tip into the root gap until a change in arc noise indicated full penetration. The 'keyhole' shape in the penetration gap confirms this (arrow). Pausing at the borders of the weave (circles) filled in the edges. The second pass features an easier H-pattern weave, again with edge pauses. But the second weave wasn't wide enough to blend with the plate's outer edges, and there is some undercut near the start caused by too-brief pauses.

1.52. Too much heat turns a vertical up weld into a mess. Gravity pulls molten metal down too far before it solidifies (arrow).

1.50. A simple crescent weave features in this quality single-pass run. Neatness and strength come from very deliberate rod tip movement, coupled with a pause at each edge to let the crater fill (circles).

1.51. Assorted weave patterns. Use number 1 for flat (down hand) work, 2-5 for vertical up. Choose whichever best suits the job in hand.

used as a step to hold fresh weld. It's like making each rung of a ladder as you climb.

Follow the arrows in pics 1.49, 1.50 and 1.51 to see the track the rod tip takes during different weaves. A good upward weld has a wrinkled, prune-like finish; it's the result of all those individual ladder rungs. One or more downward passes using a crescent weave can tidy things up if needs be, but reset the current and use the right rod (page 31).

For best weave control imagine you're a slow-motion robot, constantly tracing the same pattern on the joint at the same speed. Keep the rod horizontal; or in thick sections, just above horizontal. Center it over the joint to balance fusion between the plates, and hold arc length as short as current allows to direct metal where you want it.

If the set has more than one output voltage, use the higher to help arc establishment and smoothness when welding vertically up. Relax, taking the electrode cable's weight on surrounding

metalwork and propping yourself comfortably. When you're welding, try keeping a light grip on the electrode holder. Enjoy yourself! Repeat after me: vertical up is fun, vertical up is fun….

Overhead welds are another tightrope act. It's flat welding turned upside down, only this time gravity is working against you. Metal will transfer across the arc thanks to magnetic forces, but the molten pool wants to drip. So three rules apply: Keep the arc as short as you can to lessen the chance of losing metal during transfer; keep the current as low as possible so weld metal can freeze before it sags; and travel as fast as you can so heat build-up is low. All this has to be balanced against achieving good fusion and penetration – hence the tightrope act. A visual clue on how well you're doing is in the bead shape. If the center hangs down, you're a little too hot or too slow.

SMAW HELPLINE

Everybody (but everybody) makes mistakes. There's no shame in it. But if you want to improve it helps to be able to spot faults, assess their seriousness and know where you went wrong. Pictures A-H deal with common problems and ways around them. (All pictures courtesy of The Welding Institute).

A. Slag traps (arrow) are a pain. Avoid them by keeping the four variables right — use enough current and the appropriate rod angle, hold arc length fairly short and don't travel too fast. The one above came from using too little heat or a long arc. Rod metal took the shortest path to the vertical plate, leaving a hole for slag to fill. Dealing with traps is covered on page 30.

B. This weld seemed fine on the surface, but a peek inside shows unequal length legs and a slag trap instead of root fusion. Low current, a too-long arc and the wrong rod angle were the cause.

C. This T-fillet, welded with the right current, rod angle and arc length, shows equal leg lengths and good fusion in both plates. A second, weaved run was added – spot its coarse, grainy look. The first run has been normalized by the heat of the second, leaving its grains smaller and improving strength. The small hole at the root isn't a problem: it comes from the vertical plate's original rounded profile. If you're not convinced, lay a rule along the right-hand edge.

D. Two faults in one here: incomplete penetration despite the gap between plates, plus a circular slag inclusion at eight o'clock. A smaller diameter rod, run at a reasonable current, would have helped penetration and provided enough heat to prevent trap formation. Just winding up the current on a big rod wouldn't do, as its girth would still stop it reaching the bottom of the joint.

SMAW HELPLINE

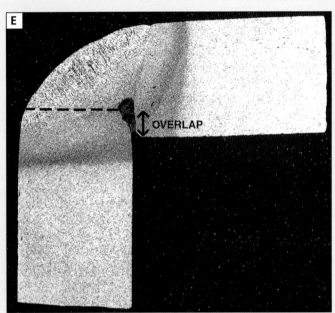

E. Poor preparation sank all hope for this outside corner joint. The plate edges were overlapped rather than kept parallel (dotted line), which kept arc heat from the joint root and allowed slag to flow in instead. Aligning the edges so there's no overlap and maybe leaving a small penetration gap is the answer.

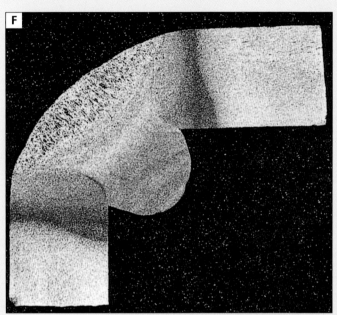

F. Another outside corner, only this time with too much penetration. Weld metal from the first of two runs has oozed right through the joint, either because the gap was too big, the current too high or travel too slow. The sudden change of section at the inner corners will concentrate stress, giving a site for breakage.

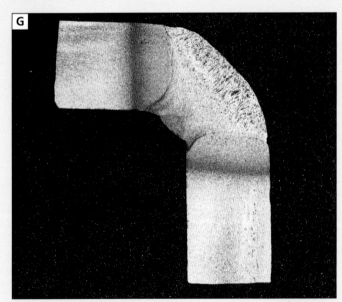

G. That's better. This T-fillet's two runs penetrate, fuse to full depth and preserve the parent plate's section.

H. Nothing much wrong with this lap joint. But if it's loaded heavily, failure is likely in the narrow heat-affected zone where grains are coarse and relatively weak (arrow). The torn surface would show a characteristic crystalline structure. There's not much that can be done, short of post-welding heat treatment to relieve stress and normalize the grain. It's a common cause of unexpected breakage in welds that otherwise look good.

Section 2

Gas Metal Arc Welding (GMAW)

Now for something newer. GMAW equipment was developed for industrial production, where its speedy work offsets the originally-fierce equipment cost. Now very capable sets are offered by a whole range of manufacturers, so farms too can exploit the process's benefits in fabrication and repair.

Here we'll deal with the sort of unit most likely to be bought new by an average farm workshop … whatever that may be. Typically it'll be a single phase set, running welding wire from 0.023-.052" (0.6-1.2mm) diameter. A higher-capacity plant is likely to need three-phase power (which limits mobility) and will be more expensive. Although such units offer more sophisticated control, their basic operating principles are the same.

So what is GMAW, and why the peculiar name? It's an arc welding process in which the stick electrode is replaced by continuously-fed wire, and shield gas takes over from an electrode coating.

The common shorthand for GMAW is MIG, which stands for Metal Inert Gas. But the only truly inert (i.e. non-chemically reactive) shield gases are argon and helium, which are reserved exclusively for welding aluminum or other non-ferrous metals and their alloys. So strictly speaking, MIG welding refers just to that.

Here, though, we're talking mainly about welding steels, using either carbon dioxide (CO_2) or a CO_2/argon mix as the shield gas. As carbon dioxide is not inert, the process can't rightfully be called MIG. Instead, Metal Active Gas (MAG) welding is the proper term. So which to use? Although GMAW is the proper moniker, it's a bit of a mouthful. So we'll settle for the common name – MIG – on the understanding that it's bending the truth.

Convert or beginner?

MIG welding has a reputation for being easy, and it is if approached the right way. Yet it's equally easy to make big mistakes.

If you're coming to MIG from a stick welding (SMAW) background, be prepared for change. Applying SMAW rules to MIG just doesn't work, as the new technique stands most things on its head. For instance:

- MIG is always a DC (direct current) process.

- The operator is not manually in charge of arc length. This is changed by altering voltage at the set.

- Current is adjusted indirectly by altering wire feed speed.

- Travel is substantially faster and the gun is usually pushed, not pulled.

- There's effectively no help from flux.

The only really constant thing between SMAW and MIG welding is the everlasting importance of penetration and fusion. That never changes, no matter whether the weld is made by SMAW, MIG, flame or mind over matter.

MIG's benefits

MIG welding offers a fair selection of advantages over SMAW.

- MIG's small filler wires carry similar current to SMAW electrodes, only on much thinner wires: for example, 130A on 0.035" (1mm) filler instead of a ⅛" (3.25mm) electrode. So there's great potential for excellent fusion and penetration so long as technique is good.

- MIG is faster, in both speed of travel and post-welding clean-up.

- MIG operation requires less manual skill, as arc length is controlled by the set rather than the operator. Stacked against this is the need for more careful setting of welding conditions, i.e. the fine-tuning of voltage and current.

- The joint area is easier to see as there's no slag coat, so potential problems can be spotted sooner while you're welding.

- There's no slag to control.

- Given a reasonable volume of work, MIG is potentially cheaper, even considering the cost of cylinder rental and shield gas.

The last point has to be looked at carefully in a farm context. MIG plant is more expensive than the equivalent SMAW gear, thanks to its wire-feed mechanism and AC-DC rectifier. Extra complexity means more potential for going wrong. Thus buying a MIG set for occasional use makes little sense. But once you've got one, it'll probably take over the bulk of the work. For some jobs SMAW's wide electrode choice, (relative) contamination tolerance and immunity to nature's breezes make it the better choice. Also, small SMAW sets (particularly inverters) are lighter and far more portable than MIG. Thus relying solely on MIG for the whole spectrum of farm work isn't a good idea, but MIG with SMAW backup is.

What's involved - more detail

MIG uses bulk electrode wire on a spool. The user holds a gun-like torch, whose trigger starts and stops wire feed, welding current and shield gas flow. Real bargain-basement sets leave the welding wire live all the time, so there's always the risk of accidental arcing. Don't bother with these.

Wire is fed continuously to the weld pool by a motor and roller arrangement, with feed speed varied by a control on the set (2.1). The wire

2.1

BUTTERS

275

2.1. This upmarket single-phase MIG set has click switches to change voltage in coarse and fine steps, plus a rotary knob for wire speed. Other rotaries look after burn-back control (how long the arc stays on after the trigger is released, and thus how far the wire burns back) and arc on/off times for spot- and stitch-welding. The spool gun socket (center) is for a remote wire feed unit.

passes through a copper contact tip as it leaves the gun, picking up electrical power en route. A copper coating on the wire improves electrical contact and delays surface rusting.

Compressed gas shields the weld pool. A regulator or flow meter on a bulk supply cylinder (2.2) varies gas delivery pressure, passing it up to the gun through a flexible tube. Flow is started and stopped by an electrical solenoid valve activated by the gun's trigger.

The gun – aka torch – ends in a nozzle. Usually height-adjustable, this directs the gas over the weld area to ward off atmospheric contaminants (2.3).

How about the filler wire? Apart from steel, it includes small quantities of deoxidants (silicon, manganese and perhaps aluminum, titanium and

2.2. Three ways to control shield gas flow. Budget MIG welders often come with a simple flow-meter (left). The single-stage regulator (center) shows cylinder pressure on its dial and gas flow on its graduated barrel, while a two-stage regulator (right) adds precise control over delivery pressure. For normal work, a single-stage regulator is a good compromise between cost and control. Note: Any regulator must match the gas it's used with. Oxygen equipment is shown here simply as an example of a regulator type – it must never be used with MIG shield gases!

2.3. Shield gas flows from the gun (A) before passing through the nozzle (B), and then to the weld area. Filler wire (C) is fed to the weld pool mechanically via the torch liner, picking up electrical energy from a copper contact tip (D) as it leaves the gun.

zirconium) to help counter the effect of shield-gas derived oxidants on the weld pool. But these can't match a SMAW rod's flux coat in cleaning effectiveness, leaving MIG much more contamination-sensitive than stick welding.

The set's front panel carries more controls than a stick welder. Along with the on/off switch you'll find either buttons or switches to change voltage,

and a rotary knob to vary wire speed. More complex sets offer functions like spot weld timing, burn-back control and variable inductance. Page 38 has more on these.

Voltage and wire speed – an intimate relationship

Before going into the nuts and bolts of setting up a MIG set, we'll see what happens when you change voltage and wire speed. Understanding how these two interact is important, and there's more detail on pages 37-38. But if you don't fancy that and if just contemplating electricity gives you the willies, here's the basics.

Changing voltage

With MIG, arc length and voltage are directly related. The more voltage you dial in at the control panel, the longer the arc gets. Think of it as a hosepipe being lifted over a vegetable patch: the more you lift, the longer the water jet gets and the wider it fans out. If you keep on increasing voltage without stepping up wire speed, the arc eventually ends up right back at the contact tip, fusing the filler wire in it – have a go and see. *To recap: more voltage produces a longer arc, which heats a wider area. Dropping voltage shortens the arc and heats a narrower strip.*

Changing current

There's no knob on a MIG set to vary welding current. Instead you do it indirectly by altering wire feed speed.

But how? The power unit is designed to hold voltage (arc length) to the operator's pre-set value, but is free to vary current within limits. At any instant, it delivers just enough current to melt filler wire at the rate needed to hold arc length steady. If you increase wire speed, the set delivers more current to keep the wire burning back at the same rate and thus hold arc length the same. If you slow wire speed down, the set still pegs arc length by delivering

less current so the wire doesn't burn back as fast. Thus changing wire speed varies the (average) current.

But only within limits. If you keep lowering wire speed, there comes a point where the set can't compensate any more. From here on, wire will be burnt back faster than it's fed to the weld pool and you'll notice arc noise and appearance change. On the other hand, if you wind up speed to the point where the set can't deliver enough extra current to burn off the incoming wire, that wire starts to rush into the weld pool more or less un-melted. You'll feel this through the torch as juddering or 'stubbing' as it hits the underlying plate.

To sum up: *voltage has by far the most effect on arc length, though wire speed alteration also affects it a little.*

Changing wire speed alters average current, though the available variation isn't huge.

Practical points to emerge from all this are:

- In MIG, the operator pre-selects voltage and thus arc length.

- Higher voltage gives longer and wider arcs. By choosing wire speed and diameter to exploit the higher energy available, thicker sections can be welded.

- Lower voltages give shorter arcs and narrower bands of heating, so are used with thinner wires on thinner work.

- At any given voltage setting the operator can vary average current via wire speed. Faster feeds mean more current, slower feeds mean less current.

(Thinking) Caps On

To really get the most from MIG it's necessary to twig how the process works. Figure A shows what's going on in the weld zone. A key point to start: a long electric arc needs more voltage to sustain it than a short one. Why? There's more electrical resistance in a long arc, which takes more volts (electrical pressure) to overcome. As arc length grows, voltage goes up and current drops.

SMAW and MIG power supplies are quite different animals, with the way they work making it possible to control the two forms of welding. We'll start by looking at what goes on inside a stick welding (SMAW) plant. The user sets welding current to give the required heat input, then fine-tunes this manually by altering arc length. The set's initial voltage output is fixed at one or more levels depending on the equipment, with 50 and 80V lines common.

For consistent fusion and penetration, welding current needs to remain as

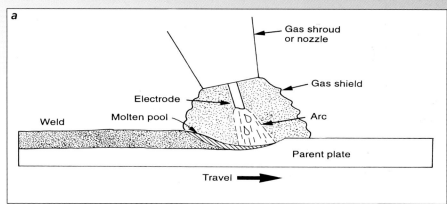

A. MIG in action. Shield gas keeps air from the molten pool, mechanically-fed wire is the electrode. Filler metal can get to the pool in several ways, giving practical implications – page 41 explains.

constant as possible during work. But current varies with arc length, and the SMAW operator's more-or-less unsteady hand means that arc length is always shifting a little. As it lengthens, arc voltage goes up. As it shortens, voltage drops. So welding current wants to change too.

The stick set's internals try to minimize current change. They are designed so that a large change in arc length (and thus voltage) produces only a small change in current. This minimizes the effect of operator unsteadiness on welding heat. The power unit behaves like an elastic band between voltage and current, holding one end steady (current) while you pull the other by changing arc length (voltage). Figure B puts this in graph form.

SMAW electrodes burn back fairly slowly, giving the operator time to spot and counter changes in arc length. But when the operator is half-asleep, the power supply helps by holding current as steady as it can – which minimizes the effect on weld quality and rod burn-back until the operator wakes up again. Despite this, SMAW welding still largely depends on the user's ability to feed rod steadily to the joint.

(As an aside, you might fall to wondering – in a bored moment – why an AC welding set can work at all. After all, AC voltage and current cycle repeatedly through zero, which ought to stop the arc. The day is saved by reactance in the power unit. This electrical phenomenon introduces a designed-for lag between AC voltage and current. As a result, they don't fall to zero together, and the arc keeps running. MIG sets are always DC so don't have the same potential problem).

MIG power

By contrast, MIG's thinner filler wire burns back far faster than a rod, to the point that even Superman would be hard pushed to keep arc length constant. So it needs an automatic control system.

This small miracle is achieved by reversing the 'elastic band' effect inside the power unit. Voltage is pegged while current is stretched to and fro. If the operator lifts the torch from the work, arc length tries to grow and voltage wants to climb. But the power unit is designed so that as soon as voltage shifts, current changes even more. Compare Fig C with Fig B to see what's happening.

What does this quick-shifting current achieve? Think again about the

B. Power supply characteristic for SMAW. On striking the arc, voltage falls from the open circuit value (A) to the running voltage band (B). Alterations in arc length produce voltage variations in this band. See how the curve's shape produces only corresponding small changes in welding current (C)? The set actively helps to maintain current – and hence weld quality – when the operator's arm wobbles.

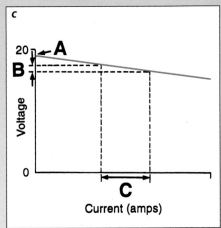

C. The MIG power supply holds voltage and thus arc length (B) relatively constant for a large change in current (C). As the operator wobbles, arc length tries to shift. But the rapid change in current burns off more or less wire, returning length to where it was. This makes MIG intrinsically easier to use than SMAW.

operator lifting the torch. Arc voltage tries to go up, but current drops faster. The filler wire immediately burns back more slowly – and as it's being fed mechanically at a constant rate toward the weld pool, the arc gets shorter. This shorter arc needs less voltage to run, so the power unit raises current a little to burn back the wire faster. The result is an arc that maintains a constant average length, self-adjusting quicker than you can notice.

Automatic arc adjustment also brings a bonus. A longer or shorter arc would fan out more or less on the work – remember water spraying from a garden hose. Left unchecked this would increase or decrease weld pool width, but MIG's self-adjustment tends to keep pool and bead width steady.

Some MIG sets also offer **slope control.** By changing the slope of the power supply's volt/amps curve (blue line, C), this gives a way to fine-tune spatter. At any given working voltage, a shallow slope lets short-circuit current rise more than a steep one does. High short-circuit

current practically explodes the molten drop from the wire tip, while lower current lets it part more slowly. So dialling in more slope limits short-circuit current, and thus reduces spatter. Lower cost sets tend to have slope fixed.

You might also find **variable inductance** on more capable sets, usually achieved by plugging the return lead into alternative outlet(s) on the front panel. This controls the rate of current rise during short circuit transfer's short circuits, with more inductance giving a slower rise and gentler pinching of droplets from the welding wire. One result is less spatter; others are a longer 'arc on' time (and thus a more fluid weld pool) and a flatter, smoother bead. If you have it, use variable inductance to control spatter and improve finish: but bear in mind that too much inductance for a given voltage produces poor starting. Experiment in both short circuit and spray modes to see its effects.

Which wire?

Smaller single-phase sets handle at least 0.023-.030" (0.6 and 0.8mm) diameter wires, while bigger-capacity sets take 0.035, 0.045 and maybe ¹⁄₁₆" (1.0, 1.2 and 1.6mm) sizes as well. Keep stocks of all the sizes your set can use, buying big-name brands for reliability.

Wires come in different grades. For fabrication or repair in mild and low-alloy steels, double-deoxidized wire to grade ER70S-6 of the appropriate AWS standard is fine. Note the low-alloy coverage: using standard wire, MIG can deal with semi-special steels like weld-on power harrow tips. Unless you specify otherwise, ER70S-6 is what your supplier will probably provide. If you don't mind paying a little extra, precision-wound spools give a smoother feed than random-wound versions.

Triple-deoxidized wire to grade AWS ER70S-7 handles contamination better but is significantly more expensive. Other wire grades cover high-alloy and stainless steels but these don't feature much in farm work.

Steel filler wire is generally copper-coated to resist corrosion and improve current transfer. Prolonged damp affects performance. MIG wire has a big surface area in relation to its diameter, so even light surface rust interferes with smooth feeding and produces lower-strength welds. If the set won't be used for a while in winter it's best to take off the wire spool and keep it somewhere dry – spare spools should always be stored this way.

Clean filler wire always feeds and welds best. A simple fit-up with wire wool, cloth and a couple of clips will scrub the filler, helping feed rollers get a grip and minimising contaminant build-up in the torch's guide tube (2.4 a, b and c).

Which gas, and how much?

For mild steel, use either CO_2 or a CO_2/argon mix.

CO_2 gives narrower, deeper penetration and a less fluid molten pool that's easier to control on positional work. It's cheaper, a cylinder lasts longer and

2.4. In winter damp, the top coils of MIG wire pick up a thin, patchy layer of rust. Steel wool and a piece of rag help produce a smooth feed and consistent work (a, above). Don't clamp the wire too tight, and change the pad material occasionally. If wire feed is erratic look at spool friction drag (b, below) and feed roller adjustment (c). Wire drives come with alternative rollers to match different filler diameters.

2.5. Shield gas effects. No gas (A) leaves mousse-like bead with some pinholing. Inadequate gas flow (B) gives heavy pinholing, and weld zone contamination will give the same effect. Adequate gas flow (C) shields the weld completely.

2.6. Contamination produces a weld that looks like a Hershey's Air Delight chocolate bar and has about the same strength (A). This CO_2-shielded weld improved as the plate got cleaner (B).

the extra penetration can be a boon on thick section steels. But CO_2 produces a rougher weld finish with more spatter. The arc is harsher and spray transfer can never be achieved. Globular transfer is the norm so spatter can't be tuned out by the operator. Ideally, triple-deoxidized wire should be used with CO_2 shield gas to counter the gas's oxidizing tendency and thus maximize weld strength.

Argon/CO_2 mixes give a hotter, more fluid molten pool and support true spray transfer. Penetration is broader but shallower, making argon mixtures better for thin-section material. Spatter is reduced, the weld surface is smoother, the arc more stable and plant setting is less critical. Gas mixtures with 5% – 20% CO_2 are on offer, though not necessarily in all cylinder sizes. A 20% mix gives a slightly cooler pool better suited to positional work and helps penetration, while the 5% variety is best on thinner sections. For general farm work, a 15% – 20% gas mix is good.

Gas supply rates are often quoted, with 25-30 Cubic Feet per Hour (10 liters/min) or 3-5 psi typical. In practice it's enough to use your ear alongside the nozzle. Set wire speed to zero (so you don't get an earful of wire), pull the torch trigger and increase flow at the regulator until a steady, soft hiss is heard. Then, once work has started, decrease flow as much as possible. Too little shield gas gives the weld a rough, mousse-like look: make a run with and without gas to see the effect (2.5). Contamination in the weld zone also produces a poor bead, which is usually riddled with holes (2.6).

When welding in a draught or at high voltages, increase gas flow. Using a sheet of tin to keep the gale off the work area will help, but MIG can't cope with much airflow; the gas shield is blown away.

In normal work, using 'a little more gas just to be sure' is a waste. The shield gas has absolutely no effect on the arc's ability to handle rust and other contaminants, so there's no point in using more if the arc isn't behaving. In such cases stop, find the problem and put it right. Using too much shield gas runs the risk of actually lowering weld protection (especially with CO_2) as the stream becomes turbulent, drawing in the air that you're trying to exclude.

MIG SETUP 1
Short Circuit or Spray?

MIG sets are a bit like Janus, the two-faced Roman god. Looking one way is an inviting 'easy-to-use-me' smile. Facing the other way is the more mysterious side of 'setting up'. But twiddling the knobs to get the best from MIG isn't too hard once you've got a grip on the principles.

Unlike with SMAW, you get a choice of how to deposit the filler metal. The mode used – either short circuit transfer or spray transfer – has big implications for pool control, fusion and penetration. Whether there is a choice in practice depends on the set's maximum output, the filler wire diameter and the shield gas.

Lucky dip ...

Where work involves either thin sections, positional (i.e. not flat) work or gap filling, **short circuit transfer** is the mode to use. In this there's not enough voltage for the arc to run constantly, so it dips in and out of a weld pool that's relatively small and fast-freezing. Heat input is relatively low (so distortion can be too) and filler metal is only transferred while the wire is in the pool, never in free flight across the arc.

Plate 2.7 shows short circuit transfer. Filler wire comes out of the torch's contact tip just faster than the arc can burn it off, so travels down and touches the work. The resulting electrical short heats the wire until a length melts into the weld pool, establishing a temporary arc. The process repeats 20-200 times/sec, generating MIG's characteristic crackle.

... Unlucky globular ...

As voltage and current (wire speed) are increased, the way filler wire metal is transferred to the weld pool changes. More voltage allows a self-sustaining arc, and short circuit transfer shifts to

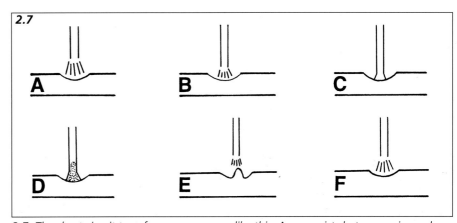

2.7. The short circuit transfer sequence runs like this. An arc exists between wire and weld pool (A). But as wire is feeding faster than the arc burns it back, the tip gets closer to the pool (B). When wire and pool meet the arc goes out (C), producing a short circuit. Current flow heats the wire (D), which melts to leave a globule in the pool (E). The cycle is then back at square one (F). MIG's characteristic crackle comes from the on/off arc.

globular transfer. In this, large blobs of molten wire move across the arc in free flight (2.8). Droplets are the same width or wider than wire diameter and break off randomly, changing the smooth ripple of arc noise into a rougher popping.

Although heat release is greater than in short circuit transfer (as the arc is 'on' continuously), globular transfer is not very good news. There's not enough magnetic energy to direct those big droplets to the weld, so either they miss it altogether or whack home like a hippo jumping into a paddling pool. Either way, metal is lost from the joint and spatter goes everywhere.

There is no off/on transition between short circuit and globular transfer, just a blending from one to the other. Where in the wire speed range this happens depends on the set and shield gas, but it'll be at higher feed speeds.

If you're using an argon/CO_2 mix, side-stepping globular transfer is a matter of spotting what's happening and tuning it out – see pages 44-46. But if you're using pure CO_2 you can only have globular transfer. Penetration will be good but the higher the current goes, the worse the spatter will get and the rougher the weld will look.

... And super spray

Spray transfer is the third way to

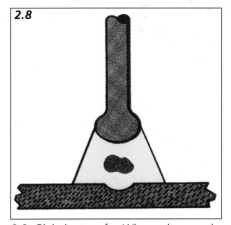

2.8. Globular transfer. When voltage and wire feed speed (current) are both high enough, a self-sustaining arc appears. But it's energy is not high enough to produce true spray transfer or channel molten filler metal straight to the weld pool. The result? Blobs of filler fall through the arc into the weld pool, or are pushed sideways and out. Spatter is high, weld finish is poor.

deliver filler metal to the weld pool, though it's available only at higher arc energies and with a mixed shield gas. Spray can't be achieved with CO_2. With smaller wires, the set must deliver at least 160A and the shield gas must have 80% argon at the minimum. Thicker wires need higher energies still.

For a given wire diameter, combining high voltage and high wire feed speed will produce globular transfer. But by winding back the wire feed speed

2.9. Spray transfer. Higher arc energies pinch off filler wire in much smaller droplets, which are taken down through the arc by magnetic field. Spatter is low, the arc long and wide, the weld pool hot and liquid. Penetration and fusion are potentially high.

a little, the wire can be burnt off in a more orderly fashion. Much smaller droplets fly across the arc in a fine spray (2.9).

The resulting long, high-voltage arc delivers heat in a wide fan. Fusion and penetration increase compared to short circuit transfer, suiting spray to heavier steel sections. The downside is that the hot, fluid weld pool limits work to the flat (or gently sloped) position and is too fierce for thinner materials. And keep an eye on the torch when spray is used, as the extra heat released can cook it.

Arc noise changes as globular transfer turns into spray. Its uneven stutter fades to a smooth, low hum. Light and heat output both go up noticeably. You can't miss it.

MIG SETUP 2

Equipment checks

There's a lot to look after with a MIG set, so here's a pre-welding list.

Contact tips are consumables. They're cheap and don't last forever (2.10). The wire picks up welding current here and good, consistent contact means a smooth arc. When wire flops about in a used item, fit another. If a tip looks so-so, try slipping a length of the next-fattest wire in it: if this goes through, throw the tip away. Spatter can part-block the exit hole which slows the wire,

and there must be good, easy-sliding contact between the two for an even feed. Unless you're desperate it's not worth trying to clear a blockage with gas nozzle reamers — the soft copper is rasped away before harder spatter, leaving an oval, oversize hole.

If the **nozzle** crusts with spatter, less shield gas will flow (2.11). Really serious crud will bridge between nozzle and tip, turning the nozzle live and risking an arc between it and the surroundings. Clear spatter with a blade or special tool – MIG pliers combine wire cutters, tip pliers and reamers in one unit (2.12). Spatter-release spray helps combat build-up, but don't let it block the gas exit

2.10. Compare a worn contact tip (bottom) with a new one. Change as soon as wire becomes a floppy fit, or after spatter damage. The wire must be a free-sliding fit, never tight.

holes below the contact tip (2.13). Looked after, a nozzle lasts a long time. During work check its condition frequently.

Adjust **nozzle height** to suit the welding process (2.14). For short circuit transfer, the contact tip can be level with or just peeking out beyond the nozzle. This minimizes electrical resistance caused by long stick-out (page 48), while maximizing welding current and the operator's view of the

2.11. Short circuit transfer at high voltages leaves a crusting of spatter in the nozzle, particularly when working vertically or overhead. This eventually cuts gas flow and can bridge to the contact tip, turning the whole nozzle 'live'. Check and clean frequently.

2.12. Cheap and very useful, MIG pliers put a nozzle reamer, wire cutters and tip spanner in one tool.

2.13. Torch gas holes (arrow) can block with spatter and sticky residue, limiting flow. Too much release spray makes it worse.

2.14a

2.14b

2.14. For short circuit transfer set the nozzle so it's level with or just below the contact tip (a) to give the best view of proceedings. For hotter spray transfer, set the nozzle so it masks the tip by about ¼" (6mm) (b).

proceedings. When working in a tight corner try exposing the tip even more, through spatter build-up will be fast – as it will when working vertically or overhead.

Be careful in short circuit transfer. The more the tip is recessed, the greater is the effective stick-out and the more you'll be tempted to make up for lost current by increasing wire speed. Bead shape and penetration then suffer.

For spray transfer draw the nozzle forward so it shrouds the tip by about ¼" (6mm) (2.14b). The tip is then held back from arc heat and the nozzle can direct shield gas for better weld pool protection.

Spare a thought for the **torch liner**, the replaceable internal spiral which

guides welding wire. An occasional blast-out with dry compressed air clears its tubes, giving a smooth wire feed and steady arc. Don't use oil! Even a good liner won't last forever, so don't overlook it if wire feed gets the jitters.

The spool spindle has an adjustable **friction control** (2.4B). Set this so the spool won't overrun when the feed motor stops. Too much friction loads the motor and can mean a jerky feed as rollers slip 'n slide. Tighten the damper before moving the set around in a vehicle, or the bumping will produce a bird's nest of wire.

Too much **feed roller pressure** can damage the wire, yet too little gives an uneven feed. The latter shows up as an unsteady arc and (perhaps) in the tendency for wire to burn back and fuse with the contact tip, even though voltage is right. Back off pressure until the rollers just start to slip as you brake wire between finger and thumb; then increase it until the slipping stops. Keep the rollers clean and free from oil – it's surprising how quickly crud builds up on them.

MIG SETUP 3

Finding good welding conditions

You've decided on the filler wire, the shield gas and picked a metal transfer mode to suit the job – short circuit for thinner stuff and positional work, spray for heavy sections if welding position allows. Now to set the set.

The idea is to balance voltage and wire speed to produce a particular transfer mode, then tweak these settings for the job in hand. Several things are important:

- There is no spot-on setting. Instead, there's a narrow band of **good welding conditions** to find and move around in.

- At the borders of good welding conditions are transition zones into bad ones. Steer clear of these.

- The calibrations on the set's controls seldom tie in with any specific voltage or wire speed. They're just markings, useful as waypoints during setting and for subsequent recall.

- Although there are tables laying down the minimum and maximum currents usable with each wire size, these are not much good unless the set has read-outs for volts and amps. Most farm-level sets don't run to such things, so unless you rig up your own meters you must fly by the seat of your pants. Table 2.1, on page 48 has values for those who can use them.

- How do you know when to change wire size? As joint width and material thickness increase, extra filler wire and heat are needed to make a weld.

Simply increasing wire speed to boost current and put more metal into the joint will succeed for a start, but only until short circuit transfer shifts to untidy, inefficient globular mode. That aside, once a given wire's current-carrying capacity is reached, any further increase in feed speed just lays down a fatter bead – it can't put more heat into the joint. If you want to stay with short circuit transfer the only way to deliver extra metal and current is to shift to a thicker filler wire and reset wire feed speed to suit it.

It's possible to come at good welding conditions from two directions. The precise way is to set wire speed to a given value and then use tables and experiment to find the right voltage to burn it off, which is ideal where all the variables are known.

But in the suck-it-and-see farm workshop it's easier to pick a voltage that delivers the heat you want, then find the wire speed range to suit it.

Until you know your set inside out, tune up first on a bit of clean scrap steel of the same thickness as the job. Short circuit transfer is a low arc-energy

2.15. The voltage effect. In runs 1 and 2 voltage is too low; the weld bead is narrow and fusion poor. Increasing voltage through runs 3-6 produces good welding conditions: the bead is widening and flattening, fusion is fine and spatter disappears. Run 3 shows cool short circuit transfer, run 6 hot short circuit transfer. By runs 7 and 8 there's not enough wire arriving to satisfy the lengthening arc, which burns progressively back toward the contact tip. The bead is wide and very shallow, undercut appears and spatter comes back.

2.16. The flip side of 2.15. Moving up from low voltage (bottom) to high shows increasing penetration.

mode, so pick a voltage toward the lower end of the scale and set wire speed to about one-third of maximum. Adjust voltage until you're happy with bead width and penetration, using picture 2.15 as a guide. Then fine-tune current with the wire speed control (2.17). Two important points: while it's okay to alter wire speed while the arc is running, don't change voltage as there's a good chance that you'll blow the set. And to minimize confusion, only alter one variable at a time.

Setup, step-by-step

Here's the process:

1. Adjust voltage

Pics 2.15 and 2.16 show a series of runs on 0.08" (2mm) plate, made with 0.030" (0.8mm) wire and 20% CO_2 shield gas. The only thing changed between each run was voltage; wire speed was left alone. Each run corresponds to one voltage step on the set, starting low and working up. See how bead shape and spatter level change?

In MIG, voltage controls arc length – the more volts you dial in, the longer and wider the arc grows. In runs 1 and 2, voltage is too low to burn off the incoming wire. The bead is thin, uneven, humped and shows little sign of fusing with the parent plate, as heat is lacking. There's a lot of spatter from weld metal being physically splashed from the pool, and the operator could feel 'stubbing' through the torch as wire is jabbed down into the plate.

With increasing voltage, runs 3-6 blossom into good welding conditions. Now there's enough energy to burn off the wire, so the bead is regular and fuses to the plate. With each step up in voltage, the arc lengthens and widens a little so the bead flattens. By runs 4 and 5 short circuit transfer is in full swing, the arc is sizzling nicely and spatter has died clean away.

By run 7 the party is nearly over. There's so much voltage that the arc is burning well back up the wire. The wider arc produces a wider melt zone. And could you but hear it, your ears would tell you that the rate of sizzle is slowing right down.

2.17. The effect of changing wire speed (current) while voltage stays constant. Speed starts off high (bottom) and is gradually slowed. In runs 1 and 2 speed is too high. Runs 3-9 are all good welding conditions, run 10 looks OK on the surface but has no penetration; see text for explanation. All runs are short circuit transfer with 0.030" (0.8mm) wire, argon/CO$_2$ shield gas on 0.08" (2mm) plate.

2.18. The flip side of 2.17 shows how a drop in wire speed reduces penetration, as a result of reduced current.

In run 8 (maximum voltage) the arc is burning right back to the contact tip in a series of fuzzy-sounding pops and whooshes. The melt zone is wider than the filler could fill, leaving undercut at the edges. Spatter is back and the whole area has a powdery brown coat.

This bad-to-good-to-bad sequence happens at any wire diameter as voltage is wound up. 2.16 reinforces the point. Turning over the plate shows how penetration rises and widens with voltage. Using the above as a guide, take a bit of plate and run the experiment yourself. In short, pick a voltage that suits the work.

2. Adjust wire speed (current)

Once you've settled on a good voltage,

bring wire speed into balance with it so penetration and bead shape are right. We've already seen in theory how current goes up with wire speed, and 2.17 and 2.18 confirm it. These show a series of short circuit transfer runs in which wire speed starts fast, then is slowed a little each time. Voltage setting stays the same throughout.

When wire speed is too high for the voltage (runs 1 – 3), the arc can't burn off incoming wire fast enough. The torch jumps, the arc stutters and pops, spatter flies everywhere. The weld bead (such as it is) is humped and pinched, coming and going between bouts of wire stubbing. Transfer is globular.

By run 4, wire speed has slowed enough for short circuit transfer to start. Spatter

has almost gone and the weld bead starts to look respectable. Relatively fast feed means high current, so fusion is good; check the corresponding penetration in 2.18.

Lowering feed speed progressively through runs 4-8 sees the bead gradually narrowing as current drops, but welding conditions are still good. Arc noise softens and the rate of ripping crackle slows with it.

By run 9, current is getting low. Short circuit transfer is still happening but short circuit rate is slow. The arc comes and goes, the bead is noticeably narrower and starting to hump as heat input drops.

2.19. Wire speed adjustment involves fine tuning. On the Butters set and with the wire/gas used, 2.15's full range of welding conditions was delivered in the narrow arc between H and L. Other sets are calibrated differently. It's all part of the joy of welding.

In run 10 short circuit transfer has more or less stopped. The arc is burning back up toward the contact tip and wire falls as blobs into the pool, so the narrow bead's width varies as a result. From here, all it takes to get back to good welding conditions is a nudge up in feed speed.

Turning the plate over (2.18) shows how wire speed (current) affects penetration. After steady short circuit transfer is established (everything after run 4) current goes down as feed speed drops, so penetration declines. By run 10 it's gone altogether.

Depending on the set, these changes will happen in a bigger or smaller arc of speed knob movement (2.19). Run the sequence for yourself – the examples used 0.08" (2mm) plate, 0.030" (0.8mm) wire and 20% CO_2 gas. With quality sets like the Murex Tradesmig and Butters Merlyn used to produce the samples shown here, small changes in feed speed deliver very obvious results. With a cheap set, adjustment effects can be less clear-cut.

Summary

The foregoing shows that once you've settled on a voltage that gives enough fusion for a given job, more wire speed delivers more current and penetration.

It's also clear that there's a definite band of good welding conditions (bounded on either side by settings that deliver duff results) and that it's possible to move around the good band by tweaking wire speed.

Pick voltage and wire speed to tailor a weld to the job, knowing what your own set can do. For instance, to produce a flatter bead with minimum surface build-up, use a higher voltage and lower wire speed to give **hot short circuit transfer** (2.15). For a narrow bead on thin sheet joints, limit arc length by lowering voltage and keeping feed speed down to minimize current – **cool short circuit transfer**. Or to reduce bead volume in a particular joint, increase voltage for a set wire speed or reduce wire speed for a given voltage.

Conditions for spray transfer

Spray transfer involves higher energies and produces more light and heat than short circuit transfer. Allow for these by using an 11EW mask filter minimum, and adjusting the torch nozzle so the tip sits about ¼" (6mm) up inside it.

If you're using 0.030" (0.8mm) wire and a 160-180A set, start by dialling in maximum voltage and half wire speed. Thicker wires will need more volts, so smaller-capacity sets may not deliver spray with them. To see if spray is happening run a short bead on a piece of scrap, which needs to be at least ¼" (6mm) thick to take the heat.

At these high voltage levels the physics of the arc/wire system won't allow short circuit transfer. So if the arc crackles hard and there's a lot of spatter about, globular transfer is going on.

To move into spray, lower the wire speed a little and try again. Keep lowering it until the arc suddenly widens and lengthens: at the same time light output will jump, arc noise shifts to a quiet humming and spatter dies away as metal transfer becomes more orderly.

2.20. Three transfer modes, all produced with 0.04" (1.2mm) wire on ¼" (6mm) plate. Run 1 is low-voltage short circuit transfer; cool, orderly and spatter-free. For runs 2 and 3, wire speed and voltage were both increased until globular transfer appeared. Although sounding something like short circuit, the arc's smooth crackle harshens and shifts to a more staccato popping. A lot more spatter leaves the arc, as the bead area shows; metal transfer has become disordered. Run 4 shows spray transfer, generated by slowing wire speed until the arc lengthens and fans out. Noise changes to a smooth, quiet hum and light output increases. The jump in heat produces a wide, smooth bead. Orderly metal transfer across the arc leaves little spatter.

Now you've hit spray transfer (2.20).

The arc fans out to generate a wide, fluid and slow-freezing pool. If this is too wide for the job, drop wire speed just a touch. The arc will narrow and start to crackle faintly. This tighter spray is good for fillet joints, as it puts more metal into the area where the two plates meet.

Check penetration and fusion. Both will be much better than with short circuit transfer. If they're excessive for the job, try a lower voltage. But you can only go down so far and maintain true spray conditions. When voltage drops too low for the wire in use, transfer will move back to globular mode, spatter will increase substantially and the arc will splutter.

Conclusion?

All this business of setting one thing and adjusting the other looks complicated on paper, and sometimes isn't that much better when you've got the torch in your hand. But persistence and experiments pay off. Settings are never quite the same on different jobs; get to know what you want and what you're seeing and hearing, then fiddle until the set delivers the goods.

Watch Out – Dodgy Combination About

Careful plant setting and good technique will produce a fine-looking weld, but you still need to think about what's going on. A joint can look a treat but have the strength of a stick of Brighton rock (a and b).

What's wrong with this fillet? Looking at the bead surface in (a), not much. But when stressed, the joint failed suddenly under light load. See how little fusion there was in the vertical plate wall (b), and none in the root? Thin filler wire, delivered by short circuit transfer, couldn't put in enough heat for good fusion/penetration.

2.21. A subsoiler wing, welded with spray transfer using a 180A set and 0.030" (0.8mm) wire. Short circuit transfer wouldn't have produced the required penetration, given the foot's big heat sink effect.

Getting penetration takes heat. The thicker the section, the more heat it absorbs before melting. So for a strong job in thick sections, the arc must deliver enough energy to satisfy the steel's heat-swallowing tendency and still have enough left over for a good, deep melt in the weld zone. With MIG, voltage is arc width and wire speed is current. Only the bigger wire sizes can handle the voltage and current needed to guarantee penetration in thicker stuff.

So the message is simple. If you try welding heavy sections with small wires and short circuit transfer, low energy input can produce a joint that looks good but is inherently weak. So what are your options if you're stuck with a small set and limited fillers?

- Restrict 0.023" (0.6mm) filler wire to material under ⅛" (3mm) thick.

- With thicker-section steel use the highest possible voltage and wire speed that still maintains short circuit transfer, but don't edge into globular.

- Travel at a speed which keeps the arc at the front edge of the weld pool. This is a balancing act. Work too slowly and the arc fires more into the weld pool than the parent plate, so penetration is reduced. Work too fast and there's not enough time either for a thorough melt or to fill the arc path, so penetration again takes a hit and undercut can be a problem.

- If in doubt and where set output, shield gas and welding position allow, use spray transfer on the thickest wire the set allows.

- Where spray isn't an option, weld the joint vertically upwards with short circuit transfer. The slower travel helps heat build up, and gravity drains the pool so the arc can puts its energy into the parent plates.

• IF NONE OF THE ABOVE IS POSSIBLE, DON'T USE MIG. Switch to stick electrodes or take the job to someone with a more capable set. Sudden failure of a safety-related item can be terminal.

Table 2.1 Wire Sizes, Voltages and Currents

Wire diameter	Voltage (V)	Current (A)
(0.6 mm) 0.023"	16-20	50-100
(0.8mm) 0.030"	18-24	60-185
(1.0mm) 0.035"	18-32	80-300
(1.2mm) 0.045"	18-32	120-380
Typical operating ranges		
Short circuit transfer	16-20V	
Globular transfer	22-28V	
Spray transfer	24-32V	

Note: *Values will vary with equipment, shield gas and welding position.*

MIG'S VARIOUS VARIABLES

That's adjusted the equipment; now to do the same for the operator.

Which variables affect weld strength? To three of SMAW's originals (current, speed of travel and angle), MIG adds voltage and wire extension.

One of MIG's selling points is that it's easy to make a reasonable job with very little practice. And indeed it is, because the very thing that most people find hardest with SMAW – holding arc length steady – is controlled by the set. But for consistent, strong welds all the variables still have to be right.

Arc Length. The more volts or less wire speed, the longer the arc. But that's it; the operator can't adjust arc length manually during work because the set's power supply is designed to hold it constant. More voltage lengthens the arc and increases total heat input to the work, and vise versa.

Current. At a given voltage, altering wire feed speed changes current. But as we've seen, not by all that much. For large changes in penetration and fusion it's necessary to alter voltage and/or swap to a different wire diameter. Each time the operator must again fine-tune feed speed according to conditions.

Stickout or extension should be kept short, to minimize electrical resistance downstream of the contact tip and maximize welding current at the arc (2.22). In practice, use ¼"-⅜" (6-10mm) visible extension depending on welding voltage (2.23).

Welding with too much wire beyond the contact tip will hit weld strength. To see how, try this: with the arc running normally, gradually raise the gun. As stickout grows the arc gets weaker, until finally the filler wire just glows red and won't fuse with the work. By lengthening stickout you've progressively increased electrical resistance between the contact tip and arc, so energy is diverted into heating the wire (2.24).

Eventually there's not enough current left to run an arc. On top of that, increasing the stickout moves the arc farther and farther away from the gas shield, potentially adding porosity to the weld's woes. SMAW electrodes don't suffer from the stickout effect. Being fatter they offer much less electrical resistance, so can carry normal welding currents without overheating.

There's a big temptation to use extra stickout when trying to weld in a deep, narrow groove or somewhere that you (or the gun) can't quite reach. But don't do it. Though the joint may seem to be welded, reduced current means that it's likely to be only stuck together.

Having said that, and as long as you stay within limits, it's OK to use stickout as a quick'n dirty way to control current; for example on a very thin-section butt joint

2.22. Wire stick-out or extension. Visual stick-out is what's actually seen by the operator, which is the length of filler wire outside the nozzle (A). The power supply, though, senses the whole length of resistance-creating wire between the contact tip and arc (arrow, B). The more recessed the contact tip is in the nozzle and the greater the visual stick-out used in work, the greater is this resistance. Arc energy is lost to heating the narrow wire, so fusion drops.

2.23. Generally use about ¼" (6mm) extension for short circuit transfer (a), rising to ⅜" (10mm) where current needs to be lowered a little to control burn-through. For the best view, the contact tip can poke slightly beyond the nozzle if welding heat won't cook it.

2.24. What happens when stickout gets too long? Each bead was run from right to left, starting and finishing with normal stickout. For the section between the arrows, stickout was doubled. Current dropped and the gas shield was left behind: fusion was hit, bead profile suffered and porosity and spatter grew. It doesn't take much to turn a good MIG weld into a weak one.

2.25. Travelling too fast (top) leaves a thin, stringy bead. Travelling too slowly leaves a heavy bead with the risk of poor fusion underneath (bottom), while travelling at a reasonable speed - which will be faster than with SMAW – is just right (center).

when burn-through looks imminent. Here a little more stickout will reduce current and prevent disaster. But don't use it as a substitute for thoughtful selection of voltage and wire speed.

Speed of travel is at the root of some big problems with MIG. Going too fast leaves a stringy bead with reduced fusion and penetration (2.25). That's easy to spot. Going too slowly is harder to see and if anything, is worse for strength. There's a very high risk of poor fusion and penetration, even though the weld may look fine.

Why? Rather than biting into the underlying joint metal, the arc plays on the weld pool; or worse, on a ball of molten filler rolling over the potential weld zone. Heat doesn't reach the joint's root and sidewalls so fusion suffers.

Here's a guide to travel speed. Once you've dialled into good welding conditions, travel at a speed that lays down a relatively flat weld with good fusion. This will be significantly faster than you're used to travelling with SMAW. Watch the departing new-laid bead for height, and the joint's floor, walls and edges for fusion. Aim to keep the wire arcing at the front of a slightly sunken molten pool.

Direction of travel. With MIG there's a choice: pull or push. Normally the gun is pushed in the direction of travel, while angled at 70-80° to the work. This is **forehand** operation (2.26a), which has

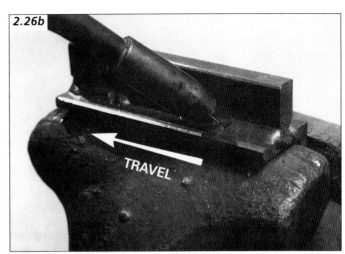

2.26. Forehand operation is normal for MIG, i.e. the gun is pushed along in the direction of travel. This gives the wire a clear feed to the front of the weld pool, while the operator gets a good view of what's happening (a). In backhand operation (b) the gun is pulled along, leaving the bead behind. Penetration is better but the weld pool can be harder to see.

2.27. Stickout increases if gun angle gets too shallow (arrow). Current and fusion drop, and the arc tends to edge out of the shield gas envelope.

a couple of advantages. If travel speed is right the filler wire feeds directly into the weld pool's forward edge so there is less danger of the 'rolling ball' effect described previously. Compared to SMAW, the operator gets a very good view of what's happening. In forehand operation the weld is wider and flatter, with reduced penetration.

Backhand operation is the alternative (2.26b). Now the gun is pulled in the direction of travel, giving deeper penetration and a narrower bead. The arc tends to be more stable and spatter is reduced.

Compared with SMAW, MIG is more tolerant of angle variation during work. But don't use too shallow an angle (2.27). This not only reduces current through increased stickout, but also tends to carry the arc away from its gas shield.

A couple of comments on visibility and masks. When welding thin sheet with MIG, there's not much arc light about and it can be hard to see where you're going.

2.28. True progress. A self-darkening filter lets you see to line up parts for tacking. Pay a little more for shade adjustability and manual/auto operation: both are well worth having.

Changing the mask filter to a relatively transparent grade (9EW) helps, but be very sure to swap this for a darker item when using currents in excess of 40A: that's equivalent to 15-16V with 0.023" (0.6mm) wire. If the bank balance can stand it, keep a clearly marked mask for low-voltage MIG work and a darker one for higher voltage MIG and SMAW. A better solution is to splash out on a shade-adjustable, automatically darkening filter. It's an extravagance you won't regret (2.28).

MIG - GETTING DOWN TO IT

After all the preamble, time to do some work! We'll start right next to

Godliness. **Cleanliness** in MIG work is much more critical than with SMAW, as MIG wire is very short on contamination-beating ingredients. If it's true that time spent on preparation before SMAW welding is never wasted, then it's doubly true for MIG. The process can handle light surface rusting and mill scale, but that's all.

The safest bet is to grind everything back to bright metal, which is often easier said than done. Where possible, get rid of all paint, significant rust, grease, mud and plating from the weld area. Where a grinder won't reach, try flame heating and a wire brush.

Most jobs can be prepared well enough. But if joint strength is critical and you

can't get rid of the crud, recognize and accept MIG's limitations by switching to SMAW and hoping a lot. Contamination is contamination, whatever the welding process.

Where preparation is skimpy, the MIG arc will pop and miss, sound harsh and the weld pool will 'boil'. Stop and you'll probably find porosity. The only thing to do is to grind out the affected section and re-weld it.

You may notice a little porosity close to a start. If this is not down to contamination, it comes from a temporary shortage of shield gas. When the gun hasn't been used for several minutes, the supply pipework can empty. Give the trigger a quick squeeze

2.29. Tiny blob-tacks (a) in anything other than sheet steel won't be much good. There's little leeway for realignment (that is, belting the bits with a hammer) and poor fusion leaves a weak spot after welding. Tacks at least ⅜" (10mm) long are much better (b).

2.30. Long stickout and a burnt bulb-end on the filler wire will delay arc establishment and hurt fusion at the start of a weld run (a). For fast, clean starts and restarts, snip filler wire off at an sharp angle (b).

2.31. Gun control is better where two hands are used. Lay one over the swan neck (a) or rest swan neck between the first and second fingers (b).

to refill the gas line before you start, which also pushes out a little clean wire for snipping back.

MIG tacks: No differences here to SMAW tacks (page 30).

Starts and stops. On non-critical work you can get away with leaving the wire's burnt bulb-end intact (2.30A), but always chop it off where high strength is important. Poor fusion at the start of a weld concentrates stress wonderfully and is a prime site for failure. A clean, fast start needs high local current which implies good electrical contact, so first see that the welding return path is sound. Then snip off filler wire at an acute angle to leave a fine, sharp point; this will carry high current density and promote quick arcing (2.30B).

Snip the wire close to the contact tip to leave minimum current-draining stickout. The shorter the initial stickout the cleaner the start, but the greater the chance of filler fusing with the contact tip as the trigger is pulled, particularly at high voltages.

It may seem a good idea to begin a run by physically touching the filler wire on the start point and pulling the trigger, but this is not good practice. As the filler wire 'prop' collapses, the contact tip can touch the work and wire will want to burn back and fuse with it. If nothing else you end up wasting time while sorting out the mess. Neither is it a good idea to deal with excess stick-out

by putting a 90° bend in the wire. Arc establishment will be slower as current is not concentrated into a point area, and a nasty-looking 'whisker' is usually left behind.

For good control during starts use two hands. Lay the non-trigger hand over the gun's swan neck (2.31) for maximum control. Keep the gun upright to minimize stick-out and maximize heat input, then bring it smartly to working angle as you move off.

No matter what precautions are taken, MIG starts are prone to lack of fusion. It's a fast-moving process, so you can't wait around and weave while heat builds up as you can with SMAW. If you try, the arc is likely to play on a molten lump of filler and fusion will suffer anyway. To get the best fusion at the start of a joint, use a run-on plate — a piece of scrap alongside the start area on which the arc is first established.

Restarts along an existing weld can also suffer from initial lack of fusion. To make the best job, use the SMAW technique of starting just beyond the existing run's end, backtracking around the crater and continuing on down the joint (page 28). Where appearances are important, taper-grinding the start area to a hollow pad helps. It's harder to make undetectable restarts with MIG: they don't often

pass the fingernail test (page 28).

On the positive side, building-up the **end of a weld** run is easier with MIG. Just stop, circle and fill the finish area. Sometimes trapped gas erupts like a tiny volcano during or just after filling, threatening to leave a crack-promoting crater (2.32). This often happens when welding old pipe or box section; coating fume or water inside turns to gas or steam, whose escape route is

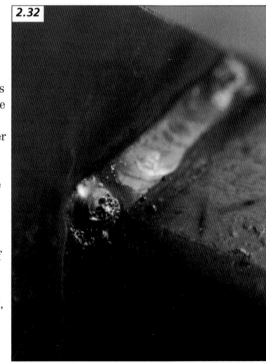

2.32. Escaping steam or gas can crater a good finish, or heave weld metal into a solidified 'pipe'. If the surrounding metal is pinholed too, grind and re-weld for a high-strength job.

finally blocked by the weld finish. Alternatively, the volcano can come from contaminants left behind after skimpy preparation. Whatever the cause, fill the crater by a short burst of weld immediately the eruption stops and the area is still semi-molten, or grind out the defect and re-weld.

MIG JOINTS

Most of the basic techniques explored with SMAW apply equally to MIG. But there are differences.

Butt joints. With unprepared square-edged sheet welded flat with no penetration or root gap, the upper thickness limit for full penetration is about 0.08" (2mm). Up to ⅛" (3mm) sheet can be handled by leaving a small gap, while vertical down work on anything but very thin sheet demands a gap to help penetration.

Material over ⅛" (3mm) thick will need edge preparation. A single Vee is OK up to ¹⁵⁄₃₂"-¹⁹⁄₃₂" (12-15mm), and a double Vee is best over this. If using the latter, balance out distortion by making one Vee double the depth of the other (a 30-60% split) and fully welding the small side first (2.33).

Leaving a small step or root face at the bottom of the Vee isn't necessary with MIG, as root penetration can be more readily controlled than with SMAW. If necessary, a small weave can be used on the root run to control penetration.

Horizontal/vertical joints (those where you're working side-to-side across a vertical plate) use the same attack as SMAW (page 26), though now arc length is not a variable. Use the minimum current and highest travel speed consistent with good fusion and penetration.

T-joints are a big heat sink, which should sound warning bells if you're using short circuit transfer and

2.33. Heavy sections can be welded with MIG given sufficient heat – which means higher voltages on thicker wires. For material over ⅝" (15mm), use asymmetrical double-Vee preparation split 30/60% as here. Weld the smaller Vee first, completing all runs before tackling the bigger part. With this technique, distortion is largely self-correcting.

thin wire. The weld is laid down on the edge of the vertical plate but usually away from the edge of the horizontal one, so in total there's more metal to absorb weld heat. Thus higher energy input is called for; one voltage step up over the equivalent-thickness flat butt is normally enough, with wire speed balanced to suit. If you're using spray transfer, weld a fillet in the flat position

so it forms a Vee under the gun. The pool is hot and fluid, and away from the flat position there's always the risk of sagging and undercut.

2.34. Fillet multi-runs (a) are sequenced the same as in SMAW work, i.e. a root pass, then a run half-overlapping the lower plate and another half-overlapping the vertical plate, and so on. Many passes went into this h/v fillet in 1" (25mm) steel (b), with no allowance made for distortion - see what the cooling weld metal has done for vertical plate alignment?

2.35. *Vertical down work with MIG is never strong, thanks to poor penetration and fusion in anything but thin sheet. But it has its uses: this long open corner joint in ½" (12.5mm) plate had a small gap at the top and a ¹⁹/₃₂" (15mm) gap at the bottom. It was welded in one pass, first with no weave and then with the gradual introduction of an inverted C-pattern to bridge the increasing gap.*

Sequence multi-run fillet passes as you would for SMAW. That's a root run first, then a half-overlap on the bottom plate and half-overlap on the top and so on (2.34). Lower the gun angle slightly to fire weld metal up on the vertical plate in run 3, keeping an eye open for undercut.

Don't slow down to try to fill a fillet, or poor fusion will be the likely result. And for the main passes don't weave if you can help it, as fillet legs are likely to end up uneven and the greater heat input risks undercut.

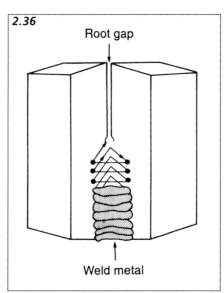

2.36. *Good penetration into a Vee comes from a triangular weave (top). The arc is taken into the root with a positive pushing movement, shown by the arrows. Move the gun rather than letting stickout grow. Work deliberately, pausing at the extremities to allow filling (see dots) and not travelling too far upwards for every traverse. In tight Vees, the nozzle can restrict access. If it looks as though you won't be able to reach the joint root without excessive stickout, use SMAW.*

Lap joints are only a different form of fillet, so the same rules apply. Use a slightly higher voltage than for the equivalent-thickness flat butt, don't work too slowly and avoid over-burning the top edge.

Vertical welding is generally easier than with SMAW, as there's no slag to complicate matters. General points first: the weld pool is easier to control if current is kept low, so work in the lower end of the 'good welding condition' wire speed range.

Gun angles are much the same as with SMAW but are less critical. Start with the nozzle at or just above horizontal when viewed from the side, and centered over the joint line when viewed from the front. Angles can be altered during the run to control fusion and penetration. Dropping the gun angle increases stickout, lowers current and makes the pool more controllable. But don't overdo it, or fusion will fall right

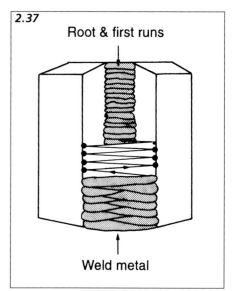

2.37. *A diagonal up-and-across weave (bottom) can be used on flatter faces, either to cover more width or to give a better-looking finish than an H-pattern movement. An inverted C gives a neat finish, too. Whichever you opt for, don't rush. Work deliberately, pausing at the black dots. Where vertical work on anything other than thin sheet is called for, travel upwards. Done properly, this guarantees penetration and strength.*

away and there's a risk that the arc will move outside the gas shield.

In general, keep the gun centered over the joint line to balance heat input into both plates. The obvious exception here is when welding thin material to thicker stuff, when heat can be biased toward the thick plate for better fusion and control. And be sure to pause at the joint edges to let the crater fill, or the weld will look as if mice have nibbled the edges.

Vertical down work has limited application with MIG. Penetration is never better than poor, so the technique is best restricted to sheet under ⅛" (3mm) or for gap-filling. On plate thicker than this there will always be a major lack of penetration and fusion.

Butt joints welded vertically down will always need a penetration (root) gap unless material is very thin indeed, and vertical down should not be used for anything other than an un-weaved root run or for filling gaps.

Gaps? No shortage of these in agricultural repair work. Here vertical down's lack of penetration can be turned into an advantage, allowing very wide holes to be filled without burn-through. Use a side-to-side weave to bridge whoppers (2.35).

2.38. Pics 2.36 and 2.37 turned into metal, using three vertical-up passes in ¹⁵⁄₃₂" (12mm) plate. The triangular-weave root run can't be seen but the following two can, and they're examples of good control. The second run was another triangular weave, while the third's necessary width came from a diagonal up-and-across movement. Heat input was controlled by using relatively low voltage and wire speed, working in the lower part of the 'good welding condition' range.

Vertical up welds are potentially very strong. Control is easier than with SMAW, so going upwards shouldn't cause too much alarm. You'll generally have to weave so there's the potential for good heat build-up and fusion. Penetration is also excellent as molten metal drains back from the weld pool, leaving clear parent plate for the arc to work on.

For vertical-up fillets, open corners and Vees, a triangular weave is good (2.36). Be very sure to push the whole nozzle into the root each time. If you let stickout grow to take the wire to the work, then fusion will suffer. As with SMAW move deliberately during all weaves, pausing at the outer corners for good infill. Don't move up too far for every traverse; aim for a compact series of weld steps. Keep the arc moving relatively quickly across the weld face, or you'll end up with a series of candle-wax blobs rather than a set of neat ladder rungs.

Subsequent run(s) can be made using a side-to-side weave, travelling only slightly upwards with each traverse, scudding faster across the face and pausing at the edges (2.37). Alternatively an inverted C-shaped weave works well, but watch for changes in stickout at the edges.

Vertical up's excellent penetration sets a lower limit to material thickness and penetration gap size. Sheet under ⅛" (3mm) is prone to undercut and eventual burn-through, while working in a gap means difficulty in controlling penetration and maintaining a continuous arc. Wire will shoot through, interrupting the arc and leaving an untidy 'whisker' on the far side.

Overhead work. Some say this isn't recommended with MIG, but using short circuit transfer it's quite feasible. Use similar settings to equivalent flat welds (perhaps with a little more wire speed), but travel a little faster to avoid excess weld metal build-up. Both straight root runs and subsequent weaves are possible. Keep a closer eye than normal on the nozzle as falling spatter blocks it very quickly, especially at higher voltages.

Faults, Problems and Remedies

Mistakes happen. The following sections cover technique, equipment setting, equipment faults and oddities.

Technique-based problems

Fault: Travelling too fast. Weld bead is 'stringy' and irregular; ripples are pulled into Vee-shapes. Fusion/ penetration is poor.

Remedy: Slow down. (page 49).

Fault: Travelling too slowly. Bead heavy and wide, ripples U-shaped. Risk of poor penetration and fusion.

Remedy: Speed up. (page 49).

Fault: Stickout too long. Bead irregular, fusion patchy, much spatter.

Remedy: Reduce stickout to ¼"-⅜" (6-10mm). (page 48)

Fault: Weld start poorly fused or not continuous with existing weld metal (2.39)

Remedies: Check return lead connection (high resistance lowers current and hence hurts fusion). Snip back old filler wire at an acute angle to ¼" (6mm) stickout before starting. Wait for arc to establish before moving off, but don't overdo it. If necessary, use a run-on plate alongside weld area to establish arc and move on to joint.

Fault: Severe undercut and sagging in vertical up work

(2.40). **Remedy:** Lower voltage to bring heat down, reduce filler wire volume by setting wire speed to low end of acceptable range. When weaving, travel smartly across weld face to avoid heavy build-up. Angle each traverse slightly upward to limit metal deposited, but still pause at edges to fill joint. 2.41 shows several faults. The weld wanders off-line. Its lower section (1) has too much upward movement for every traverse, giving weak, edges and heavy metal deposit on face. The middle section (2) is better as upward travel for each traverse is reduced. The upper

2.39. A poor MIG restart. New metal (A) hasn't overlapped the old finish (B), leaving a weak spot.

section (3) is about right, with little upward movement for each traverse and quick passage across the face. The outcome is a compact, fast weld with controlled metal deposit.

Fault: Poor joint area preparation.

Result: Arc won't run smoothly and develops 'machine-gun' staccato crackle; stubbing (page 45) may occur. Problem may clear itself along joint. Uneven weld quality with areas of pinholing. Joint strength poor. **Cause:** Patchy contamination along weld zone, typical of rust dirt, paint and oil. **Remedy:** Grind out existing poor weld, thoroughly grind unwelded area and try again. Flame-heat and wire brush areas where a grinder

2.40. This SMAW bead shows how too much heat and poor technique makes a mess of vertical up work, and the same goes for MIG. Yet see how gravity drains molten metal back from the weld pool (top)? This gives great potential for penetration when the job is done with less heat and more control.

2.41. Common vertical up weave problems (a) and their breakdown (b). Consistent weaving gives a good, strong result (c).

can't reach. If good preparation is not possible, don't use MIG where high strength is important.

Equipment setting problems

Fault: Voltage too low.

Bead is narrow, round or oval, humped on plate with very little edge fusion. Penetration and joint strength poor. **Remedies:** Increase voltage (optimising wire speed each time) until bead flattens and fuses. If only a small increase in fusion is required, supply more current by increasing wire feed speed. Upper wire speed limit is felt by the onset of stubbing. Fine heat input adjustment is possible by decreasing stickout, thus increasing current. NB: A wide humped bead can also come from too-high wire speed with correct voltage. To pinpoint this, reduce speed step by step. If bead flattens and fuses, voltage is okay.

Fault: Voltage too high.

Penetration/fusion excessive, leading to undercut. Burn-through very likely on thin sheet. Bead flat, may be irregular, looks 'burnt' with excessive spatter. Ripples pulled into exaggerated Vee-shapes. **Remedies:** Reduce voltage and re-optimize wire speed. If necessary/possible, go down to next wire size. For small heat input changes, reduce current by first reducing wire speed and then increasing stickout to maximum of ⅜" (10mm).

Fault: Weld porous.

Weld metal coarse, like mousse or Aero chocolate. **Cause 1:** Lack of shield gas. **Remedy:** Is there gas in the cylinder? Is its spindle valve open and regulator set? Otherwise, check gun and nozzle for spatter blockage. If all is OK follow gas path through set, checking for flow after solenoid valve and before gun. **Cause 2:** Contamination along weld line. Grind out and re-weld. If good clean-up is not possible, use SMAW.

Cause 3: Filler wire rusty. Strip wire off spool until clean coils are reached, then add spring clip and steel wool over wire, followed by clip and cloth pad to clean wire before feed rollers. Keep spool in dry place when not used.

Fault: Gun jumps in hand, smooth arc noise breaks up while stickout visibly lengthens and shortens.

Cause 1: Stubbing. Wire is being fed faster than it burns back, thus physically pushing gun away from weld area. **Remedy:** Reduce wire speed.

Equipment troubles

Fault: Arc unsteady.

Cause 1: Torch guide tube coiled or bent at sharp angle, especially where high wire speed is needed. Straighten and retry. **Cause 2:** Worn, damaged or loose contact tip. Check condition. **Cause 3:** Weld zone contamination. Thoroughly regrind unwelded area, grind defective weld and redo. **Cause 4:** Wire feed rollers slipping. Check roller pressure, spool drag setting and wire condition. Wire should be rust- and oil-free; spool drag set to just stop overrun when trigger is released, and roller pressure set so wire just stops when braked between fingers. **Cause 5:** Dirty torch liner. Blow out with dry compressed air; replace altogether if necessary. **Cause 6:** Wire drive motor or speed control circuitry unstable. Speak to machine supplier for fix.

Fault: No wire feed or wire speed uncontrollable.

If motor not running with trigger pressed, check that the mains power and set are on(!), that speed and voltage are selected on front panel and that fuses on mains supply and any in the set are OK. Check gun trigger contacts or microswitch. If motor operates but there's no feed, check roller setting and wire spool for tangles. If feed speed is uncontrollable, control circuitry has gone berserk. Telephone

the manufacturer.

Oddities

Fault: Joint failure from poor fusion.

Cause: low heat input. Voltage/wire speed too low, forward speed too slow, combination of thin filler wire and short circuit transfer. **Remedies:** Change to thicker wire/higher current if available. Use spray transfer, if set capacity and wire diameter allow, for flat work and horizontal/vertical fillets. Weld vertically upwards in short circuit transfer mode to increase heat build-up. Travel at speed that keeps wire arcing to front of visibly fusing molten pool. If extra heat input not possible through set output/positional limitations, switch to SMAW.

Fault: Volcano-like crater or pipe-like knob at end of run.

Snapping off projection shows pinholed weld metal underneath. Caused by contamination from escaping gas or steam. **Remedy:** Fill crater with burst of weld while still red hot or grind off projection and re-weld.

Fault: Arc wanders uncontrollably between the wire and work.

Cause: Arc blow, typical of DC processes. Strong, directional magnetic fields are pulling the arc out of shape. Typically happens when working in a tight corner or holding work with a magnetic clamp. **Remedy:** not always 100% curable. Keep the welding return lead's clamp close to the weld area. Weld directly toward or away from it. Swap magnetic clamp for mechanical one or move it further from weld area.

GASLESS MIG

Having discovered the simple joy of MIG welding, you'll find it stops once you wheel the set out of the workshop. Unless the weather is very quiet or you've cobbled together a shelter, the wind will whip away the shield gas to leave holey (and wholly) unsatisfactory joints. And that's a bummer.

But what if the welding wire could pretend to be a stick electrode and take along its own gas shield? Flux core wire does just that, as farms using it for hardfacing will already know. Rather than being solid like the usual stuff, cored wire is a hollow tube packed with flux … like a stick electrode turned inside-out. The technique is known formally as flux cored arc welding (FCAW) and informally as gasless MIG. It can be performed with conventional sets, given several limitations and some changes in setup/technique.

The box 'Roll your own' details how cored wire is made. Like Bernard Madoff it's been called several names; flux-cored, gasless or self-shielded wire are the most common. Developed first in the 1950s for shipyards and other heavy industries that can't wait until the breeze stops blowing, cored wire can join most materials and do pretty much everything that a stick electrode can, including handling more contamination than solid MIG wire.

But don't shout 'eureka' and bring out the dancing girls. Most cored welding wires are designed for DC negative sets…while the smaller single-phase units found on farms are universally DC positive. On top of this, cored wire is expensive: a roll costs about five times more than solid wire. So while it can bring some of MIG's speed and ease of use to the great outdoors, cored wire is far from a magic bullet.

Witches' brew

Much of cored wire's ability comes from the flux, whose main jobs are to shield the molten weld from oxygen and nitrogen, stabilize the arc, squirrel away impurities in the slag and then protect the cooling weld.

Sound familiar? It should – the core powder is much like the flux on a stick electrode, only not bound into a solid mass. De-oxidizers and de-nitrifiers handle contamination from the air, other components help wetting and cleaning, while metals like chromium and molybdenum can go in to boost weld toughness.

Being packed with flux, core wires are bulkier than their solid equivalent. The smallest diameter on offer is 0.035" (1.0mm) – compared to 0.023" (0.6mm) in solid wire – with sizes more normally spanning 1/16-5/32" (1.6-2.4mm). This affects the minimum welding current required and the minimum material thickness that can be joined, as we'll see later.

Cored wire comes in many grades. But many won't work without a separate booster supply of shielding, usually CO_2 or an argon/CO_2 mix from a cylinder. Of those that can go solo most need to run DC negative; that is, with the torch plugged into the negative side of the power supply. Which, as we've said, run-of-the-mill MIG sets can't handle.

Cross off wire types that won't work in farming and the choice is cut dramatically. For example ESAB offers one wire – 7100 Ultra, with equivalents on offer from other brands. It's a very simple beast, able to run DC positive and join mild, medium-tensile and cast steels in a moderate breeze. Comparable to basic ER70S-6 wire and more versatile than a general-purpose mild steel rod, it's close in nature to a E7018 low hydrogen stick electrode. The snag is that this wire is not happy on vertical or overhead joints, which limits usefulness in stockyard and machinery repair.

Setup and technique

Three areas change on switching to cored wire – the torch, welding technique and plant settings. We'll start at the business end and work out from there.

- **The torch**. With no shield gas there's no need for a nozzle, so off it can come. This leaves the torch tip exposed like a skinned rabbit. Access into tight places is much better, but you'll need to watch tip positioning (as of course it's live when the arc is running) and take care not to ding any torch threads left exposed. If you're feeling flush, buy a specific cored-wire torch. The set's existing feed rolls and torch liner can probably be used as they stand, remembering to change rolls to suit the new wire diameter. If these can't deliver an even feed without major pressure increase, replacement knurled rollers will do the business without crushing the wire.

- **Technique.** Here (as always) preparation comes first. Thanks to it's scouring abilities, cored wire can handle as much contamination as a good mild steel stick electrode. This makes it particularly good for joints where poor access renders 100% cleaning impossible. Grind off paint and platings where you can and don't skimp, but cored wire can put up with modest rust and mill scale if it must.

- Next comes **travel direction.** Cored wires work best when the torch is pulled, rather than pushed. That is, the tip trails the operator's hand, as with stick welding. Pulling the torch keeps molten weld metal more where you want it, maintains the best gas cover and produces a fuller, more even slag coat on the weld. Travel speed is set by the same considerations as for all MIG: keep the arc concentrated more on parent metal than the molten pool, and look to fill the joint and fuse the edges.

- **Stickout.** See page 48 for definition. Stickout must change dramatically. The flux in a cored wire needs to be warmed before it reaches the arc or it won't do its best. The more stickout you give, the hotter flux gets through resistance heating of the wire. Try 1-1 ¼"(25-30mm) as a starting point

2.42. *Cored wire brings changes from conventional MIG technique. The torch is best pulled; that is when the welder's hand leads the arc, as here. And see how visual wire stickout (the distance between the contact tip and arc) is much longer? Use 1-1 ³⁄₁₆" (25-30mm) rather than the usual ¼"-³⁄₈"(6-10mm). This torch still wears its nozzle, though shield gas isn't flowing. Take it off for better access into tight spots.*

2.43. *Stickout matters with cored wire. This H-V fillet in ¼" (6mm) plate shows what happens when it strays too far. Holding stickout at 1-1 ¼" (25-30mm) allows good flux pre-heating and produces a tidy result (left). Halving stickout cuts flux effectiveness and leaves a weak pinholed weld (center). Extending stickout too far drops arc current so there's not enough heat to burn off the wire: the bead is humped with poor fusion and penetration (right).*

(2.42). Here's yet another of welding's balancing acts. Too little stickout stops the flux working properly, so gas cover breaks down and you get pinholes in the weld. Too much stickout bleeds off energy into heating the wire, so there's less to run the arc and penetration/fusion suffers. Take a look at 2.43 to see all this in action.

- **Voltage and wire speed.** Compared with a solid wire, the cored version's thin walls have a much smaller cross-section to carry current. Lower voltages and wire speeds are needed, yet the high current concentration still gives good potential penetration. On the other hand, burning off the flux takes substantial energy. So the welding set has to be able to put out about 200A minimum for ¹⁄₁₆" (1.6mm) cored wire.

As with normal MIG operation, each voltage step on the set links to a corresponding band of feed speed to deliver good welding conditions. In this band, voltage and wire feed are in balance. Expect to use lower speeds and voltages than with solid wire, and as usual your ears and eyes confirm when you've hit the sweet spot – the arc pops and crackles, albeit more softly than with solid wire, and spatter is at a minimum.

Cored wire should feed into the weld pool steadily without whooshing or stubbing, though there's usually a dewdrop or 'boot' of molten material at the tip. Compared with conventional short circuit-transfer MIG work there will be more spatter as some metal is transferred across the arc in a globular way; but otherwise the joint should be neat and tidy (2.44). Slag is thinner than with stick electrodes, lifting off easily (2.45). Chip and wire brush between runs. Slag traps are less likely than with stick electrodes if voltage and wire speed are right.

Other limitations

The minimum diameter of ESAB 7100 Ultra wire is 0.035" (0.09mm), so it needs a fair whack of current to run properly. This calls for a capable welding plant. It also defines the minimum material thickness weldable without burn-through; about ⅛" (3mm). Having said that, the process's high tolerance to variable stickout length and freedom from a separate shield gas blanket means that thinner stuff and irregular gaps can be tackled; adjust welding current on the hoof, by varying stickout. Heavy sections can be welded with appropriate preparation and multiple passes. No special pre-heating or cooling is needed with mild steel.

Here's a caution to finish. Welding with cored wire produces a lot of fume, which is definitely not good stuff to breathe. Outdoor work on a breezy day should be fine, and is the very time when you'll want to exploit cored wire anyway. Indoors, weld as close as possible to an open door or in moving air from a window. Ideally use a fume extractor. If that's not possible, wear a disposable respirator under your welding helmet or invest in an aspirated filter unit.

2.44. Cored wire MIG produces smart beads marked out by spatter. The latter is inevitable as metal transfer is partly by short circuit and partly across the arc, so some gets lost on the way.

2.45. Flux coating is much thinner than with stick electrodes, lifting away very easily from a tidy bead.

Roll Your Own

How do you make welding wire that thinks it's a sausage roll? By sneaking up on it in small steps. Steel arrives at the factory as rolls of flat sheet. This is cut into smaller and smaller strips by drawing it through roller guillotines. Once the strip is the right width a series of shaped rollers form it into a U-tube, which then passes at right angles just below a wide conveyor belt.

Down the belt comes a stream of powdered flux, spread in a thin layer the width of the belt. Flux rains in a steady curtain on to the U-tube whizzing by below, partly filling it. More rollers then curl the tube closed.

By now the wire is about 0.2" (5mm) in diameter. To bring it down to the final size of 0.035-3/32" (1.0–2.4mm) it's drawn progressively through several sizing dies, compressing the flux core and getting mighty warm along the way. All this happens on a long, humming machinery line. Finally, the sized wire is wound on to big spools before taking the short hop across to the spooling area, where it's dispensed either on to consumer-sized reels or big 550lb (250kg) packs for use with unattended robot welders.

2.46. A disposable respirator.

Gas Welding and Cutting

As MIG sets come down in price and move into farming, buyers seem less interested in gas welding. This is a real pity. For after a credit card, oxyacetylene actually is your 'flexible friend'. Nothing else can fusion weld, bronze weld, braze, cut and heat. Even if gas gear's welding ability is ignored, having a flame for bending, straightening, cutting, unseizing bolts and creating general mayhem is more than just convenient. In any serious workshop it's essential.

Buying: new or second-hand?

Unless you're quite sure what you're looking for and at, buying second-hand gas equipment is not a good idea. With any of this stuff it's quite possible to blow yourself up, and using worn-out gear is an easy way to go about it. So tread warily around a farm-sale set, internet or local-paper bargain. With any gas equipment the motto has to be 'If in doubt, don't buy'. Let someone else have the bonfire: safety must come first.

If you're still tempted, look for manky fittings; cracked, bent or otherwise knocked-about gauges; damaged seatings on all hardware and split or cracked hoses. Some sizes of oxygen cylinders are now being filled to 3,450psi (230bar) pressure, so it's essential to be sure that a second-hand regulator is marked either '3,450psi service' or '4350psi service' ('230bar service' or '300bar service'). Older regulators will only be rated to 3000 psi (200bar) and must not be used where there is the slightest risk of connection to higher-pressure cylinders.

Be aware that gas cylinders remain the property of the supplying company so won't be the vendor's to sell. Before equipment changes hands, the existing cylinders should go back to the nearest depot and any outstanding rental should be settled. The remaining hardware can then be sold, with the buyer renting fresh cylinders in his/her name.

The best way to own gas gear is to buy new. Looked after, it'll last a very long while. Work out your requirement in terms of material thickness for welding and cutting, then trundle off to a reputable supplier. He'll fit you up with quality kit and be there when service is needed.

The big bang... don't have one

Picture 3.1 covers naming of parts. As it's wholly possible to do yourself and others mortal damage with oxyacetylene equipment, no excuses are offered for devoting space to the ground rules.

Please don't flick through this section. Understand exactly what's what before trying out new or second-hand gear. If in doubt over any procedure, ask the gas or equipment supplier for advice.

Gas cylinders are best treated as potential bombs. A cylinder explosion in a workshop doesn't leave many

3.1a
Adjusting screw
Regulator
Regulator safety valve
Flashback arrestor
Spindle valve
Spindle key
Spark gun
Cutting nozzle
Welding nozzles
Goggles
Hoses
Oxygen cylinder (black)
Acetylene cylinder (maroon)

3.1b
Cutting oxygen needle valve
Cutting lever
Blowpipe
Needle valves
Check valve
Welding mixing chamber
Cutting nozzle
Welding nozzle

3.1. Equipment for oxyacetylene welding and cutting. Note the flashback arrestors in (a). These are required on new models and very much advisable on existing ones, both for secondary safety and to fulfil the farm's duty of care to employees.

pieces to be picked up, and you get no second chance. The cylinder supplier is required by law to inspect and pressure-test each unit regularly, so although a fresh cylinder may have leaked away some of its contents before coming home, it's intrinsically safe. Explosions and fires are thus down to bad practice or equipment neglect. Safety is solely the operator's business.

So how best to look after the kit and (by implication) yourself? The rules aren't hard, though they may seem many.

Cylinder care is a good place to start. Acetylene gas is only slightly compressible before it goes bang, so it's sold dissolved in acetone. The acetone is held in an inert matrix but isn't fixed by it, so laying a cylinder down lets liquid collect in the neck. If this acetone is allowed to reach regulator diaphragms and hoses, it attacks them with eventual safety consequences.

Thus cylinders must be used upright, and ideally moved and stored upright. But it's not always practical to move a cylinder without laying it down. To let acetone drain back where it belongs, a cylinder that's been horizontal for more than a few minutes should be left vertical for at least a couple of hours before use, and eight or more hours is better. And yes, people do get away without doing this. But acetone gnaws away at rubber parts over time, unseen. Eventually equipment will fail, always with expensive (and potentially nasty) consequences.

Fitting regulators to cylinders is straightforward. New cylinders arrive with plastic protectors on their outlets, so these must come off. Regulators and fittings for the fuel gases acetylene and propane have left-hand threads, while oxygen threads are right-handed. Thus the two can't be mixed up. But don't be tempted to swap fittings between different fuel gases: the threads may allow it, but gases vary in delivery pressures and permissible flow rates. Using inappropriate bits can end in tears.

With regulators to hand that match both the gases and maximum cylinder pressures, clear the cylinder necks of water and insect life by a quick 'snift' – that is, crack open the spindle valve a little so gas can blast out debris. Then fit the regulators so that their dial faces can be easily seen and their hose outlets don't interfere with spindle key action. Tighten regulators and hose connections with the spanner supplied. If this has long since gone into a tractor driver's tool box, use a normal-length spanner. *If any joint leaks after reasonable tightening, find out why rather than over-tightening or bodging leaks with tape.*

Regulator life will be longer if the central pressure-adjusting screw is backed off after use. Not between jobs, but overnight or through the weekend. If left screwed in, the underlying diaphragm and spring will slowly take on a permanent 'set' and accurate adjustment eventually won't be possible. There's a safety angle, too. With the regulator screw backed right off, gas can't escape down the hoses when forgetfulness or a leaky spindle valve leaves gas in the regulator.

Oxygen regulator gauges carry the warning 'Use no oil.' This is not whimsy: ignore it at your peril. High-pressure oxygen meeting oil or grease anywhere in the system (including the blowpipe) can give a tidy explosion. If you must lubricate sticky fittings, use only dry graphite.

Should an oxygen cylinder regulator blow or be sheared off, it's a bit like letting go of the neck of a huge balloon. But this balloon is made of steel, and nothing will stand in its way; not walls, not equipment and certainly not a human body. For this reason it's

3.2

3.2. Portability comes from small cylinders on trolleys, which accept normal peripherals. Cylinder life is OK for welding, but cutting quickly empties the oxygen.

major folly to carry or lift a cylinder by foreloader or forklift, and hoisting with slippery chains or weak rope is right out. Keep your cylinders (including spares) chained into a trolley or tied back against a wall.

More shock horror

We haven't finished yet. Bodging hose connections can lead to trouble through leaks, as can using old, perished hoses. Keep hoses looped in gentle bends while out of use, as wrapping them tightly accelerates cracking.

Don't be tempted to repair a hose with a length of copper pipe, as copper reacts with acetylene to produce unstable, explosive acetylide compounds.

Check hose and blowpipe connections now and again for tightness. Acetylene's distinctive whiff is easily picked up, so nose round the regulator and pipework; the gas smells like someone's breath the morning after a particularly significant curry. Only a true dumbo would use a match to find an acetylene leak, and then they'd only do it once.

Oxygen has no smell, so track down leaks by ear or by using a dilute soap solution. Brush it on and watch for bubbles. Leaks from spindle or needle valves can usually be cured by controlled tightening of the gland nut, but don't overdo the spannering.

Though not inflammable itself, oxygen very actively supports burning. Oxygen-impregnated clothing will flare like a beacon if a spark lands on it, and people have died this way. *It follows that oxygen must never be used in place of compressed air to blow down clothing, to clear a bench or to power air tools.*

Finally, for anything short of very heavy cutting, don't open either cylinder valve more than one full turn or it can't be shut quickly in an emergency. Less is usually plenty for normal gas delivery. And always park the spindle key on the acetylene cylinder's valve, for this is the one that must be shut first in case of trouble.

That's a run-through of the main safety points. Others will be covered as they come up.

Backfires, flashbacks and arrestors

Backfires. You'll hear occasional pops and bangs during welding or cutting. At best the pop makes you jump; at worst you're on the way to trouble. What's happening? Small-scale bangs are backfires. Gas is igniting uncontrollably, rather than burning steadily at the nozzle. Common backfire causes are:

• The nozzle touching the work or temporarily blocking with spatter. Gas flow stops, the flame goes out and then

reignites with a bang. If this blows the flame out, don't try relighting with both gases flowing or another, possibly bigger bang may result. Shut off acetylene first at the blowpipe needle valve, then oxygen. Purge both gas lines and relight, follow the steps on page 64.

• The nozzle overheating through working in a confined space, so the gas mix fires off inside it. To cool it down, turn off the acetylene flow and plunge the whole nozzle into warm water: a cold bath can cause cracks. Oxygen flow will keep water out while the torch head is pretending to be a submarine. Check nozzle tightness afterwards as thermal shock can loosen it.

• A worn nozzle. When the gas exit hole(s) wear, backfire risk goes up. Reface or replace the tip (page 76).

• Low gas pressures. If the gas column is moving out of the nozzle too slowly, the flame will burn back down it. In marginal pressure conditions the result is isolated 'pops' or sometimes a machine-gun string of mini-explosions.

In worse cases this popping escalates into a sustained backfire. The flame disappears down into the blowpipe's mixing chamber and burns there; you'll hear a thin screeching noise and see a stream of black smoke coming from the nozzle. Act quickly now, or the blowpipe can melt. *Shut off oxygen to starve the flame* (the only time when oxygen is shut down first) and then the fuel gas. Purge both lines (see page 64) before relighting. To stop the banging increase pressures a little, keeping them balanced if appropriate.

Don't let backfiring go on as it may lead to worse things. Normally, gas is fed down two hoses into the blowpipe. Where feed pressures are not exactly equal (and they seldom are), gas from the higher pressure line wants to push

3.3. Check valves are a legal requirement at the blowpipe end of hoses. Test often by blowing through them – an arrow (top right) shows direction of gas flow.

into the lower pressure one. If it does the result is a potentially explosive mix in one hose, which could be triggered by a backfire's flame front. To stop this, OSHA requires that **check valves** (3.3) are fitted at the blowpipe end of each hose. These are one-way valves which close when gas tries to backtrack. A backfire's relatively low-pressure, cool flame front is stopped by check valves.

Test the valves occasionally as carbon build-up can make them leaky. Unscrew the hose, put the valve end under water and blow down the other. If the check valve is OK, no air should pass in the regulator direction but flow should be free toward the blowpipe.

Flashback. Check valves are only a first line of defence which can't handle all eventualities. It's possible in normal use to generate extreme pressure imbalance; perhaps when something steps, falls or drives onto a hose, when it kinks, or when one cylinder runs empty of gas. At this point you can be heading toward a flashback.

With one hose blocked or out of gas, any backfire will be much more severe. If the flame is fast enough to jump the check valve(s) and enter the hose(s), these can burst. The associated high pressure wave can destroy the regulator(s) and detonate the acetylene cylinder contents,

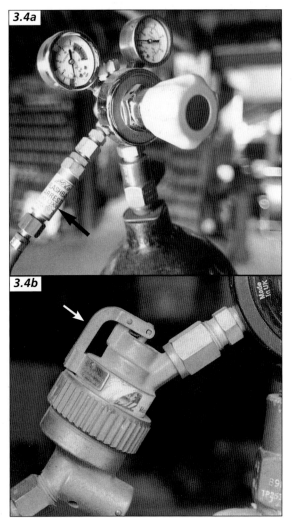

3.4a

3.4b

3.4. A simple flashback arrestor (a) snuffs out a high-velocity flame front before it can reach a cylinder. Some also have an internal link that melts in flame heat to cut off gas flow. Others can reset automatically. More expensive varieties (b) have pressure-sensitive valving and are re-settable via an external arm (arrow).

producing a lethal explosion.

So flashbacks are very bad news. Good working practice is the key to avoiding trouble, but both common sense and OSHA strongly recommend fitting **flashback arrestors** to both regulators (3.4). These snuff out a flame front before it can get to the regulator, with some designs also tripping a valve to stop gas flow. Costing from $20-$60 at the time of writing, they are recommended for all farm gas equipment.

Mind you, such mechanical backup should never be needed. Sort out the cause of backfires before they grow, watch hoses around stock and machinery and don't run cylinders right down to their last dregs. *And before lighting or relighting a blowpipe, purge each line to make sure it contains only the gas it should.*

Table 3.1: **Safe start-up/shutdown procedure for oxyacetylene welding equipment.**

1. Make sure blowpipe needle valves are closed. Back off regulator screws if necessary. Check all connections are tight, especially at the blowpipe.
2. Stand facing regulator dials. These usually have blow-out backs, so facing the dial is safest. Open acetylene cylinder spindle valve slowly to a maximum of one turn; slow opening means no pressure shock to regulators. Ditto oxygen spindle valve. Leave key in acetylene spindle valve.
3. Gas is now into both regulators. Two-stage models will show pressure on one dial.
4. Purging and pressure setting are combined. Open the blowpipe acetylene needle valve. Adjust pressure regulating screw so gauge shows nominal pressure required by nozzle (table 3.3). Let gas flow for a few seconds to purge system, then close needle valve. Repeat the procedure for oxygen. NB: Pressures can be set accurately only under free-flow conditions. Back pressure from a closed needle valve gives false reading.
5. With the nozzle pointed upwards, open acetylene needle valve a little and light gas. Use spark igniter; matches or a lighter risk burning fingers.
6. Open the needle valve further until acetylene flame is 'bright' – smoke at tip is all but gone. If this can't be achieved, increase pressure at the regulator until it can. If flame separates from nozzle tip, gas speed is too high. Close needle valve until it rejoins.
7. Gently open oxygen needle valve and feed in gas until required flame type is achieved (page 66). Again, slightly increase pressure at regulator if necessary. Fine control of flame type comes only from the blowpipe needle valves.
8. To shut down, close acetylene needle valve first. Flame thus goes out quickly. Turning off oxygen first leaves a smoky acetylene flame, able to burn up to – and perhaps inside – the nozzle. The only exception is in the case of sustained backfire, where the nozzle squeals and puts out black smoke. In this case turn off oxygen first to starve the fire.
9. Close oxygen needle valve.
10. Close acetylene cylinder spindle valve, then ditto for oxygen. This traps gas inside cylinders.
11. Drain gas from rest of system by opening blowpipe acetylene needle valve. Line pressure gauge will fall to zero. Repeat for oxygen.
12. If welding has finished for more than a couple of hours, back off regulator adjusting screws. This prolongs regulator life as well as stopping the progress of any gas leaking past cylinder spindle valve. NB: Cylinder pressure gauge may creep back up over time if spindle valve is leaking. Don't be tempted to jam valve shut by hammering the key or using pipe for extra leverage!

Note: Accurate flame balancing is possible only with nozzle in good physical condition.

Lighting and shutdown: One step at a time

Tables 3.1 and 3.2 lay out the safe step-by-step procedure for lighting and shutting down gas equipment. Follow it to be sure that gas flow through equipment is under control and that lines contain only one gas. **Purging** means clearing the system of any mixed gas.

Getting Started

First, eye protection. The intense glare from gas welding/cutting plus the risk of physical eye damage from flying sparks makes good goggles essential, even for the briefest operation. Lenses should be made to ANSI Z71, with shade density chosen for the job. When the lenses have pitted and the strap has as much elasticity as a piece of string, give your eyes a treat and buy new goggles.

With those sorted out, the equipment safely set up and the lighting/shut down procedures understood, all that's left is to choose a nozzle, set the pressures and adjust the flame. Welding comes first, cutting on page 75.

Which nozzle to use? Table 3.3 relates material thickness to size. But experience soon shows that thickness isn't all that matters. The idea is to find a nozzle that brings work quickly up to heat, yet isn't so big that the weld pool is hard to control.

Most farms will use oxyacetylene welding on steel sheet. Work on stuff thicker than ⅛" (3mm) gets increasingly slow, takes a lot of heat, causes considerable distortion and uses more and more gas, so arc welding takes over. Most jobs will be covered with nozzle sizes 1, 2, 3, 5 and possibly 7, though one-offs may call for something bigger.

Nozzles are usually stamped with their size (1-90) and the maximum gas volume delivered per hour. So a number 1 nozzle is also stamped '26', a number 2 '57' and so on. The smallest nozzles are used where modest heat input is enough, while a number 90 will roast chickens at a distance and empties cylinders in minutes.

Table 3.2: **Safe start-up/shutdown procedure for oxyacetylene cutting equipment.**

Start with all three blowpipe needle valves shut. Then follow points 1–5 in Table 3.1 to purge hoses, set initial pressures and light the acetylene flame.
6. If the acetylene flame still smokes with needle valve fully open, increase regulator pressure a little until it stops.
8. Feed in oxygen using cutting head spindle valve until flame is neutral.
9. Operate cutting lever and check flame stays neutral. If not, bring to neutrality while holding down cutting lever, using attachment's needle valve. If one or more pre-heater flames are shorter than the others, shut down. Slacken the nozzle nut and turn the nozzle so its inlet holes are not in line with those in the head. Tighten, purge and relight.
10. Shutdown is the same as table 3.1. After draining oxygen line of gas, close both oxygen needle valves.

Table 3.3: **Welding nozzle sizes, recommended pressure settings and material thickness weldable.** (Courtesy Murex).
See how gas pressures rise with nozzle size but stay balanced. Figures are a guide only, and refer to clean mild steel worked indoors.

Mild Steel		Thickness	Nozzle	Operating Pressure				Gas Consumption			
				Acetylene		Oxygen		Acetylene		Oxygen	
mm	in	swg	size	bar	psi	bar	psi	l/h	ft3/h	l/h	ft3/h
0.9	0.0354	20	1	0.14	2	0.14	2	28	1	28	1
1.2	0.045	18	2	0.14	2	0.14	2	57	1	57	2
2	0.0787	14	3	0.14	2	0.14	2	86	3	86	3
2.6	0.1024	12	5	0.14	2	0.14	2	140	5	140	5
3.2	1/8	10	7	0.14	2	0.14	2	200	7	200	7
4	3/32	8	10	0.21	3	0.21	3	280	10	280	10
5	3/16	6	13	0.28	4	0.28	4	370	13	370	13
6.5	1/4	3	18	0.28	4	0.28	4	520	18	520	18
8.2	5/16	0	25	0.42	6	0.42	6	710	25	710	25
10	3/8	4/0	35	0.63	9	0.63	9	1000	35	1000	35
13	1/2	7/0	45	0.35	5	0.35	5	1300	45	1300	45
19	3/4		55	0.43	6	0.43	6	1600	55	1600	55
23	1		70	0.49	7	0.49	7	2000	70	2000	70
25	1+		90	0.63	9	0.63	9	2500	90	2500	90

psi = lb/in² or lbf/in²

Table 3.4: **Nozzles and pressures for flame cleaning, acetylene fuel gas**

Nozzle	Fuel gas pressure		Oxygen pressure	
	Bar	psi	Bar	psi
2" (50mm) flat	0.49	7	0.57	8
4" (100mm) flat	0.70	10	0.70	10
6" (150mm) flat	0.85	12	0.85	12

3.5. Nozzles to extend equipment usefulness. The flame cleaner (top) is good where a diffuse heat source is required, like taking off paint or surface rust from otherwise unreachable areas prior to welding. A gouging nozzle (center) cuts grooves, also useful prior to welding where a grinder can't reach. For rapid, economical heating prior to unseizing or straightening something, the heating nozzle (bottom) is best. All the above come in different sizes and may need a different mixer for the blowpipe.

Where thin mild steel is to be welded, start with a number 1 nozzle. First you'll need to set the flame.

Flame setting

A gas flame's nature changes with the balance of oxygen and acetylene being

3.6. Storing spare nozzles in a wood block keeps them out of harm's way – and you'll know where to find them.

burnt, with different flame types suited to different jobs (3.7). Most welding needs a neutral flame; bronze welding and brazing calls for a slightly oxidizing flame, while aluminum and some hard-facing applications need a gently carburizing flame.

The three types are easily produced by twiddling the blowpipe needle valves, with differences best seen through gas goggles. Here's how they run.

But first, have a peek at the nozzle's

tip – it needs to be clean, with a square-edged round hole. If it's worn, re-face it (pages 75-76). Set regulator pressures using Table 3.3, purge hoses and light the acetylene. Open the blowpipe needle valve until smoke at the flame tip all but disappears. If this doesn't happen, increase acetylene pressure at the regulator until the flame just separates from the nozzle tip. Then reduce pressure until the flame just sits back on the tip. (3.7e).

Feed in some oxygen from the needle valve; the flame turns from yellow to white. Adding a little more oxygen resolves the flame into three sections – a blue central cone next to the nozzle, a white 'feather' beyond it and an outer, less distinct envelope.

Opening the oxygen needle valve shortens the feather. All the time you can see it there's more carbon-rich acetylene in the mix than oxygen, so the flame is **carburizing.** It's also cool. Working with such a flame leaves a weld that's hard but brittle.

As oxygen supply is increased the feather blends down into the central cone, which turns soft-edged and hazy. Oxygen and acetylene are now being burnt in equal volumes, leaving a hotter **neutral** flame. Neither carbon nor oxygen is left over to combine with weld pool metal, so potential weld strength is good.

3.7. The right flame matters. With no oxygen, acetylene burns ragged yellow with much soot and smoke at low flow rates (a). If flow rate is too high, the flame separates from the nozzle (e). Feeding in some oxygen quietens the flame and produces a long, white central feather beyond a small central cone (b) – a carburizing flame. Adding more oxygen sees the feather shrinking until it's just merged with the central cone, leaving a faintly fuzzy outline (c). This neutral flame is used for most work. Dialling in more oxygen sees the flame shortening and getting noisier with a tiny, pointed cone (d). There's now an excess of oxygen - an oxidizing flame. To check for neutrality, take out oxygen via the needle valve until a feather appears, then add it until neutrality is achieved. Watch flame condition during welding as it's prone to change.

3.7a

3.7b

3.7c

3.7d

3.7e

Feeding in yet more oxygen tips the balance again. With an excess of O2 the cone gets smaller, harder-edged, more pointed, lighter in color and takes on a spiteful 'hiss'. Now it's an **oxidizing** flame, which – where not wanted – will produce showers of sparks and convert molten metal into weld-weakening oxides. If this flame can't be produced with the oxygen needle right open, increase regulator pressure a touch until it can. Then close the needle valve until the flame is neutral.

Play around with flame types so that you can produce each at will, aiming to set the regulators so that final flame tuning is done with the blowpipe needle valves. As equipment warms up a neutral flame tends to become oxidizing, which needs watching during work. Cheaper single-stage regulators can't hold pressure as constant as two-stage versions, so pressure drift can also unbalance the flame. If it changes with a regular pulsing rhythm, watch out: gas pressure is too low on one of the lines, making a check valve oscillate. Correct this before backfiring starts.

GAS WELDING

With the smaller nozzles at least, welding by flame is a much quieter process than SMAW's sound and fury. Part science, part art, it best suits men of easy temperament.

For mild steel there's a choice of processes, either fusion welding or bronze welding/brazing. **In fusion**, metals are taken to melting point and flow together in a liquid pool. If necessary, filler rod of similar composition is added to build up or fill the joint. But in **bronze welding and brazing**, the parent plates are not melted. Instead they're brought to red heat, then a relatively low melting point copper/zinc alloy is flowed on to the surface. This acts like a metallic 'glue', hooking into tiny surface hills and valleys and locking the joint together. To promote cleanliness and surface wetting, bronze work needs a flux. This either comes from a pot, or is carried on (or in) the welding rod (3.8). Each process has

3.8. Bronze welding flux can come in a pot (a) or as part of the rod (b). Here, small notches in the rod's flank hold it.

its advantages, disadvantages and place.

Fusion welding needs slightly less preparation, and (given good execution) is stronger than a bronze weld. But the process puts more heat into the job, increasing distortion.

Bronze welding calls for very thorough preparation, but its lower heat input minimizes distortion. Different thicknesses are easily joined, and (given the right rod) dissimilar metals can be welded. And it's easy to do.

Brazing uses the same fillers as bronze welding, but exploits the liquid alloy's ability to move between close-fitting plates or tubes. Capillary action sucks in the hot bronze, producing an extremely strong joint with no external build-up (3.9). Traditional bicycle frame joints are an example of the technique's use,

though today's aluminum and alloy steel frames are more often TIG-welded. Plumber's solderable fittings also exploit the capillary principle.

Table 3.5 shows common types and sizes of filler rod for fusion and bronze work. Each manufacturer's range differs slightly, but all brands have the main types. Fusion welding needs a filler rod of similar material to the parent plates. If in doubt over which rod to use, ask a supplier or the rod maker.

3.9. Brazing relies on liquid bronze's ability to be sucked into a joint by capillary action.

Table 3.5: **Commonly used gas welding rods for steels.**
(Examples from the Murex range)

Trade Name	Suited to	Diameters (in)
Process: Fusion welding		
Saffire mild steel	Low carbon steels	1/16, 0.08, 3/32, 1/8, 3/16 (mm: 1.6, 2.0, 2.4, 3.2, 5.0)
Saffire Medium Carbon Steel	Most low-alloy steels	1/16, 3/32, 1/8, 3/16 (mm: 1.6, 2.4, 3.2, 5.0)
Process: Bronze welding and brazing		
Saffire silicon-bronze	Steel, copper, brass	1/16, 3/32, 1/8, 3/16, 1/4 (mm: 1.6, 2.4, 3.2, 5.0, 6.0)
Saffire nickle-bronze	Steel, malleable iron	1/16, 1/8 (mm: 1.6, 3.2)
Saffire manganese-bronze	Cast or malleable iron	1/8, 3/16 (mm: 3.2, 5.0)
Self-fluxing rod for bronze/brazing		
Saffire Fluxobronze K for silicon-bronze	Steel, copper, brass	3/32, 1/8 (mm: 2.4, 3.2)

FUSION IN PRACTICE

For mild steel sheet work up to 0.0591" (1.5mm), start with a number 1 nozzle and ¹⁄₁₆" (1.6mm) mild steel filler rod. Cut a chunk of sheet to roughly 6x3⅞" (150x100mm), resting it on two lengths of angle iron so it's off the bench and away from any chilling effect.

Comfort is essential, so lean on any support or (ideally) sit down. Take the time to unwind any twists in the supply hoses as fighting these is a mug's game. Also rotate the blowpipe mixing chamber so the nozzle points down at the work. The blowpipe's acetylene needle valve should be under your thumb, ready for quick shut-off in case of backfire (3.10).

Check your goggles. These should be green-tinted and marked 'GW4'. Use the darker GW5 tint if glare is troublesome.

Set a neutral flame. Position the nozzle so the hottest part of the flame – which lies about ⅛" (3mm) over the inner cone's tip – plays on the plate (3.11). If the nozzle is big enough, within a few seconds a clear liquid pool will magically appear under the flame cone. Flying sparks mean oxides are about. If the pool is part-covered by a shifting, sparkling skin, check the flame is still neutral and that the parent steel or the rod is not rusted.

When a pool is reluctant to appear or flame heat very rapidly burns through the plate, experiment with flame and nozzle sizes as follows.

Any given nozzle can deliver a range of heat. To increase it, add more acetylene via the needle valve and rebalance to neutral. The flame is now harder – longer and hotter, so will produce a molten weld pool more quickly. If burn-through is your problem, produce a cooler, softer flame by taking out a little acetylene and rebalancing.

Understand, though, that there are limits. The more acetylene you feed in, the higher its velocity. Eventually it's rushing out so fast that the flame will separate from the nozzle, and the weld pool will probably be pushed out of shape by the high-speed steam. If either thing happens, switch to

3.10. Turn the mixing chamber/nozzle so you're holding the blowpipe with one thumb over the acetylene needle valve. This way, fuel gas can be quickly shut off in an emergency. Don't forget to retighten fittings after an adjustment.

⅛" (3mm) ⁵⁄₃₂"-¼" (4-6mm)

3.11. For maximum heating keep the flame's inner cone about ⅛" (3mm) above the target. Holding the blowpipe parallel to the work gives the proper nozzle-to-plate angle, thanks to the nozzle's cranked end.

3.12. Filler rod is best balanced between stretched fingers. Feeding in and rocking the wrist then takes the tip controllably to and from the weld pool (arrow).

the next-bigger nozzle: this will give the required heat at a lower flow rate so the flame and pool stay happy.

Coaxing a smaller, cooler flame from a given nozzle means closing needle valves, thus dropping gas velocities. Again, watch out: below a critical flow rate, backfiring will begin. Not only will this blow the weld pool to the four winds, but backfires are a potentially lethal precursor to a

flashback. *So don't persist when a nozzle starts to pop and bang.* If you need a cooler flame, go down one nozzle size.

The aim is to weld with a flame that you are controlling, rather than one that's controlling you. So having found a nozzle/flame size that produces a molten pool fairly quickly, experiment by 'pushing' that pool across the plate. Move the nozzle so the pool travels

3.13

20°

3.13. Filler rod is held at a much shallower angle than the nozzle, allowing it to dip cleanly under the latter's tip; about 20° is fine. Keeping filler in the flame envelope during work makes sure it's close to melting point and away from oxidizing air.

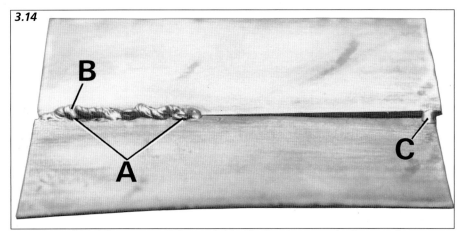

3.14

B

A

C

3.14. A small bird flew over and dropped this. The bead constantly changes shape, suggesting uneven rod/flame work. Fusion was poor, as rod was melted by flame heat rather than being added to a molten pool. Where rod solidified on the underlying plate, cold laps are evident (A). Rather than one continuous bead, unsteady progress gave un-fused cold shuts (B). Slapdash preparation left the plate edges misaligned (C), giving little chance of equal fusion.

3.15a

3.15b

forward, setting a speed that keeps it ⁵⁄₃₂-¼" (4-6mm) wide (3.11). Righthanders should work from right to left, keeping the nozzle pointing straight down the line of advance and held at 60-70° to the horizontal. Lefthanders should work from left to right.

When you're happy with this, try adding filler rod. Snip a fresh ¹⁄₁₆" (1.6mm) mild steel rod in two and bend one end over so it won't jab in anyone's eye. The bent end is also a clue when you pick it up: the straight end is the hot bit. Righthanders, balance the rod between spread fingers and thumb of the left hand (3.12). Position the hand so the rod lies along the line of the weld and makes a 20°-30° angle with the plate (3.13).

Make a molten pool, and then rock the left wrist so the rod tip dips in and out of the pool. Move the blowpipe and rod together across the plate, dipping as you go: travel to maintain pool width at about ¼" (6mm). Keep the rod low and within the flame's protective outer envelope, sliding it in under the flame's inner cone.

Keep the rod rocking in and out of the pool like a nodding donkey. Try to hit the middle of the pool each time; if you catch the front edge or leave the rod in too long, it'll stick. Don't worry – just hold it still until flame heat frees it.

Whatever you do, don't use the flame to melt and drop bits of rod on to the plates. This only produces the renowned 'bird dropping' effect (3.14), which has no fusion and thus zero strength.

Good gas welding is a relatively fast, continuous process in which rod is always added to the center of a molten pool. The result of tidy rod/flame work

3.15. Steady work with flame and rod leaves an even-width bead with fairly consistent ripples (a). Edge fusion is good, suggesting that flame heat was about right for plate thickness and desired speed of travel. The reverse of the joint (b) shows pretty consistent penetration, suggesting careful preparation (plate edges aligned and tacked, in this case with a small gap) and steady, controlled progress. See how heat blueing is equal on both plates, confirming good flame position?

looks like 3.15. If yours is closer to 3.16, not to worry – use the caption to sort out the reason(s). You may need several tries to get the moving pool, dipping rod act together, but once the penny drops it's not forgotten.

SIMPLE JOINTS

Filler rod isn't always needed. Where design and metal thickness allow, edges can be melted together in a pool and carried along by flame heat. These are autogenous or self-making joints.

Open corner joints in sheet are great for this. To practice, take two 6x1½" (150 x 40mm) bits of ¹⁄₁₆" or 0.08" (1.6 or 2mm) plate. Tack them into a right-angled roof shape (3.17), keeping edges parallel and close together. This is vital, for misalignment will limit fusion and any big gaps will just let the pool sag through. Make tacks with a neutral flame, fusing filler metal first into one plate then

3.16. Travelling too fast or using too small a nozzle leaves a narrow weld pool with little heat available for fusion (a, 1). The resulting bead is thin, humped and not fused into the plate at its edges. Slowing down (or increasing flame size) lets the weld pool grow to about 1/4" (6mm) wide, improving fusion and bead appearance (a, 2). But too much heat or too slow forward progress results in a wide, sagging weld area, excessive penetration and a fighting chance of burn-through (a, 3). The reverse of the job (b) shows corresponding penetration: see how it increases as speed of travel comes down. NB: Example produced by decreasing speed of travel between 1 and 3.

3.17. Open-corner joints are quick and easy in thin sheet. Start by tacking so inner edges just touch all along their length and plates are at 90° (a). Overlapping the edges hides one from flame heat so it can't fuse. Make a molten pool from an end tack and run it down the

joint (b). No filler should be needed if set-up was good. Penetration should be complete (c) and the result can be flattened with a hammer without breaking (d).

bridging across to the other. Finish the tack by heating the whole tack so fuses flat into both plates. This is vital or the tack will be weak.

Bring a neutral flame down on an end tack and re-melt it into a pool. Now move forward at a speed that allows the plate edges to melt inward. If you've got it right, a beautifully smooth, rounded weld will result (3.17b). Turning over should reveal even penetration (3.17c).

Butt joints generally need filler rod. Take two more bits of ¹⁄₁₆ or 0.08" (1.6 or 2mm) mild steel plate, laying them out with a penetration gap equal to (or just greater than) plate thickness. Tack one end as above then re-gap the plates, which will have moved through distortion. Tack the center and the other end.

Now weld the joint from right to left, using nozzle and flame sizes that let you work quickly but controllably. The plates will want to close up just in front of the flame, which is why a good-size penetration gap and plenty of tacks are needed. If you have to wait around for a pool to form or if it wants to freeze on adding rod, there's not enough heat going into the work for good penetration. But if holes keep appearing, you're either working too slowly or with a flame that's too hot. Watch the molten pool very closely: it'll sag just before burn-through, so good penetration is certain if the pool is kept on the point of sagging as it's moved along the joint.

As the joint end approaches you'll have to work faster. Heat has travelled up the plates, so the finish area will be very hot by the time you get there. Add to this the fact that metal left to absorb that heat is decreasing, and melt-through is a distinct possibility...so be prepared for

3.18. Building up the finish of a gas weld (arrow) is just as important as with arc. Leaving it hollow is an invitation for cracks to start. Just hold the flame steady and add rod until the crater fills to bead height.

it. Speed up as the joint end approaches. At the finish, add filler rod really quickly to build up a pad (3.18). Lift the nozzle straight up when you're done so the weld cools in the flame envelope, which protects it from oxygen and hydrogen in the air.

Flip the finished job over and check penetration. There should be an even bead right along the back. If there's not, either the penetration gap closed right up or your heat/technique was wrong.

Distortion control... fat chance?

All the following applies as much to SMAW and MIG as to gas welding.

Why do welded parts distort? The weld metal itself starts off fluid and in its most-expanded state. As it cools it contracts, pulling at the cooler metal around it. If joint parts can move, they will – pulling out of line or distorting them.

Where you reckon that distortion will make trouble, work as fast as you can while maintaining good fusion and penetration. If you can get away with it, don't weld all the joint: think about where strength will be needed and share out welds accordingly. If you must weld the whole thing, tack every 2" (50mm) or so. Still no good? Try a lower heat technique like bronze welding or brazing.

A couple of operational techniques help spread heat around. **Skip welding** does just this. Tack up, then chalk-mark the joint into sections 1 ¼-2" (30-50mm) long. Picking and choosing at random, weld one section then another. The idea is not to let heat build up in any area of the joint.

Or there's **backstepping**. Mark out the joint as before, but this time weld the far left-hand section first. Then move to the

right, welding one section at a time. Localized heat build-up is not so great as it would be with one continuous right–left weld. Neither of these methods will be 100% successful, but they do help.

Clamping parts so they simply can't move works pretty well. But there is a snag – isn't there always? The bending forces don't go away: they stay locked up in the metal. It usually yields (or stretches) to accommodate them but where it can't, it cracks. Such hidden forces pre-stress the job, using up some of the metal's ability to stand a load and maybe making it fail earlier in service than it otherwise would.

One solution is to bring a repair or fabrication up to dull red heat, hold it there for a while then cool it very slowly under sand or a heat-resisting blanket. This should release the stress and ready the part for an arduous life. But be warned: stress relieving is an art in itself. If you think it's essential, ask a specialist.

Backstepping (top) helps minimize distortion in any form of welding. Chalk off the sections then weld each in turn, travelling from right to left. In skip welding, sections 1-7 are welded in random order, again from right to left. When building up a worn shaft or joining a broken one, lay beads on opposite sides to balance heat input and hence distortion (bottom).

Don't try DIY on any safety-related part.

Distortion builds up as work progresses. When working with sheet, stop now and again and dress down buckled or separated plates with a hammer. Otherwise, trying to weld these is a mug's game.

3.19. It's very easy to leave a fillet root unwelded, especially when the job is resting on a cold bench. But good fusion in the joint walls still left this T-joint (a) with adequate strength, despite the problem arrowed (b). Weld one and flatten it with a hammer to see. But be aware that vibration fatigue will destroy an incomplete joint faster than one with 100% root fusion.

And you'll find that the plates have bowed – distortion is a big problem with gas fusion welding, as relatively slow travel brings great heat input. Fast work minimizes the problem but can't beat it.

How about a **fillet joint?** The trick here is to supply enough heat, as the joint zone presents a bigger total heat sink than a butt's simple edges. Move up at least one nozzle size over the equivalent butt, adjusting flame size so a molten pool appears fairly quickly and is easily maintained. Ideally, support the joint so it's not resting on anything cold which will add to the heat sink effect.

Tack plates together on the side of the vertical plate that's not to be welded, biasing a neutral flame toward the heat-hungry bottom plate. Start the joint itself by building a fillet of weld metal across the plates, making sure it fuses with the parent metal and bites down into the joint root. Then using this fillet as a starting point, move a molten pool slowly along the joint. The vertical plate is most at risk from burn-through and undercut, so be sparing with the flame up there. Adding filler rod to the top of the pool also helps cool the vertical plate locally.

The vital thing is not to rush. Be certain that fusion reaches right down into the joint root before moving forward. You'll see the pool go hollow and molten metal flow into the root area as fusion happens. If the pool is pushed along before this is seen, all you're doing is building a bridge between the plates: the root won't be filled at all (3.19). This may not matter with thin sheet because, so long as fusion is good, the bridge is enough. But a joint without root fusion will always fail before one with it.

Common fillet problems come from several sources (3.20).

Using too small a flame gives a tiny, fast-freezing pool that won't flow, with the result that root fusion is near-impossible.

Too little heat also gives **cold laps**, where molten metal is just laid on top of the parent plate(s) rather than fusing in.

Cold shuts are the same problem, only this time happening where weld metal joins weld metal. If the flame is too small or the operator too keen to get on, you'll find trouble where work restarts, on overlapping runs, or where tacks aren't fused into the main weld.

Too much fillet joint heat produces burn-through or undercut of the vertical plate. One or both turns up when travel is too slow, if the flame spends too much time away from the joint root, or if a big heat-sink under the work forces the operator to use an oversize nozzle.

Lap joints are just miniature fillets. Work fast, overcoming the bottom plate's heat-sink effect by using a stronger flame or bigger nozzle than for the equivalent butt.

3.20. Not the best of fillets. Using a small flame and travelling at varying speed produced a jumble of poor fusion and misses. But things improved a bit as work progressed leftward along the joint; short sections (A and B) are better, though undercut is on show at the top edge of (A).

Judge filler quantity and speed of travel so that the upper plate's top edge is just fused in to the joint.

Going vertical with gas

This isn't too hard. The preferred direction of travel is upward since gravity makes a mess of the pool when travelling down, and unlike with arc processes there are no magnetic forces to help hold weld metal in place and direct it to the pool.

Butt joints are prepared as for flat work, leaving a penetration gap equal to or just bigger than plate thickness. Rod and flame angles stay much as they were, only shifted through 90° (3.21). Bend the rod into a hook shape and hold it alongside the joint so the tip points down to the weld pool: this avoids burnt fingers.

Use the bottom tack as a starting point. Make a pool from this and add a little rod. Once an onion-shaped hole appears over the pool you know penetration is complete, though in thin sheet an 'onion' might not be necessary. If one doesn't magically pop up, either steepen the flame or physically push it down into the joint root to open up a hole.

From soft solder to hard

Bronze welding, brazing, silver soldering and soldering are all related. The big difference from fusion work is that the parent metals are never melted. Instead, the filler acts like a glue to bond surfaces to each other. The various filler alloys are arranged on a temperature and hardness scale. At the bottom is soft and bendable solder in its various forms (tinman's, plumber's, pewterer's), containing tin and lead and melting at temperatures from 205° to 482°F (96° to 250°C). Silver solders come next, melting between 1,130° and 1,382°F (610° and 750°C) depending on what's in them. Joint strength and service temperatures are higher than with solder. The bronze alloys (also called 'hard solders') are at the top of the temperature tree, melting at about 1,616°F (880°C) – which is well below steel's melting point.

When the 'onion' appears, move upwards at a rate that maintains it, adding filler rod to the pool as you go. This may sound difficult, but it's easier to do than to read about.

Overhead gas welding

This isn't so simple. There's no magnetic transfer of filler, so gravity wants to dump the weld pool into your lap.

This painful tendency is reduced by keeping nozzle size to the minimum consistent with good fusion, and working quickly. Rod and blowpipe angles can be steeper than normal; try bringing them toward a right-angle with the work.

If you're not happy with the notion of welding uphill or overhead, time won't be wasted by dismantling something so you can weld it on the flat. Better to spend a while with the spanners than have a job fail in use.

BRONZE WELDING

A soft, quiet and thoroughly enjoyable pastime is this. Rather than melting parent metals, bronze welding uses a copper/zinc alloy as a 'glue' to hold things together or build up worn surfaces. The bond is formed partly from the filler metal hooking into tiny surface features on the joint faces, and partly from controlled local diffusion – through never melting – into the base metal.

Bronze alloys melt at a lower temperature than steel (850 – 900°C against 1500°C) so are good for joining very thin sheet. There are other bonuses: lower heat means less distortion, thick things can be joined to thin things (3.24) and different metals can be welded to each other.

Five inputs are needed for a good result:

- The right preparation
- The right flame
- The right heat
- The right rod, and (wait for it)
- The right flux.

3.21(a). Welding vertically up with gas isn't hard. Use the same rod/flame angles as on the flat. To avoid burning fingers, either hook the filler rod and hold it from the joint side, or hold it above the flame (A). Where necessary, leave a penetration gap. 13.21(b) To be really sure of welding full-depth, use flame heat and/or physical pressure to blow an 'onion' or 'keyhole' through the plates (A). For certain penetration, maintain the onion as the weld marches upwards.

Preparation is the single most important thing in any form of non-fusion welding. Surfaces must be really clean, physically and chemically, if the filler material is to flow over and 'hook' into them, so elbow grease is called for. Hit rust, dirt or paint gently with an angle grinder, then follow this up with emery cloth. Don't leave the surfaces too coarse or bronze will wet only the high points. Stop preparing only when the weld area is shiny and squeaky-clean. The final job stands or falls by effort put in at this stage.

Flame setting. Though bronze itself hates oxygen, a neutral or just-oxidizing flame is actually used. Why is this? Surplus oxygen in the flame encourages an oxide skin to form over the molten bronze, keeping its zinc content from volatilizing off. But if too much oxygen is around then the bronze won't flow.

Heat. The work will be brought only to red heat, so start with a small nozzle and soft flame to control heat input. If the joint won't come to temperature fairly quickly, increase flame size or go up one nozzle size. Set a very slightly oxidizing flame.

Filler rod type varies with the metals to be joined. All bronze rods are copper/zinc alloys, though exact composition is varied to change their strength and application. **Silicon bronze** fillers are good for general-purpose work on mild steel, copper and brass, although as the latter melts at much the same temperature as the bronze filler, it's effectively fusion welded.

Where more toughness and/or wear resistance is called for, switch to more expensive **nickel bronze** rods. The material work-hardens, so is good for building up small worn parts as well as welding steel.

Last of the commonly farm-used rod materials is **manganese bronze**. Priced much as silicon bronze, it offers more tensile strength and is good for joining cast/malleable irons as well as low- and medium-carbon steels.

Flux is essential to chemically clean the surfaces and keep slag, oxides and gases from the weld. No matter whether it's contained in the filler or comes from a pot, the flux had better be fresh. Chuck out any that's gone hard or crumbles away from the rod. A general-purpose bronze flux will do for all three fillers above.

Flowing the bronze

This is where it starts to get good. Bring those oh-so-clean joint components up to dull red heat. Then start adding bronze. First melt a little onto the surface. Then work along it, dipping the rod to the hot metal to melt more as needed.

If the preparation and temperature control are right, yellow liquid filler will spread quietly and without fuss. Experiment with heat input: see how the bronze only tracks over areas which are hot enough? This temperature-sensitivity lets you keep close control over bronze movement by varying joint heat.

The chances are that first attempts will see the filler spitting and fuming. It's too hot; the zinc is vaporizing in a huff, leaving behind a weak, copper-colored layer (3.22). Less severe overheating doesn't destroy the bead, but the departing zinc leaves weld-weakening pinholes. A carburizing flame produces the same effect.

If a weld shows pinholing, grind off the old deposit and try again. Either use a softer flame, or if this brings on backfiring, switch to a smaller nozzle. If you're already on a number 1, control heat input by playing the flame on and off the work. It might also be an idea to recheck preparation – sharp corners and projections quickly overheat, giving local pinhole problems.

Like other forms of welding, achieving good bronze work is like walking a tightrope. Aim for a rapid, controlled process that leaves a finely rippled weld surface (3.22). A smooth, featureless bead shows you were working too hot.

Sometimes molten filler just sits around in a ball (3.23). This is telling you that the work is either too cold or too dirty. Either way, the bronze won't wet the underlying metal. Re-clean the plates and use a little more heat, then it'll flow where you want.

Dead flux should be cleaned off after welding. The glassy beads of oxide can be chipped gently away (mind your eyes) or, if the work can stand it, be shocked off by cooling in cold water.

3.22. The right heat input, good fluxing and steady forward travel produces an even-width bronze bead with fine surface ripples (A). Slight overheating pushes the bead out wider and the ripples disappear (B), while greater overheating drives off zinc in a spitting huff, leaving a pin-holed and mottled copper-colored mess (C). Experiment to see how hot bronze follows flame heat over a clean plate. It'll run where the substrate is hot enough and clean enough.

3.23. Where work is too cool, bronze sits as a ball and won't flow. The same happens if the plate underneath is dirty.

BRAZING

Brazing uses the same fillers, flame and fluxes as bronze welding. So what's the difference? Bronze welding leaves an external build-up, whereas, in brazing all the filler is sucked into the joint by capillary action. So brazing only works where a small gap exists between joint components, for only here can capillary action draw in liquid filler. It follows that the two processes aren't mutually exclusive. If conditions are right for capillarity, a bronze weld can have a brazed region too.

Excellent preparation is no less vital to brazing. Any dirt will stop the alloy flowing, and if this happens up inside the joint, you'll never know. So prepare the ground by pre-fluxing the components: either sprinkle a layer on them or make flux into a paste and wipe it on.

3.24. A bronze welding bonus – you can easily join thick things to thin. This joint's even, fine surface ripples (arrow) suggest temperature was held in check and rod was added steadily.

Then bring both components up to red heat, watching to see that all areas are equally hot. Melt a little filler rod at the joint edge. If the parts are close together, hot enough and clean enough, bronze will be quickly sucked out of sight. Carry on until the joint is full.

The nut and plate example (3.25) shows how thick and thin items can be brazed to leave a neat, zero-build-up finish. Normal surface roughness and fluxing between the bits provides the gap for capillary action.

CUTTING, PIERCING HOLES

Chopping things up is an everyday task. Slicing steel relies on oxygen's keenness to combine with preheated metal, giving out extra heat in the process.

The fuel gas can be either propane or acetylene, with propane being the cheaper but more oxygen-hungry option. Here we'll consider only oxyacetylene cutting, as welding requires acetylene fuel gas which is likely to be on the farm already.

All but sheet metal cutting nozzles have a central hole surrounded by a ring of preheaters (3.26). This is the central cutting hole diameter, and the bigger the hole, the thicker the plate that can be cut (Table 3.6). Sheet nozzles come in one size only, have a single heater hole and

are stamped ASNM (3.27).

The cutting process itself is straightforward. Set a neutral flame (page 66). Let the preheat flame(s) bring the material up to red heat, then use the torch cutting lever to feed neat oxygen into the area. The steel actually ignites, turning into liquid iron oxide and giving out more heat to keep the process going. Physical pressure from the oxygen stream clears this liquid away from the cut line,

3.26. A new gas cutting nozzle shows off its round, square-edged pre-heater holes (A) and central cutting orifice (B). With use the hole's edges degrade, but can be returned to pristine condition with a file and nozzle reamers. Keep your nozzles looking like this and cutting will be easy. The same goes for welding nozzles.

3.25. Brazing is very strong if done properly – this joint has been attacked with hammer and chisel. The nut was set on a thin bed of flux and brought to red heat, then the flame moved to the plate. With both red hot, a little bronze was melted at each nut flat. It disappeared under the nut to emerge on the thread side. With any bronze work don't spend too long getting everything hot, as oxides will build up and hinder filler flow.

3.27. A sheet metal nozzle has only two holes – the higher for preheating and the lower for the cutting stream. Used with a guide it'll work well in material up to ⅛" (3mm) thick, though cutting heat produces distortion.

3.28. *Bell-mouthing in worn nozzles (a, arrow) causes turbulent gas flow and ruins cutting ability. Nozzle (b) has been dropped, flattening the soft copper alloy tip and deforming holes. It won't cut properly until refaced with a file and reamed.*

Table 3.6: **Nozzles and pressures for heating, acetylene fuel gas.**

Nozzle	Approx heat, BTU	Fuel gas pressure		Oxygen pressure	
		Bar	psi	Bar	psi
A-LHT500L	(62kW) 211,550	0.49	7	0.70	10
A-HT 25	(176kW) 600,530	0.35	4	0.35	4
A-HT 50	(309kW) 1,054,350	0.43	6	0.43	6
A-HT 100	(472kW) 1,610,530	0.49	7	0.70	10

Table 3.7: **Nozzles and pressures for cutting mild steel, acetylene fuel gas.**

Thickness	Nozzle	Fuel gas pressure		Oxygen pressure	
		Bar	psi	Bar	psi
6mm	1/32	0.14	2	2	30
13mm	3/64	0.20	3	3	30
25mm	1/16	0.28	4	3	45
50mm	1/16	0.35	5	3.8	55
Sheet	ASFN	0.40	6	1.7	25

leaving a gap or kerf.

Cutting is the only job in which different oxygen and acetylene pressures are used (Table 3.6). Thus hose check-valves must be in good working order!

Compared with welding, gas cutting needs little skill. Instead a *good cut comes down to equipment condition and settings.* Clean cuts just can't be made with poorly-maintained gear – so here's how to look after it.

Housekeeping for a good cut

For quality cutting or welding, the nozzle needs to be like 3.26 – with holes of the right diameter, all round and sharp-edged. In time the central hole turns bell-mouthed, so the cutting stream isn't blasted out as a straight-edged

gas column (3.28). Instead it swirls and tumbles, clearing only a rough, shallow hole. The result is a ragged cut that easily seals up underneath, and more likelihood of backfire.

Helpfully, nozzle makers build extra depth into welding and cutting tips so you can reface them. Do this a little and often, dressing the tip flat with a smooth file and/or fine-grade emery block, then gently reaming the holes. Go steady with the reamers; you're only aiming to clear away burrs. Don't rasp so hard that the holes end up bigger or turn oval, and keep the reamer parallel so a backfire-producing bell end isn't produced. Resist the temptation (strong though it is) to force in a reamer that's just a gnat's wing too big, or it'll probably snap off and junk the nozzle.

Proof of a proper re-facing job comes on lighting up. Set a neutral flame. With a good nozzle either welding or cutting the flame envelope will be symmetrical when looked at from the side and from above. For cutting nozzles, recheck with the cutting lever held down. If the flame is odd-shaped (or if one heater flame shows a feather or is more oxidizing than its mates), first try moving the nozzle round in the torch seat so it sits in a different spot. If this has no effect, grumble and ream again.

With cutting tips, uneven heat-bluing at the face will confirm which hole was misbehaving. See also that a cutting nozzle's internal drillings are clear: with the nozzle held up to the light and angled, you can generally see through them.

Sometimes a smoky acetylene flame appears at the cutting head's nozzle-holding ring. This is an irritation which shouldn't continue. The cause is poor seating between the nozzle and head, which can sometimes be cured by very gently dressing the nozzle seats with worn-out emery cloth or rotating the nozzle in its seat. But where this doesn't help, there's no option but to buy another nozzle.

*When a smoky flame creeps out from the joint between a **welding** (not cutting) nozzle and the blowpipe, bad seating is again the cause. Remedial action needs to be much more immediate.* There's a high probability of a backfire, which can jump straight into the nearby blowpipe mixing chamber.

A couple of other points. Because nozzles are made from a soft copper alloy, their internal passages can easily be flattened if you whack them loose from the cutting head. A tap with a softwood block is the kinder thing to do. Keep spare welding and cutting nozzles in a hardwood block, out of harm's way.

Flame setting

A balanced flame is the other half of a good cut. Set pressures one at a time with the appropriate blowpipe needle valve(s) open. Table 3.6 shows initial values. If the material to be sliced up is really rusty, increase pressures a little. Outside work on a windy day robs heat, so nozzle choice and setting will need to account for that.

Close all needle valves. Light acetylene first as normal, and adjust flame size so it's 'bright'. Then open the oxygen valve completely so that it plays no further part in proceedings. Feed in oxygen via the cutting attachment's own needle valve until the pre-heater flames are neutral.

Now hold down the cutting lever. The chances are that the flame balance will shift slightly away from neutral, so rebalance it from the cutting attachment's needle valve. The critical thing is that the flame is neutral when in cutting mode, that is, with the lever held down.

A nice slice

To make a cut, hover the nozzle completely over the start point. Keep heater flame cones about ⅛" (3mm) from the surface to maximize heat input and bring the steel to red heat as fast as possible.

Then swing the nozzle clear of the work. Feed in cutting oxygen full-tilt and quickly bring the nozzle back on target. The cut will start cleanly with a splash of molten metal: move off down the cut line. But with thick sections don't move off straight away. Wait until you see molten spatter steam from under the cut, which shows it's penetrated to full depth. Concentrate hard on keeping the nozzle centered side-to-side over the cut line: any tilt produces a bevelled edge which won't usually be wanted. Having said that, it can help to tilt the nozzle along the line of cut so the tip is just forward of the head – experiment and see.

With the cut going well, move as smoothly as the trembling hand allows while keeping those heater cones about ⅛" (3mm) from the surface. How fast do you go? Just fast enough to keep molten metal flooding from the cut's underside.

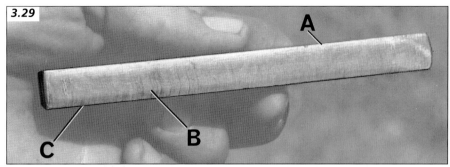

3.29. Halves of a gas-cut plate should separate by gravity rather than needing to be belted apart. A good cut's clean, un-melted top edge (A) shows that preheat flames were not too big or moving too slowly. Draglines just curving at the bottom (B) suggest that the speed of travel was as fast as possible – much faster and the cut would have stopped. A clean lower edge (C) shows heat input was right for material thickness.

3.30. A poor cut. The melted top edge (A) and crusty slag clinging to the lower edge (B) suggest too much heat, either through using too-big a nozzle or too large a flame. Cuts like this won't part of their own accord as slag holds the kerf together.

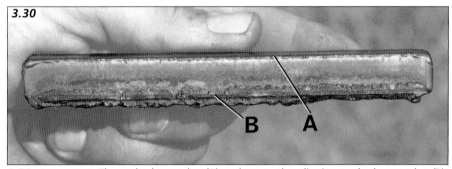

3.31. Where cutting oxygen pressure is too high, the cut face is hollowed by turbulent gas flow (A) and slag again clings to the bottom (B).

3.32. Nothing much wrong here. Only the beading on the top edge shows pre-heater flames were too low (arrows).

If travel is too slow the cut's top edges will melt away under preheat. If you go too fast, the cut either stops completely or oxide splashes back out. The first happens when pre-heating is lost, the second when the cut hasn't time to penetrate to full depth. Either slow down, set a harder flame or use a bigger nozzle.

Once a cut has stopped you'll have to pre-heat a little to get it going again. Where the job has wanted and unwanted halves, restart on the scrap side to preserve one clean edge. If you're cutting up to a square corner or want to leave the cut for a moment, make a small loop out into the unwanted material at the change of direction or re-start point. This gives space to rejoin without chewing into the good edge.

3.29–3.32 show a good cut and a selection of problems. A clean cut shows smooth drag lines and has little or no oxide on the bottom edges. Any there is will chip off easily.

A very common fault is using a nozzle that's too big or a flame that's too hard. Both put too much heat into the cut, which seals up with foamy, harder-to-remove oxide. Even the smallest nozzle will cut thicker stuff than you think: try it and see. Most work can be handled by $\frac{1}{32}$" and $\frac{1}{16}$" sizes if they're in good order.

As with gas welding, a cutting flame can be 'softened' by reducing acetylene flow until popping starts, then dialling in a little more again. Softening the flame (then rebalancing it to neutral) cuts the heat input, so is a good ruse for curing underplate oxide build-up in thinner-section plate.

Ten Tips for Faster, Easier Cutting

3.33

- Before cutting heavily rusted or painted material, use flame heat and a wire brush to clean it. This makes marking-out much simpler.

- A soapstone stick (3.33) leaves a marking-out line that doesn't vanish under flame heat as chalk does.

- A row of center-punched dots make an easily seen guide for cutting circles. Start the cut near the center, then move outwards in a circle. Slice away until the inner half of each dot disappears and the hole will be about the right size (3.34).

- Cuts are straighter when a length of angle iron is clamped alongside the line. Choose a size that puts the heater flame cones the right height above the work when you rest the nozzle clamp nut on the upturned edge. Be prepared to make new guides fairly often as heat warps them.

- Start cutting a hole from the center. A punch mark's raised edges come quickly up to heat so target these with the heaters. When they're red-hot, lift the nozzle well clear of the plate before gently feeding in the cutting stream – this way the initial splash is less likely to part-block it. Angling the nozzle once the hole starts also lessens the chances of blocking.

- Working in a confined space can quickly overheat a cutting nozzle, causing backfiring. Kill the flame then plunge-cool it in a bucket of warm water, but leave oxygen flowing to stop passages filling up. Check the nozzle ring afterwards in case contraction has loosened it.

- If at any time the nozzle starts to whistle, either spatter or too-low gas flow has led to one or more preheater flames striking back and burning up inside it. Shut off quickly and find the cause, or the nozzle will soon melt.

- Stainless steel or high-chromium welds won't cut, only melt. The stream of cutting oxygen can't combine with them. After all, the whole point of these steels is to stay stainless — that is, non-oxidizing.

- Cast iron will cut, but poorly. Use a carburizing flame and be prepared for a hot, messy job. Let the cut penetrate to full-depth before starting, weave to leave a wide kerf and keep the nozzle high to minimize blocks.

- Gas cuts stop very quickly if there's the smallest gap between parts. This works to your advantage when (say) slicing a bearing off its shaft or housing, or the head from a bolt while it's still screwed home. The downside is that stacks of plates can't sensibly be cut.

3.33. A soapstone stick and holder cost pennies. Unlike chalk, the line it leaves doesn't disappear under flame heat.

3.34. When cutting circles, punch-dot the center for an easier start. More dots round the edge are easy to see during work. For higher accuracy, make or buy a pointed pivot which clips to the cutting head. Sit this in the center dot, then use the torch like a pair of compasses.

3.34

Section 4

TIG Welding

TIG is the slowest and most skill-requiring of the welding processes. To do it well calls for concentration, patience and fine manual control. Men, with their rush and great fumbling fingers, are outclassed by women on all three counts. So the next time the other half starts looking for a new challenge, shepherd her gently toward the workshop...

Meanwhile, back on planet Earth, the sexes will probably carry on as normal. The TIG sets that are slowly turning up in agriculture have their roots back in the 1940s. Then the pressure was on to weld relatively exotic metals – aluminum, stainless steel, magnesium – by a high-quality process, and TIG (tungsten inert gas) did the business. Today's farm requirements are more modest, most likely being thin sheet steel, stainless and aluminum.

Over time, electronics have brought sets down in size, increased their flexibility and dropped the price to something relatively affordable. Makers now offer multi-role units based on inverter technology, which, by putting stick welding and TIG capability into a lightweight and sometimes generator-friendly package, have definite attractions.

If you're not familiar with the process, the panel **'What's TIG About?'** on page 82 has the basics. Before getting all excitable it's worth checking both sides of the coin, so for the sensibly sceptical the box **'For and against'** on page 83 puts TIG's arguments in a farming context. Be clear on one thing: TIG is not a replacement for SMAW (stick) welding or MIG. Rather, it's a technique akin to gas welding which, if you have the need, can sit alongside existing methods to broaden a farm's repair/fabrication armory.

At buying time the choice is between a DC set and a more expensive, more capable AC–DC unit. As many farms are likely to first explore TIG as an add-on to a portable SMAW (stick welding) set, we'll deal mainly with the setup and use of single-phase DC units. As there's a lot of kit to sort out before welding starts, we'll begin there.

Setting up shop

Kindly nip across and read the panel **'Stay Safe'**. This is important as there's more to TIG safety than meets the eye.

OK? Now to setting up the plant. The tungsten electrode puts the 'T' in TIG so comes first, bringing with it several words not usually uttered in the farm workshop.

Electrode type. Originally, electrodes were made from pure tungsten. Though these still have a use, better arc striking, arc stability and electrode durability all come from adding a pinch of thorium, lanthium, cerium or zirconium. For DC welding mild and stainless steels, use a 2% thoriated or 1% lanthanated electrode. For AC welding or for DC welding aluminum, use a 1% zirconiated electrode. Price and quality vary and a poor tungsten will not hold its shape for long; stay with big-name brands for best effect. Lanthanated electrodes like Sylvania's Tungsten AC/DC ones can be used with both AC and DC: these and ceriated electrodes contain no radioactive thorium.

Identification and storage. Electrodes carry a color code. The standard is green for pure tungsten, red for 2% thoriated, white for zirconiated, grey for ceriated and black for lanthanated (4.1). Whatever their makeup, TIG electrodes are best stored in a box or wallet away from grease and dirt.

Polarity. In DC welding, two-thirds of the heat is generated at the circuit's anode or positive side. To let the electrode run relatively cool and to put most heat into the work for best fusion/penetration, plug the torch into the set's negative outlet (DCEN – Direct Current Electrode – for welding mild and stainless steels. But to DC-weld aluminum, use the positive outlet (electrode positive: DCEP – Direct Current Electrode Positive [reverse polarity]). Much less heat goes into the work so control is easier and as a spin-off, oxides are cleared from the weld. The bad news is that the electrode now has to take two-thirds of the heat, so maximum welding current must be limited and a much fatter tungsten has to be used.

4.1 Electrodes are color-coded. These four are typical – 1% thoriated (A), 2% thoriated (B), zirconiated (C) and Murex's multi-purpose Arcrite (D). Don't grind the colored end or you'll not know which one's which.

Stay Safe

Flux is not used with TIG. While that minimizes fume production, high levels of ozone – a lung irritant – are produced by the arc. On top of this, if common platings like nickel, cadmium, zinc and chromium are not ground from the weld zone, very toxic metal fume will result from heating. At minimum, TIG weld only in areas where air interchanges freely. Ideally, take out fume at source by extraction.

Thorium is a low-level radioactive source. Storing and using farm quantities of electrodes is not a problem, but a small risk exists if dust is inhaled when grinding thoriated tungstens. Intact electrodes or those with other included elements pose less risk, so guidelines suggest using alternatives to thoriated items where possible. If not, either buy a purpose-built electrode grinder (see picture) or dedicate a conventional unit to the job. With the latter, either extract dust on-the-go or damp it before sweeping into a sealable plastic container. Dispose of dust in an approved landfill site.

High-frequency-start sets produce pulses of several thousand volts during arc initiation. Clearly it's daft to put a finger – or any other bit of your anatomy, come to that – between the electrode and work. It follows that an HF-start set is best switched off before changing or adjusting tungstens.

HF voltage can play merry hell with even distant electronic systems. Unplug or remove these where possible before welding on tractors, on implements like a modern sprayer or spreader attached to them, or on dairy equipment. Disconnect a vehicle's battery. Electromagnetic pulses from HF can also

For anyone grinding a lot of tungstens, a dedicated unit like this one from ESAB takes out the guesswork. Dust is caught by a water bath, cancelling the small radioactivity risk from thoriated electrodes.

travel down power cables and are transmitted like radio waves, potentially upsetting vital electronics.

Last but by no means least, TIG is an arc process so eye protection demands a quality arc filter – gas welding goggles offer no protection whatever. Currents are generally low and the arc small, so for good weld area visibility try shade EW9. If you're contemplating a self-darkening filter, go for one which offers a higher-sensitivity to the TIG setting range. Higher-current work with aluminum puts out more UV and light, so move up to shade EW10 or EW11.

Diameter. Common electrode diameters are 0.04, ¹⁄₁₆, ³⁄₃₂ and ⅛" (1, 1.6, 2.4 and 3.2mm). Smaller and larger ones are on offer but those listed cover normal work. Use the thinnest electrode possible for a given welding current, as this produces the most concentrated arc and the smallest, most controllable weld pool. New tungstens are usually 6" (150mm) long and can be ground back to about 2" (50mm), below which it's hard to mount them in the torch.

Take care over grinding

In AC welding, the heat generated turns the tungsten's tip into a semi-molten ball. Careful preparation isn't needed – just grind a slight bevel on the flat tip.

But in DC TIG, the **shape** and **condition** of the tip are pivotal factors. Although electrodes can be bought pre-ground, you'll need to refinish them sooner or later – definitely sooner when brushing up welding technique.

When do you need to re-grind? After the tip has been contaminated by touching hot weld metal or the filler rod; when a thoriated electrode grows a little nodule behind the tip, or if the arc kicks off at an angle rather than flowing straight down.

Tip shape decides arc stability, and so affects the ease of work and the

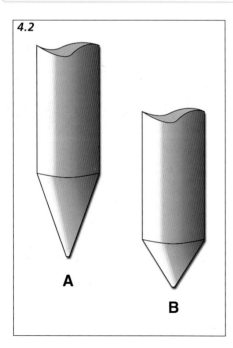

4.2

A

B

4.2 Low DC welding currents call for a gentle tip taper (A), while higher amps need a blunter taper (B) – Table 4.1 has details. Grind a tiny flat on the tip to maximize service life.

4.3 For farm work, a small bench grinder with a fine-grit aluminum oxide wheel is OK for tip grinding. Keep the electrode in line with the wheel's long side, as here. This sets up the tip to deliver the most stable arc. (See 4.4)

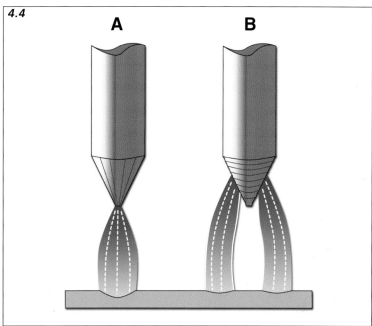

4.4 Grinding lines running parallel with the electrode's length (A) concentrate the arc at the very tip, boosting stability and delivering concentrated heat input to the work. Radial grinding (B) leads to a less stable arc and uneven heat input.

Table 4.1: **Current and electrode tip angle**

Welding current (A)	Tip Angle (°)
1-20	30
20-100	60-90
100-200	90-120
Over 200	120

evenness of heat input. Low currents need a long, thin and pointy tip, whereas higher currents need a blunter taper (4.2). A blunter tip handles more current, gives a narrower arc, keeps its shape better and helps penetration, but starting can be harder and arc wander is more likely.

Grind on a fine grit aluminum oxide wheel intended for hard metals. As a rough rule of thumb, grind a long 30° taper for currents of 20A or less, and shorten it to about 80° as current goes up. Table 4.1 gives finer detail. Don't make a needle tip unless arc starting is hard or the job is physically very small. Instead, grind a tiny flat at the end to maximize service life and minimize the chance of the point flaking into the weld, where it will form a very brittle inclusion.

Odd though it may seem, exactly how you grind the tip matters. Holding the tungsten parallel to the grinding wheel's long side (4.3) produces mini-gouge marks running toward the tip. These promote a directional, stable arc. Holding the tungsten across the stone leaves radial grinding marks which will unsettle the arc (4.4, B).

Cups, cowls or nozzles – all the same thing

Heavier-than-air shield gas is funnelled over the weld zone by a brittle ceramic or aluminum oxide cup, cowl or nozzle. This comes in various shapes and lengths (4.5).

4.5 Ceramic nozzles may carry an identifying number. Match nozzle bore to electrode size for good gas flow.

4.6 A gas lens can replace the torch's standard collet body. The fine mesh outlet directs and organizes flow, helping carry shield gas into deep corners or offset draughts.

What's TIG About?

TIG (tungsten inert gas) welding brings together elements from conventional stick welding (SMAW), MIG and gas techniques. Heat from an arc (A) is used to fuse joint components. This arc forms between the work and a pointed tungsten-based electrode (B), the twist being that the electrode is not melted into the joint. Instead, it remains intact or non-consumed. Where needed, filler metal is added manually from a rod (C).

An inert gas (generally heavier-than-air argon [D]) shields the hot electrode and molten weld pool to stop oxidation, and gives a conducting path for current. Gas makeup affects arc characteristics and heat.

TIG's small, intense arc suits it to high-quality, precision welding on steel, stainless steel, alloy steels, aluminum and other metals.

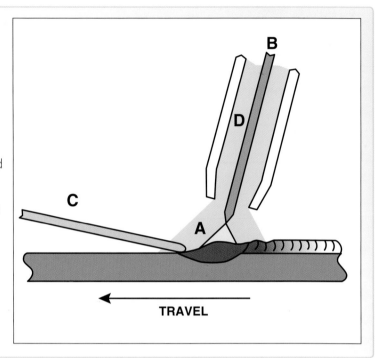

TRAVEL

Which nozzle do you use for a given job? If the nozzle is too small for the tungsten and welding current used, it'll glow red hot. Worse, the limited space inside is likely to make the shield gas tumble, which affects arc stability, pulls air into the stream and can expose the weld zone to oxidation. On the other hand, a nozzle that's too big limits sight of the weld pool and doesn't concentrate gas effectively. As a starter, pick an internal bore that's about 4x electrode diameter. Then match nozzle length to the job: shorter ones give better access into tight corners, longer ones carry the shield gas down into deep joints.

Adding a gas lens (4.6) can be a good move where work has to be of top quality or where you're forced to work in a draft. The lens replaces the standard collet body and carries a fine grid through which gas flows, rather than just a ring of holes. Gas reaches the weld in a more orderly way, forming a better blanket round the electrode and pool. Apart from buffering the work against draughts, a gas lens can let you reduce flow (thus saving money) or increase electrode stickout – the latter boosting joint access and weld pool visibility. The bad news is that a separate lens

has to be bought to suit each electrode diameter, and needs a specific gas nozzle to go with it.

Mechanic's course

So we've got a TIG tungsten sharpened, a gas cup selected and a generally expectant air. The next step – putting together the torch – is easier than Meccano, although there are a couple of things to watch.

Picture 4.7 shows how the bits screw together. The sample is an air-cooled torch: water-cooling is generally needed for sustained work with welding currents over 200A, with the main visible difference between units being coolant flow and return lines at the handle.

Check out the nylon nozzle gasket and the back cap's O-ring seal. Both need to be in good order or shield gas will leak and not flow where it's needed. The collet and body/diffuser usually come as a pair, with the required tungsten diameter stamped on the body (4.8). As the back cap is tightened, the collet is pushed into the body and grips the tungsten. Store collet and body together to avoid time-wasting rummaging.

Back caps come in long or short forms, and it's worth keeping a short one for

jobs where access is limited. Screw in the cap until its O-ring seats in the body. Slip the collet inside the collet body/ diffuser then run the unit into the torch finger-tight. Slide in the tungsten and add the gas cup, snugging this down on its seal.

Then set visible electrode stick-out. This is the distance between the business end of the gas cup and the tungsten's tip (4.9), which for normal work needs to be ⅛-¼" (3-6mm). Clamp the electrode in place by tightening the back cap. Where you need to see more of what's going on or to reach down into a joint, increase stick-out to a maximum of ⅜" (10mm) – but if you do, think about using a gas lens to be sure that gas shielding doesn't suffer.

Consumables

With filler rod and some **shield gas** you'll be ready to rock 'n roll. Picking the shield gas is a bit of a no-brainer, as pure argon works well with all farming's metals and is the cheapest choice. Argon is heavier than air, so in down-hand (flat) work tends to sink helpfully round the weld zone. Sold under various trade names, it comes in the usual cylinder sizes but isn't the

4.7

4.7 The nozzle gasket (A) and back cap O-ring (B) stop shield gas leaking so need to be in good fettle. The collet (C) slips inside the collet body (D), which in turn is finger-tightened into the torch body. Gas cup (E) threads over the body. The electrode (F) is gripped by the split-sided collet as the back cap is screwed down.

4.8

4.8 Collet bodies have holes for gas exit which need to be kept clear. Each is stamped with a size (arrow) matching it to an electrode diameter, and pairs with a collet of the same size.

4.9

3mm-6mm

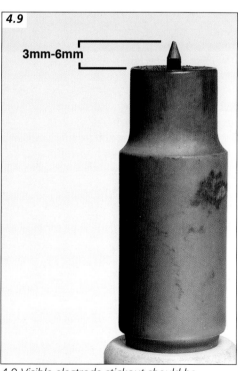

4.9 Visible electrode stickout should be ⅛"-¼" (3-6mm), though it can rise to ⅜" (10mm) for better joint access. If gas shielding suffers from longer stickouts, use a gas lens in place of the standard collet body.

TIG:
For and Against

For

- Very low current operation possible
- Low distortion, small heat-affected zone
- High quality welds possible
- Ability to join aluminum/stainless or very thin sheet steel
- Joints can be made with or without filler metal
- With filler, can build across gaps
- Slow travel speed helps with complex joint shapes
- Precise control of welding heat
- Small torch can reach tight spaces
- No spatter.

Against

- Equipment cost
- Slow compared to SMAW or MIG
- Best on material under ¼" (6mm)
- Parts must be clean
- Wind-sensitive
- Needs more skill than MIG or stick welding.

only game in town. Mixtures containing a little helium or hydrogen bring better penetration in thick sections, faster welding speeds and lower ozone emission; but at a substantial cost premium. For normal work, pure argon is just fine.

Cylinders hold compressed gas at up to 3381psi (230bar) so the usual safety rules apply. Strap or chain the cylinder vertically to a solid support so it can't topple over. Use a regulator designed for argon, rated for the cylinder pressure and known to be good. Open the cylinder spindle valve slowly so as not to shock the regulator internals. If the unit has a built-in flowmeter, set gas flow at 20-40 cubic feet per hour (4-10 liters/min) depending on torch gas cup size and any local draughts. If not, set flow to a steady soft hiss at the cup. As with MIG welding, using a flow higher than needed brings no cleaning effect to dirty, rough-prepared work: it just empties the cylinder faster.

What about the **filler metal**? As always, this has to match the material welded.

Mild and low alloy steels. Don't use ordinary gas welding filler rod for TIG, as it won't wet the parent plate very well and the weld pool won't flow easily. General-purpose TIG filler comes in low- or medium-carbon forms, is easier to use, gives a better result and has AWS grade number ER70S-2 stamped on a flattened end. The more expensive triple-deoxidized fillers are better where the joint can't be completely cleaned, or for joining low alloy steels.

Stainless steel. A wide selection of stainless fillers can be had. For repair and fabrication of common 18/8 or 18/3 stainless steels, go for grades AWS ER308L or ER316L; again the grade will be stamped on the rod (4.10). If in doubt check with your welding supplier.

Aluminum. Fillers can be pure aluminum or contain a spicing of silicon or magnesium. Each suits

4.10 One or both ends of TIG filler wire usually carries an identifying code, though you might need your specs on to see it. The top rod is aluminum 5% silicon, the bottom one ER316L stainless.

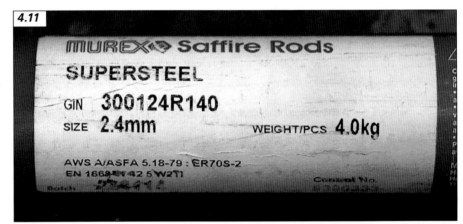

4.11. The rod pack sums up electrode capability. Store it so labelling stays readable, mice allowing.

a particular job – pure aluminum for joining pure aluminum (rare in farming), silicon for silicon-containing aluminum alloys and magnesium for magnesium-containing alloys. Unless you're fabricating with new metal it's unlikely that you'll know which aluminum grade you're dealing with, in which case the safest bet is to use a 5% silicon filler like ESAB's Tigrod 18.04 (AWS ER4043). This is the most forgiving choice, suitable for castings, sheet and extrusions. Magnesium-containing filler is more likely to centerline-crack if used on the wrong base material. At a pinch and if the job allows, it's possible to cut a thin strip of parent metal and use that as a filler.

Dissimilar and cast steels. If you need to join mild or low carbon steels to alloy steels or have material prone to cold cracking, try a chromium/nickel

filler like ESAB's OK Tigrod 16.53 (AWS grade ER309).

Cast iron. TIG's potentially localized heat input suits it to fusion welding thin-section cast iron. Either find a specific TIG filler or flake the flux from a small-diameter stick welding electrode and use that.

As usual the rod pack is the fount of all wisdom, so hang on to it (4.11).

Take control

Simple DC sets with either scratch- or lift-arc start won't have complicated controls. Welding current adjustment is usually the only thing.

HF-start sets are more complex, giving the user very fine control over gas flow and current at different stages of the weld. This is both good and bad news: good because

4.12 Some sets have a forest of adjusting knobs, others include one or more displays.

everything is tuneable to suit the work, bad because setup can get complicated, especially when you're starting out.

Knobs and buttons may be on the set's front panel, or settings might be scrolled through on an LCD screen. Either way, there will be plenty to fiddle with (4.12). Depending on the set, the options could include gas pre-flow, start current, current slope in/up, base current, pulse current, current slope out/down, crater current, crater time and gas post-flow – *take a deep breath, not done yet* – plus switches to turn HF start on/off, toggle the torch trigger function and allow remote control by foot pedal.

AC-DC sets may add wave balance control and more. But thankfully we're only concerned with DC units here.

The easiest way to sort it all out is to deal with the peripherals first, then follow the sequence of control events and their effects during a weld. So here goes.

To make torch operation less tiring, some TIG sets let you change the way the torch trigger works. The normal setup is **two-stroke** operation, in which the trigger button is pushed to start welding, held down during work and released to cut the arc or start a slope-down sequence. The alternative is **four-stroke** operation, where the trigger acts as a latch. A push-and-hold starts gas pre-flow and then the arc; then once the arc is running the trigger can be released to make torch control easier. As the end of the joint comes close, a second trigger push starts the slope-down crater-fill

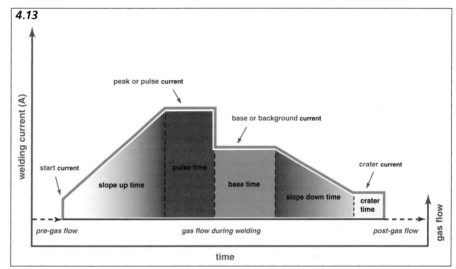

4.13 Time, current and gas flow during a pulsed TIG weld.

post-gas sequence. Four-stroke triggering is good once you've got the knack of it.

Better still is a remote foot control (4.14). Plugged into the set and used like a rock star's waa-waa pedal, the remote takes over from the torch trigger and brings stepless variation of welding current during work. Just how it interacts with settings made on the front panel depends on the unit. Apart from giving current variation on-the-move, the remote cuts out trigger operation altogether to reduce fatigue and boost physical control of the torch and arc.

Now for the various adjustments on the set – see 4.13.

Gas pre-flow sets the time in seconds that gas flows before the arc starts. The idea is to purge the torch and completely blanket the weld zone with argon, so a pre-flow of 2–3 seconds is

about right.

Start current, where adjustable, is set at a level which gives clean, fast arc initiation.

Slope up (also called slope in) sets the time in seconds over which welding current ramps up from start value to the base level. The longer the slope up time, the longer the operator has to see what's happening, position the filler rod and control fusion on a thin edge.

Peak or pulse current forms a team with **base or background current.** Between them they control heat input to the joint, potentially allowing good penetration without burn-through. The idea is simple, though the terminology and systems vary. During welding, pulses of higher current are laid over a lower background current. The extra heat produces a deeper melt; then between high pulses, the lower background temperature lets the pool

4.14

4.14 An option on some sets, foot pedal operation takes over from the torch switch to give ultimate controllability once mastered. Use it to start the arc, swell or cut the current during the weld, then trigger a slope-down sequence.

TIG Start — Scratch, Lift or HF?

Since TIG appeared in the 1940s, starting the arc has been a potential problem. If the tungsten electrode tip loses its shape through contact with the work the arc suffers, and if it sticks to the work the hard, brittle chunk of tungsten left behind upsets weld strength.

The simplest, cheapest technique is **scratch starting,** during which the operator tickles the tungsten over the work and the arc initiates as the short-circuit is broken. Tip damage and sticking are both strong possibilities, particularly for beginners.

Slightly more upmarket sets offer **lift arc starting.** This still involves contact between tungsten and the job, but the power supply gives more help. The user either touches and lifts a 'live' tungsten, or makes contact then triggers current and gas flow. This causes the set to deliver a precise low-current dose; not enough to spot-weld the electrode to the work, but enough to create a small spark as the torch is lifted. As the tungsten moves upwards the arc begins, and the power supply quickly ramps current up to the full welding value. Lift arc is easier on the operator and brings less risk of tungsten damage.

The most sophisticated option is **high-frequency (HF) starting.** The electrode is poised just above the job and current/gas flow triggered. The power unit delivers a short, sharp jolt of very high-frequency voltage, which generates a shower of sparks between the tungsten and the work. This breaks down air in the gap, ionizing it so welding current can flow. As there's no physical contact between tungsten and plate the risk of damage disappears, and starting is easier still. HF starting produces a burst of electromagnetic radiation which, although only present for a few milliseconds, can upset nearby electronic control systems.

---

solidify slightly to control burn-through.

Pulsed current operation is a little trickier to get right than one-step setting, but the added layer of control makes welding easier for the operator. Generally base and pulse current levels are set independently, as are the duration or frequency of each. To limit penetration in very thin material, set lower, less frequent pulse values on a low background. In thicker work, use higher, longer or more frequent pulses on a higher background. Pulse setting has a big impact on controllability and weld quality, so suck it and see.

Slope down (or slope out) is a decay in current from the welding values,

prompted by the operator releasing or re-clicking the torch trigger. Variable from less than one second to several seconds, it's used to limit heat input toward the end of a joint where temperatures are rising fast and the mass of metal able to sink the heat is shrinking.

Crater current and time may be adjustable separately from slope down. Set at a lower value than base current, crater current and duration should be just enough to let the operator maintain and fill the weld finish. If this is not done, the hollow pad left behind will be a focus for cracks.

Post-welding gas flow is also important to resist cracking and to let the tungsten

cool in an inert shield. If gas is cut off as the arc is broken, the molten weld pool will take up nitrogen, hydrogen and oxygen from the air and turn brittle. Setting gas post-flow time to 3–4 seconds is enough for the weld pool to solidify in thin material…and naturally the torch has to be held over the weld until flow stops.

So the more complex DC TIG sets have plenty to play with. Even more than with MIG, it pays to understand the basics then experiment while you're learning, first changing one variable at a time before seeing how different settings interact. And as with any technique, don't even think about welding safety-related items unless you're completely sure of the outcome.

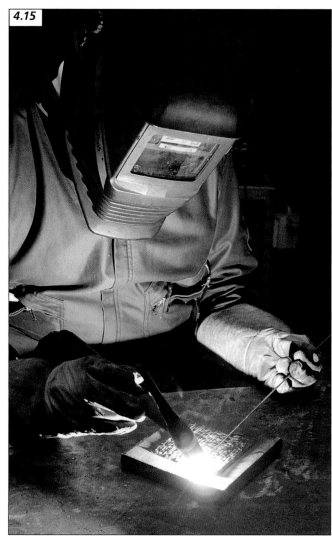

4.15 Physical relaxation is the first step toward control. Angle the work so it falls comfortably under your hands; rest your forearms or elbows on anything that's handy; or loop the torch lead over a support so you're not fighting its weight.

4.16 Grip one: Holding the torch like a pencil with your index finger on the trigger gives most control, though it's harder initially.

4.17 Grip two: The 'handshake' grip with thumb on trigger helps with T-fillet joints.

MAKING THE WELD 1
Comfort first

TIG is second cousin to gas welding, in that the operator has to control a heat source with one hand and probably add a filler rod with the other. If you can gas weld, you're off to a flying start with TIG. Mind you, gas is less demanding – the flame cone can touch the work without dire consequences, and if the weld area gets too hot you can lift the flame to cool it. TIG isn't so forgiving so operator skill must rack up another notch. And self help is the place to start.

All welding is easier if you're physically relaxed and not fighting the equipment, which produces the first rule of TIG: get ultra-comfortable before you begin. If you haven't got a welding bench, knock one up and bring portable jobs to it. There you can rest any or all of your anatomy on props assembled for the purpose – a stool for the bum, support for the elbows, something to take the weight of the torch leads (4.15). Angle the job so it falls naturally under your hands, and try relaxing your whole body before starting the arc. If you don't subsequently fall off the stool, you'll find control is much easier.

When the welder has to go to the work, stick to the same principles. It may take a while to get settled, but better that than rushing – torch control is hard enough without external complications.

A key element in comfort and control is the way you hold the torch. There's no right or wrong here, just alternatives. One tack is to grip it like a pen, with the index finger working the on/off button and it's neck supported by the fourth and little fingers (4.16). This takes a bit of getting used to, though the payoff is better control and easier change in electrode angle. The other option is to just grab the torch handle like you'd shake somebody's hand, using the thumb for the trigger (4.17). Easier to begin with, this grip is also best for fillet joints. Whichever way you choose, hold the torch gently (as tension generates wobbles) and invest in a pair of thin-leather TIG gloves for better feel (4.18).

4.18

4.18 TIG gloves – made from thinner leather than normal welder's gauntlets – give more feel.

Preparation is essential, not optional

Workshops steeped in stick welding tend to be a bit cavalier over preparation. A good rod flux usually floats gunk from the weld pool and locks it up in the slag, leaving the weld wholesome, or wholesome enough.

TIG fillers have no flux; just different levels of de-oxidants, depending on specification. And the process's argon shield gas only keeps weld-weakening gases in the air at bay. So how much surface contamination can TIG tolerate? Not a lot, and if you're after a top-quality result, none at all.

MIG's litany of grot-removal remedies applies to TIG. A little surface oil or grease is OK; it'll melt in the approaching arc heat. The thicker the layer, the more likely it is to spit and contaminate the tungsten. You'll see and hear this. A TIG electrode contaminated from any source produces a misshapen arc, which in turn means uneven joint heating, difficult weld pool control and potentially poor fusion and penetration. If you see trouble don't carry on. The

tungsten tip will discolor too, perhaps turning blue.

Paint in the weld area should be ground off completely. Where that's not possible, heat the joint area with a gas flame or the TIG arc until paint blisters, then wire brush clean. Platings can contaminate the weld, and some – yellow cadmium and galvanizing's zinc especially – are potentially evil when inhaled; as said before, cadmium fume can be fatal. Grind platings right off and avoid breathing the dust. If you've a lot of work to do with galvanized steel, think about using TIG braze-welding rather than straight fusion: more on that later.

Rust tolerance depends on how much of it there is. Flaky stuff has to be got rid of, no argument. Filler wire de-oxidants should float light surface rusting from a joint, though if there's any doubt and where maximum joint strength is essential, either abrade rust away or switch to triple de-oxidized rods. On thin sheet, an emery flap wheel or disc is kinder than an angle grinder.

When preparation has been skimped or the wire can't cope you'll soon know. As with gas fusion welding, a warning sign is a sparkling scum of oxide around, and sometimes on, the weld pool. In more severe cases the tungsten will pick up contaminants or the weld will turn visibly porous, in which case the only option is to grind it out and start again. Unlike other arc processes, TIG running in good conditions is almost silent and produces no sparks.

Keep gassing

Which brings us, if only by the most tenuous of routes, to shield gas flow and working outdoors. The first truth is that as with MIG, winding up gas flow can't (and won't) make up for poor surface preparation, and is likely to make things worse. Argon acts only as a blanket to keep air off; it can't react with weld pool contaminants and clear them away. So how much flow is enough, and why is too much a bad thing?

Argon regulators are usually calibrated in cubic feet per hour (liters/min) (4.19). Suggested flows run from 8.5 to 25.5 cubic feet per minute (4 to 12 liters/min), depending on material type, plate thickness and joint design. Roughly set and then fine-tune flow at the regulator with the torch's trigger pressed.

Lower flows go with the smaller weld pools and lower currents used to join thinner material, while bigger pools needed by thicker sections need more gas to shield them. Aluminum needs higher flows than steels, as it's welded with chunky electrodes and relatively wide weld pools. Flat-surface joints like butts and laps are more sensitive to low flows than fillets and inside corners, which through their cupped-hands shape tend to hold the gas blanket in place.

Table 4.1 gives general recommendations. Too little gas shows itself in several ways: the arc can wander if air gets alongside it; the weld pool is harder to form and carry forward, and the weld turns porous from oxidation. At the other extreme, too much flow produces high velocities in the ceramic. Turbulence can then pull air into the argon stream, again producing an unstable arc and porosity. In extreme cases the gas column will physically push the weld pool about, just like a gas flame that's too hard for the nozzle. If that's happening, do the

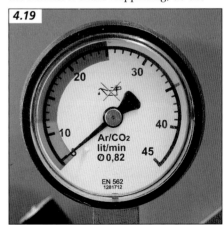

4.19

4.19 Argon regulators often show gas flow in liters/min. Adjust flow with the set turned on and the torch trigger pressed, or backpressure will give a false reading.

Table 4.2: **Material thickness, tungsten diameter and gas flow**

Plate thickness	Electrode dia	Argon flow (cubic feet per hour)
(1mm) 0.035"	(1mm) 0.040"	(4 l/m) 8.47
(2mm) 0.0787"	(1.5-2.0mm) 0.0591-0.08"	(4 l/m) 8.47
(3mm) ⅛"	(2mm) 0.08"	(5 l/m) 10.59
(4mm) ⁵⁄₃₂"	(2mm) 0.08"	(5 l/m) 10.59
(5mm) 0.2"	(2.0-3.0mm) 0.08"⅛"	(5 l/m) 10.59

Table 4.3: **Tungsten diameters and suggested welding currents**

Tungsten	DC			AC
	Electrode EN	Electrode EP		Zirconiated
(0.5mm) 0.020"	5-20	n/a		5-20 amps
(1.0mm) 0.040"	15-80	n/a		15-80 amps
(1.6mm) ¹⁄₁₆"	70-150	10-20		70-150 amps
(2.4mm) ³⁄₃₂"	150-250	15-30		110-180 amps
(3.2mm) ⅛"	250-400	25-40		150-200 amps

obvious – reduce flow at the regulator or switch to a bigger cup. TIG's requirement for consistent gas shielding make it very sensitive to drafts, even more so than MIG. If you have to work outdoors, use a gas lens rather than a straight ceramic (page 81) and put up as much physical cover round the job as possible.

Angles, distances and speeds

Basic torch and rod angles for DC TIG on steels are in 4.20. A fairly steep torch angle fires arc heat directly into the joint, rather than letting it play ahead of the molten weld pool and risk melting the filler early. Keep the filler rod low and close to the action, so it stays inside the protective gas shield and can be dipped squarely into the front edge of the molten pool. If exposed to the air, the filler wire tip will oxidize and take this contamination into the joint.

4.20 Angles for down-hand (flat) TIG. At the start of a joint the torch can be steeper than here; moving the tungsten in a tight circle helps fuse joint edges into a molten pool. Once this is established, tilt the torch back a little and set off down the joint line. Filler rod (right) is kept low, with the tip never far from the arc so it stays in the protective shield gas.

Hold arc length relatively short at ⅛-0.2" (3-5mm), depending on the current. The longer the arc, the wider and cooler the weld pool.

Current spotting

Without an investment in more technology, the scope to vary heat input during a TIG weld is limited. Varying travel speed is one way (as slower=hotter), changing the volume of filler added is another (as more filler=cooler). Both can compromise weld quality if taken too far. The thing you can't do is lift or lower the torch more than a little, as the power source will outwit the operator by adjusting arc current to try to keep heat input constant. The only proper way to vary heat input while welding with TIG – and then only where the set and job location allow – is to add a foot control (4.14), which works as a throttle pedal to start, stop, swell or fade welding current as you work.

Like the way you hold the torch, there is no 'right' electrode diameter for any particular job. Rather, various diameters can be used – as long as the current needed to produce a stable arc and a controllable weld pool lies in the tungsten's working range (Table 4.3). There's the physical side too – fatter electrodes and bigger gas cups

can't get to limited-access joints.

Electrodes can tolerate a surprisingly wide current range. But recognising the maximum and minimum points still matters, as these prompt a change in diameter. With thoriated electrodes on mild and stainless steels, the warning signs are:

- **Current too high for diameter.** The electrode starts to lose its fine point during work, followed by complete physical collapse.

- **Current too low for diameter.** Poor arc ignition, then the arc tends to wander. A weld pool won't form easily as the tungsten absorbs too much heat.

AC/DC welding aluminum needs zirconiated electrodes. For these the signs are:

- **Current too high for diameter.** The electrode's ball end wobbles or comes off.

- **Current too low for diameter.** The arc can't break the weld pool's oxide film, as the tungsten is absorbing too much heat.

MAKING THE JOINT 2

Bringing it all together

The simplest joints are those that don't need added filler metal. They're a particularly good place to begin, as both the operator's hands are left free to support the torch. That's always a positive thing to do where you can, as most of us need all the help we can get with any sort of welding. It's also a useful way to develop control – start with two hands, take one away.

So, these filler-free or autogenous (self-making) joints are fast, neat and often used in TIG production work. Common examples are the lap joint (4.21) and outside corner (4.22). On farms the first is handy for repair, the second when making things like guards.

As always, laps and outside corners need accurate alignment before welding. The plate edges must touch all the way along the joint line, for the technique relies on melting equal parts of each to form the joint. Where there's a gap, the weld pool wants to disappear and one plate edge tends to burn back (4.23). So start by straightening the plates, then tack them every couple of inches; close any gaps with gentle hammer work.

If you're using ⅟₁₆-0.08" (1.5-2mm) mild steel sheet, start with a ⅟₁₆" (1.6mm) thoriated tungsten and about 50A. On sets that allow it, use the following: 1sec pre-gas time, HF start, 20A start current, 1.5sec slope up, no pulse, 1.5sec slope down, 15A crater current and 3secs post-gas time. With simpler units, dial in as much of that as the set allows.

To run the weld, first find a comfortable working position. If you can reach the whole joint without shifting, so much the better. With the torch vertical, start the arc and close it down so the tungsten is about ⅛" (3mm) from the plate. If the joint halves don't melt equally, circle the torch to encourage them to form a central pool. If that pool doesn't appear quickly – remembering to allow for slope-up time – then stop and boost the current a little until it does.

4.21 Lap welds don't necessarily need filler rod, as long as the plates are in close contact with each other. Setup: ⅟₁₆" (1.6mm) thoriated tungsten, ⅟₁₆" (1.6mm) mild steel sheet, 60A

4.22a An outside corner tacked and ready to go…

4.22b …then part-finished. Edges can be fused without adding filler rod.

Once the pool's established, tilt the torch back by about 15° and move off down the joint. Travel at a speed that lets the pool melt the plate edges (for an open corner joint) or the upper plate's top edge (for a lap joint). Heat will get to the far end of the plates before you do, so take your finger off the torch button to start the cooler slope-down sequence before the finish. Hold the torch steady over the finish area – the pre-set lower

crater current should stop burn-through – then once the arc goes out, keep the torch there until the post-weld gas flow stops. That last bit is important. If air gets to the weld finish before it cools, cracking is likely. The continuing argon flow also keeps air from the tungsten while it too calms down.

Now add some filler …

Next step is to wield a filler rod. Butt joints are common so that's the

job – weld one plate to another laid alongside it, in the flat (down-hand position). As with laps and open corners, tack the plates together first. This time, though, leave a penetration gap roughly equal to plate thickness (4.24). It won't matter if the edges aren't straight and tidy, as filler will take care of them. How thick should the filler rod be? Chunky enough to build up the joint without non-stop dipping, but not so thick that adding it causes the temperature

4.23 Whoops. If plate edges aren't touching it's very hard to start a joint without filler (arrow). The weld pool will disintegrate if there's a gap part-way along, too.

to dive and the molten weld pool to nearly freeze.

The technique is this. Form a pool, add rod, use arc heat to push the pool forward into fresh metal, add rod, push the pool forward again … and so on. Shift the tungsten back a little (don't lift it more than a gnat's) before adding rod, so there's less chance of a filler-tungsten collision. If that happens you'll have to stop and re-grind the electrode tip, as the arc won't heat evenly.

Start the arc, make a pool and move off. Try very deliberately to place the filler rod directly into the pool, just like dipping a pen in an inkwell. If you're too young to know about inkwells, think of dipping the business end of a pool cue into a corner pocket. Doesn't matter if the filler sticks to the pool's front edge; leave it there and arc heat will quickly free it. The thing is not to let arc heat melt the filler ahead of the pool. If that happens, filler metal and plate won't fuse properly.

Travel speed depends on the balance between welding current, material thickness and filler addition, but as usual the idea is to work as fast as possible while still keeping control of the molten pool. As the joint end hoves into view, trigger the slope-down sequence. Make a tidy finish, adding filler so the weld bead isn't left concave and weak. Wait for post-weld gas flow to finish, and job done (4.24 and 25).

If your set allows, experiment with the two-stage current available through pulse welding. Try different pulse sizes and durations, using the high current for the melt-and-push-pool-forward phase and the cooler background time for adding filler. Pulse welding adds a lot of flexibility, and is very useful to balance penetration against burn-through on thin sheet.

… and finally fillets

Number three common joint is the T-fillet, welded in the flat (down-hand) position. The basics are the same as always: tack up, make a pool from both joint halves, add filler low and to the front of it, trigger slope-down before the end. Several detail tweaks should make this go easier.

As usual, get comfortable and use anything handy to take torch weight. Shift your grip to the handshake style (4.17), which gives better control for fillets. If you're of an economical turn of mind, gas flow can be reduced a little as joint shape retains the blanket better than butts or laps. For best access and visibility, switch to a smaller ceramic and increase tungsten stickout to a maximum of ⅜" (10mm). Pick a filler diameter that looks as if it'll build the required weld fillet without burning back like a fuse, or you'll need to shuffle rod through your fingers too often.

4.24 Butt joints in mild steel sheet need a penetration gap about as wide as the plates are thick. While it's possible to weld these without filler, penetration will probably be shallow. This one used 1/16" (1.6mm) rod and 60A.

4.25 The reverse side of 4.24 shows that where the penetration gap, heat input and speed of travel are about right, fusion will be full-depth.

Tack and dress the plates so the joint edges are touching, particularly with thin sheet. Gaps expose the vertical plate, which will burn away quickly. If this looks to be starting, drop the temperature locally by adding filler at the top of the joint.

Build a pool between both plates and move off. Keep the electrode angled into the root of the joint (4.26) rather than pointing it too far forward down the line, as this lets heat skip forward rather than putting it where most needed. Use the standard technique – melt, push forward, add rod – but be certain to hold the melt phase for long enough to let metal right at the root of the joint fuse into the pool. Again, pulsed operation can help with thin sheet. If you don't get a proper melt (and it's easy not to) then you're just building a bridge between the plates. This may do for light-duty applications, but will fail earlier than a fillet welded to full depth.

Finally, watch out for undercut. This usually turns up on the vertical plate as a weakening notch above the weld. It's the outcome of too much heat and too little filler rod. To fix undercut? Drop

the welding current, work a little faster or add more filler high in the joint to protect the vulnerable vertical plate.

The ups and downs

To weld vertically upwards with TIG, take the normal flat technique and rotate it through 90°, as you would for gas welding. That puts the torch pointing up the joint line, and the filler rod pointing down it (4.27). As with flat T-fillets, switch to the 'handshake' grip and use a little more electrode stick-out to reach into the bottom of the joint.

You can't build steps to support fresh weld metal as you can with MIG or stick work, as the weld pool is too fluid. So the pool has to be carried up the joint non-stop, which takes good physical control. As with other TIG jobs, pulsed current buys time, especially on thinner metals. Collect yourself in the cooler background pulse, then use the hot pulse to push the pool into fresh parent plate. Keep the filler wire low so it doesn't tangle up with the tungsten, and plonk the tip directly into the pool's leading edge. Which can be rather easier said than done, particularly

where the job doesn't make it easy to rest on something solid.

Current and rod diameter? As ever, heat input must walk the line between a good, fairly fast melt of the parent plates – for penetration – and producing a weld pool that's easy prey to gravity through being too big and too fluid. If the pool sags and burn-though is happening, drop the current. If the pool's hard to start and maintain, add amps. And the right filler wire helps: pick a diameter that builds the joint readily without constant dipping, as the more you dip the more control you'll need.

Welding vertically down with TIG can be very handy. Gravity can work for

4.27 Vertical TIG is about as hard as it gets. Rest body weight, relax, be happy. Travelling up or down, use the same filler/torch angles as you would for a flat butt. Relatively thick filler minimizes rod additions. If your set allows it, try a fairly long background current pulse to give a mini-breather between the higher-current pushes into fresh plate. Setup: ¼" (6mm) mild steel plate, ⅛" (3.2mm) filler, ⅛" (3.2mm) thoriated tungsten, 180A, no pulse.

4.26 Basic torch and rod angles for a flat (downhand) T-fillet. Feed the filler rod in low so it can slip under the arc. Keep the tungsten relatively square to the joint; heat then goes where it's needed, while filler rod – which is plonked straight into the weld pool – isn't melted early.

you, pulling down the molten pool so it's constantly quenched by fresh plate. It's often the best technique with thin sheet, generating strong results quickly without the need to use a filler rod. Which also means that two hands can control torch movement.

Material considerations

Now for some specifics on different metals. The steels (mild, low carbon and stainless) can all be welded easily without filler rod if the joint allows. Watch out with no-filler butts, as complete penetration is hard to achieve without using a lot of heat. Such welds have a shallow profile and centerline-crack easily, as there's not the thickness in the joint to handle stress from contraction or loading.

Tungsten composition and quality influences ease of work and joint integrity. For steels, the best all-round choice is a big-name brand of 2% thoriated electrode. Be specific when buying and if necessary spend a little more, rather than taking what comes. Multi-purpose and 1% thoriated tungstens tend to lose their tip easier, particularly in scratch-start DC TIG. In all cases – mild and stainless steels – pure argon shield gas is the best choice.

Heat travels slowly through stainless steel, which expands and contracts more than the mild stuff. As a result stainless is much more likely to distort, so that needs thinking about before starting a job. Putting in as little heat as possible will help; use pulse welding if you can. In any case, set the minimum current that gives good fusion and allows steady, consistent progress, and keep the filler rod dipping in and out regularly to balance pool heat. Using a gas lens is a good idea, as it delivers a more even argon blanket so makes a better job of excluding oxygen which, when it hits hot weld metal, turns the surface rough and black.

When you've got the balance right, the joint will show even ripples and have a fine straw color, at least on the top side (4.28). Underneath it'll probably be

4.28 Stainless steel TIG-welding with good gas shielding and about the right current shows even, small ripples and a straw-color finish. Setup: 0.0591" (1.5mm) stainless sheet, ¹⁄₁₆" (1.6mm) thoriated tungsten, ¹⁄₁₆" (1.6mm) filler, 45A base current, 55A pulse.

4.29 Underside of a butt joint in stainless steel, welded with too much current. Note the burnt, black oxide finish – shield gas can't keep oxygen away from here.

burnt-looking from oxygen attack, but not to worry; that's just a surface effect that doesn't weaken the joint (4.29). If it bothers you, cleaning with weak acid will get rid of most of it – a good welding supplier will suggest what to use. The cleaner stainless steel is before welding, the better finish you'll get. It's more contamination-sensitive than mild steel.

We've touched before on DC welding aluminum, suggesting that (with a bit of luck and a following wind) it can be used on non-critical jobs, though never where safety is involved. Here's some explanation and few thoughts.

The problem in using DC TIG to join aluminum lies in persuading two molten pools, one on each joint plate, to fuse into a single pool which can be carried along the weld line. Stopping the happy wedlock is a skin of very hard-to-melt refractory oxides on each pool, with the result that it's a bit like trying to join two footballs full of water. The buzz of alternating current (AC) more easily breaks that skin, so it's the preferred choice.

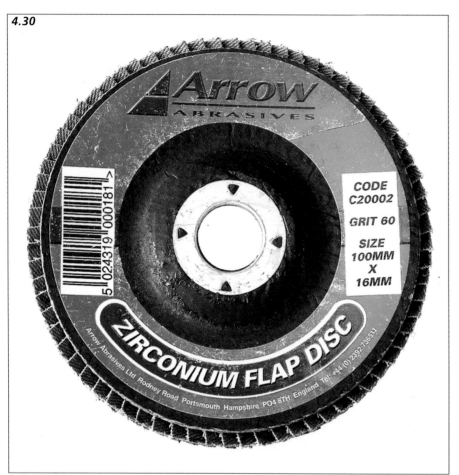

4.30

4.30 Aluminum must be cleaner than clean before welding. A zirconium flap wheel or stainless steel wire brush whisks off oxides without leaving contaminants behind.

Grind a zirconiated tungsten square, then it'll develop a rounded tip in use. Weld aluminum with the torch almost vertical, tilting it just enough to see the front edge of the weld pool. The arc from a blunt tip isn't as directional as the arc from a pointed one, and too much tilt elongates the pool and makes breaking the oxide skin harder. The filler rod will also tend to melt too early as you feed it toward the pool.

To help break the skin and get the pools to fuse, work the arc round in a tight circle as you start the weld. Once they have joined, the surface will clear to reveal bright, liquid aluminum and you're away.

Pure argon shield gas is fine. If you're only going to keep one sort of filler, go for a 10% silicon type like ESAB's OK Tigrod 18.05. These match most common sheet and castings and are usefully ductile, so are less prone to cracking as the weld solidifies.

Trying to weld with DC and the torch plugged into the negative socket as usual – DC negative – isn't good at breaking the oxide skin or cleaning oxides from the plate surfaces. Reversing the leads to make the tungsten DC positive is much better, though not as good as AC. The snag is that now the electrode carries two-thirds of the arc energy while the work takes only one third, so a fat zirconiated electrode is needed to stand the heat. This can be considerable, for although aluminum melts at a much lower temperature than steel, it conducts heat much faster so relatively high input will be needed.

Really thorough preparation is vital when trying to DC weld aluminum. The cleaner the metal, the easier it'll form a weld pool. Pre-heating up to about 100°C with a gas torch will make surface oxides easier to shift; then follow up quickly with a good scrub from a stainless steel wire brush or stainless wool pad. Using something made from mild steel will add iron oxides, so won't help. More violent cleaning comes from an aluminum oxide flap wheel or disc (4.30). Don't use a disc designed for steel as it'll only leave weakening inclusions. Keep filler rods clean and don't wear dirty old gloves in work, or the filler will pick up contamination as you handle it.

TIG brazing — sometimes a savior

When technique is less than perfect (and whose isn't?) joining thin steel sheet can give anyone a hard time, even with TIG's low currents and tiny arcs. That's when TIG brazing can lend a hand. It's also good on galvanized steel, where the heat of fusion welding destroys the coating, puts poisonous zinc fumes into the air and generally isn't much cop unless all the plating is ground off first. TIG brazing runs over galvanizing, saving time and effort; it's more pleasant to do and the joint needs only a coat of zinc-rich paint to protect against corrosion.

What's more, TIG brazing's relatively low temperatures deliver low distortion welds in mild steel. And it can join cast iron, silicon bronzes, brass and dissimilar metals, so is a very handy technique to know.

The idea is the same as gas flame brazing or bronze welding. That is, an alloy with a lower melting point than the parent metal is used as a metal-based glue. Brazing uses capillary action to suck the molten filler into a joint, so the TIG version isn't strictly that. Rather it's braze welding, where the filler metal is flowed over hot, clean surfaces to build a fillet of material (4.31).

The preliminaries parallel gas brazing. The parent metal(s) must be completely clean or the filler will blandly refuse to flow, so the usual thorough degreasing/light grinding routines apply. And the joint metal has to be hot enough, or filler laid on its surface will pull into a tight ball and go nowhere.

The filler rod can be silicon, aluminum or manganese bronze, specified for TIG work – gas filler won't do. Silicon bronze is the most ductile and flexible in service. The weld it leaves is more copper-colored than aluminum bronze's yellow finish. Manganese bronze gas rods can be used with TIG to join cast iron if joint faces are given a coat of filler

4.31 TIG brazing is good backup to fusion TIG for joints in very thin mild and stainless sheet, and in brass and bronze alloys. It's also good on galvanized steel, reducing fuming and coating loss. Yellow finish is typical. Setup: ¹⁄₁₆" (1.6mm) mild steel sheet, ¹⁄₁₆" (1.6mm) thoriated tungsten, silicon bronze filler, 40A.

4.32 A lap joint TIG-brazed at the right current and forward speed runs quiet and smooth (A), with virtually no melt of the parent plates. Deliberately slowing travel increases heat input to the point that the underlying plates fuse with the bronze filler, which promptly cracks (B) and loses strength. Speeding up again resumes normal service (C).

(buttering) before the weld is made.

Welding technique is straightforward. Use a slim thoriated tungsten, argon shield gas and just enough current to heat the joint quickly to red. Feed the bronze filler toward the arc and let it melt on the hot plates at the fringe of the arc; work quickly, using a melt, flow and move-forward sequence. Depending on the joint type and

welding current, some very limited fusion of the parent plates is OK. If the joint gets too hot you'll soon know – the bronze will spread itself thin and wide, the underlying plate will melt and dilute the filler and the work is likely to crack (4.32).

So there it is. TIG can be the most frustrating of processes, but is highly satisfying when you get it right. Minority sport or not, it's a worthwhile addition to the workshop.

Plasma Cutting

Plasma cutter: There's a name with a real Star Wars ring to it, although the technology dates back to the 1950s and isn't nearly as scary as it sounds. But it's still very clever stuff – and since the recent introduction of small inverter-based sets, plasma cutting is increasingly affordable on the farm.

What can it do for you? Traditional gas cutting kit works by oxidizing hot metal, and there lies its Achilles heel. Faced with something that won't oxidize (stainless steel, aluminum) or oxidizes poorly (cast iron), oxy-acetylene or oxy-propane can't cope. A plasma cutter, though, can slice anything which conducts electricity – so all the steels and non-ferrous metals are fair game (5.1). Using plasma takes less skill to use than oxy-fuel cutting, is potentially safer (there are no fuel gases and no flashback risk) and fillets metals with speed, surgical tidiness and precision.

Yet it's not the universal solution for agriculture. Today's sets are still very expensive compared with gas cutting kit, and consumables don't last long. Modern single-phase machines have limited capability and are tied to a compressed air supply, so aren't readily mobile. Neither can they heat, weld or offer the wide cutting thickness choice of gas. But if you have a need to make speedy, neat cuts in single items or stacks – and don't want the hassle and cost of cylinders – then plasma is definitely worth a look. To see how it works, see page 98. Before then, here are two quick definitions: a **quality** cut has a clean finish with minimal, easily-removed dross and is produced by a plasma set working within its capability. A **severed** cut will separate but needs much more cleaning up, and tells you that the set is literally working on the ragged edge. The difference between the two can be just 0.08"-⅛" (2-3mm) plate thickness (5.2).

Needs, options, costs

Plasma cutting will fit right into most workshops. All that's required is a single-phase mains outlet for smaller sets (13A is usually OK if the plug has a slow-blow fuse) or three-phase power for bigger ones, plus a reliable supply of clean compressed air. The latter may not be needed as some small plasma cutters have a compressor on board, though such sets have lower capability as the mains must feed both the compressor and the welding circuit. About 4-5cfm (120 l/min) air at 80–90psi (5.5–6bar) will serve single-phase sets; a requirement deliverable by even a modest compressor. Three-phase tackle able to sever 1¾" (45mm) mild steel needs about 5.5–6.0cfm (165 l/min) at similar pressures.

5.1

5.1 Gas can't slice aluminum or stainless steel – but plasma can.

5.2a

5.2. A little extra metal thickness turns a quality cut (5/16" [8mm] mild steel, top) into a sever cut (⅜" [10mm] mild steel, bottom).

5.2b

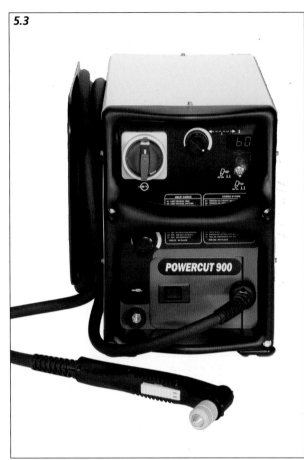

5.3

POWERCUT 900

5.3 A good single-phase inverter set has stepless control of current, warnings for over-temperature and low air pressure and a regulator/gauge for pressure setting. The air check button simulates flow to allow accurate setting.

Photo courtesy of ESAB North America.

The supplied air must be dry, as wet air leads to uncontrolled arcing in the torch which will quickly wreck it. Good sets have their own inlet air filter/regulator to back up the workshop outlet's own separator, and both of these must be serviced regularly.

Plasma can also pierce and gouge, albeit within limits. Piercing capability extends to about 60% of cutting capacity, while gouging is the preserve of three-phase sets.

The market divides into inverters (small, portable) and conventional power units. Either way, the cost/capability balance strikes hard. Most single-phase equipment is limited to quality-cutting 5/16-3/8" (8–10mm) steel, which on farms won't be enough for plasma to be the only

cutting technology.

Three-phase sets able to cut 1¾" (45mm) steel are significantly more expensive. So as usual, equipment choice depends on the depth of your pocket and planned use. Where light-gauge work features such as ducting, irrigation pipes, cladding, trailer sides, vehicle bodywork, gates, guards and decorative ironwork, an ESAB plasma cutter with ¼" (6mm) capability ($600–800) brings convenience without big capital outlay.

Or you can take the next step up. The Hypertherm (5.3) is rated at 45A and lists at $1,600 at the time of writing. It runs from a 16A socket and can sever up to ⅜" (10mm) mild steel. The latest generation single-phase sets like Hypertherm's 1650 have higher performance, severing 1¾" (44mm) in steel and quality-cutting to 1½" (38mm).

Such units – and those from other big-name makers – come with solid warranty backup and deliver what it says on the tin. Expect to pay $3,000-4000 for an 85A single-phase inverter, rising to $4,000-5,200 for a three-phase machine with 1¾" (45mm) cutting capability.

Main consumables are the electrode and tip. An hour's continuous work before replacement is normal; new electrodes are about $10-12. Outer nozzles ($15-20) wear slowly but are at risk of physical damage. The significant cost of consumables is offset for many users by plasma's speed, ease, and ability to work round a template – which comes in

very handy when making weathervanes and such.

How does it work?

A plasma is just a gas that's been superheated until it breaks down and ionizes. Plasmas are intensely hot – up to 90,032°F but typically 27,032-36,032°F (up to 50,000°C but typically 15,000–20,000°C) – and conduct electricity very readily.

Equipment varies from highly complex, mechanized industrial units to portable packs (5.4). All work on the same principle. Simple single-phase sets make their plasma from ordinary air; three-phase sets use air too, but may also add a second gas like nitrogen.

The plasma is generated inside a torch. Smaller and handier than the gas cutting equivalent, in its simplest form this holds a central electrode, a tip with a small exit hole centered over the electrode, and a surrounding ceramic/fibre cup (5.5). When the operator clicks the torch trigger, compressed air at 4–6bar (60–90psi) streams down around the electrode and exits through the tip.

After a short pause the power supply delivers a jolt of high frequency DC to the electrode, creating an internal pilot arc between the electrode and tip. This ionizes the air stream into a plasma, which pushes the pilot arc out from the tip. On contact with the work the set's main arc fires up and tracks down the plasma. The pilot arc is shut off, and main arc generates a straight, clean-edged plasma column travelling at near-supersonic speed. The combination of arc heat and plasma jet force first melts, then blows away metal to leave a narrow, clean cut line (or kerf) with very little dross. The cut continues for as long as there is metal for the arc to transfer to, or until the operator releases the trigger. Air then continues to flow for a few seconds to cool the torch.

5.4 Dense technology inside a modern inverter helps explain the price.

5.6 A plasma electrode has a central core of hafnium or tungsten (arrow), surrounded by copper. Service life is about one hour's continuous use, cost is $6.50-8.

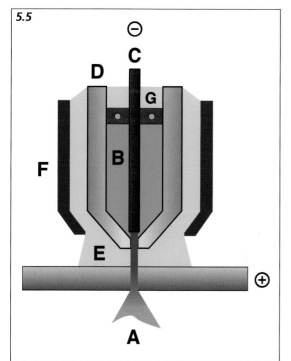

5.5 Torch operation. An intensely hot plasma jet (A) is formed from swirling high-pressure air (B) as it's ionized by an arc from the central electrode (C). The nozzle (D) concentrates the jet through a small hole. Cooling air (E) flows round the nozzle, contained by a shield cup (F). A ceramic collar around the electrode controls air swirl (G).

By varying the current, gas flow, gas type and tip hole diameter, the size and force of the plasma jet can be changed. Different thicknesses of varying materials can thus be cut. Or by using lower gas flow in dedicated kit, welding is possible.

Air is deliberately swirled into a mini-tornado as it enters the electrode chamber. The spin centers it on the electrode and forms the blast into a tight, parallel-sided column exiting the tip.

The electrode itself has a core of hafnium or tungsten sheathed in copper (5.6). Hafnium (a close relative of the zirconium used in TIG electrodes) is used with air as it can stand contact with oxygen; tungsten is used with nitrogen. The tip is also copper and would normally melt from proximity to the intensely hot plasma, but is protected by a skin of non-ionized, cooler air formed in the swirl process.

Torches vary in design. Single-gas versions (naturally enough) use one gas, typically air, but divide it into two flows internally; one swirled for the plasma and another passing around the outside of the tip to cool it (5.5). This shield flow also boosts cut quality, reduces spatter and helps when piercing. Multi-gas torches allow different gases to be used for plasma generation and shielding. Torches on bigger kits are usually single-gas and cooled by water.

Setup

The torch has an on-off trigger and in some cases, a stepped tip designed to follow a guide or template: the latter is useful when working in thin material (5.7). When precision is needed in thicker stuff, run the outer nozzle (rather than the tip) along a guide.

Torch components are few and fit together logically (5.8). Switch off mains power before delving into the innards and don't lose the ceramic swirl baffle. If

5.7

5.7 Some tips are stepped (1) so they can run round a sheet metal template. In thicker metals, rest the nozzle (2) on a guide if required – see 5.12 for an example.

5.8

5.8 Torch components are the electrode (1), ceramic swirl baffle (2), tip (3) and nozzle (4). The electrode and tip are consumables.

5.9

5.9 Compare a new tip (front, center) with worn ones. As the central hole loses size and shape, cut quality goes down.

this is not in the right place or damaged, plasma won't form properly and arcing inside the torch is likely.

The electrode and tip are both consumable. Work with an electrode until it's about 0.2" (5mm) shorter than a new one: beyond this, the pilot arc will be reluctant to jump from the electrode to the tip and the torch won't fire up.

The tip itself both squeezes and directs the plasma jet. Cutting performance will suffer as the central hole erodes. With proper setup and a good tip, the cut line or kerf will be clean, narrow – much narrower than with a gas torch – and square-shouldered. Replace a tip as soon as the center hole elongates or grows (5.9), or when the kerf widens and becomes untidy. The outer ceramic/fibre nozzle will gradually deteriorate but unless whole segments break away, this won't affect cutting performance.

Plant setting

The workshop compressor must be able to deliver ample air without flagging, or cutting performance will go rapidly downhill. About 120 l/min air (4-5cfm) should serve single-phase sets, while bigger ones need 165 l/min (5.5-6.0cfm). Fit the air supply point with a water trap and turn off or remove any air tool lubricator. If a short extension hose is needed to get the set to the job, use at least ⁵⁄₁₆" (8mm) bore.

A good plasma cutting set has its own inbuilt water trap/regulator (5.10). This, and the one on the supply outlet, must be empty and clean. Adjust air pressure to the maker's requirement on the set's own regulator, using the air check facility (where provided) to mimic cutting conditions. Typical pressure will be 5.5–6bar (80–90psi).

5.10

STAY SAFE

Plasma cutting is an arc process, so it's vital to take the usual precautions against skin burns and eye damage. Cover up exposed areas and use a welding filter specified for arc use. Gas welding goggles will not do. Arc intensity is relatively low, so shades EW5–EW10 handle all work.

In this Murex torch, the business end is isolated from the power supply by a small switch button (arrow), released as the outer cup is unscrewed.

High open circuit voltages (200V–plus) at the torch add an extra hazard. It follows that torch maintenance must never be carried out with the plasma cutter switched on. Better-designed torches have automatic backup protection in the form of an internal switch: in the Murex version pictured, a cut-out button (arrow) isolates the torch from its power supply as the nozzle is unscrewed. Such backup is there ONLY for the odd time that you make a mistake. For primary safety, switch the set off at the mains.

5.10 Good sets have their own regulator/water trap.

All that's left is to dial in the amperage required for a clean, full-depth cut in the material you're working with. Trial and error is the way forward until you've worked out what your set can do.

The thermal conductivities of aluminum and stainless steel are different to carbon and cast steels, so cutting capacity is lower in these metals. Naturally, thickness also has an effect: using high current on thin material won't cause problems as long as you speed up forward travel to suit, while in thick stuff you'll have to slow down so the cut can penetrate. The set's capacity limit is reached when the kerf won't clear and slag blows back toward the torch.

Technique

A caution or two to start. When slicing conventionally with a gas torch, even a tiny air gap stops the cut – but not

so with plasma. The positive news is that you can stack-cut several sheets at once. The negative is that when you're trying to separate one thing from another (say, a damaged bearing from its housing) you can no longer rely on the gap between parts to break the cut. On top of that you'll need to take more care when working over something you might not want damaged, like an anvil.

And watch out where you put the set's return lead. As with any arc process, if current passes through the small contact points of bearing balls or through bushings on its way back to the set, resistance heating can produce flat spots in them.

Cuts in thin materials or at currents below 45A are usually made with the torch tip resting on the work. For higher currents and thicker materials, leave a 0.08"-⅛" (2-3mm) stand-off gap between tip and work. A specially-designed stand-off nozzle can be used

where consistent top-quality results matter (5.11).

To start a cut, position yourself where you'll be able to see the tip all the while. Hold the torch so the tip's central hole is just in contact with the work (5.12): this

5.11

5.11 A stand-off nozzle helps make consistent cuts in thicker material, but limits the operator's view. The metal shield runs easily alongside a guide (bottom).

5.12 To start a cut cleanly, position the tip with its hole on the edge of the work (arrow). Working with sheet, hold the torch upright. With plate, angle it as shown – this is ⁵⁄₁₆" (8mm) mild steel.

5.13 The right travel speed sees a continuous stream of molten metal clearing the cut. Dross (arrow) will chip away easily.

5.14 Compare torch angle with the molten flow leaving the plate to see how the plasma column bends. Note the very narrow kerf width and lack of distortion – both are characteristic of plasma cutting.

allows the plasma stream to initiate quickly. Then squeeze the trigger. After a burst of compressed air, the arc fires up and the cut starts. Move off at a speed which keeps a steady stream of molten slag flowing from below.

On thin sheet hold the torch vertical. In thicker stuff the plasma column bends on its way through, so allow for this

by angling the torch slightly forward in the direction of travel (5.12). At the end of a cut, keep the trigger down until the sliced plate falls away – if you let up too soon, the plasma stream won't clear the bottom edge and a tiny island will be left uncut.

Making holes, gouging

Plasma can pierce holes in any conductive material, though maximum depth is limited to about 60% of the set's cutting thickness capability.

As when starting to pierce with gas, molten metal will splash up from the surface. If fine metal spray interferes with the magnetic field around the plasma column, the column can sway into the tip and damage it. Or, if molten metal bridges the gap between the tip and plate, high current will flow through this bridge and wreck the tip completely.

Get around both problems by starting to pierce with the torch canted over at roughly 45°. Once the initial splash subsides and a crater opens up, gradually bring the torch upright. Maintain a standoff gap of about twice the normal cutting height between tip and plate, or as much as the set will allow. Work around the embryo hole until it's the required size.

Unless you're blessed with a good eye and a steady hand – or better still, a circle cutting attachment – some modification is usually needed to tidy up the hole. While plasma lets you carve slices from the edges to round out a hole or to increase its diameter, this is not as easy as with gas. The plasma stream stops immediately when there is no conductive metal below it.

Gouging is a good way to cut a preparation U-groove before welding. Plasma is ideal for the job, but you'll need a three-phase set – most single-phase sets don't have the grunt to produce a long plasma column. Which is a pity, as gouging with plasma is faster, more effective and less fume-ridden than with a SMAW rod. Use a wide tip, hold the torch at about 40° and blow metal away, repeating if necessary until the right profile/depth is reached.

Problems, causes

Here are some common faults and their fixes.

- **Reluctant arc strike.** Poor earth return connection/path; worn electrode too short; air pressure too high.

- **Substandard cut.** Material too thick for set's capability; electrode too short; tip orifice misshapen or too big; travel too fast.

- **Heavy dross build-up.** Travel too slow; current too high; material thickness at set's upper capability limit.

- **Material distortion.** Travel too slow; current too high.

- **Internal arcing.** Ceramic anti-swirl baffle missing or damaged; water in compressed air supply.

- **Fluffy-looking plasma column.** Water in compressed air supply.

- **Reduced cutting speed/thickness.** Low air pressure or flow; current set too low.

Section 6
SPECIAL TECHNIQUES

1. Welding Cast Iron

Back in Granddad's time, cast iron and farm machinery were inseparable. These days there doesn't seem to be quite so much of it about, although now and again a broken sprocket or some such is likely to thump on the bench for repair. When it does, what are the welding options?

One thing is for sure – it's funny old stuff, as likely to crack as not and never coming with a guarantee of repair. And the dirtier the casting, the more unpredictable is the outcome. Welding problems stem from three main areas:

- **Contraction stresses.** Cast iron is brittle, and often can't put up with different rates of contraction between the weld and parent material. So just when you thought you'd got away with it, the work goes 'ping' and cracks, usually in the heat-affected zone alongside the weld. Back to the drawing board.

- **Item shape.** Castings usually have nooks and crannies, changes

of section and complicated shape, all of which make good preparation difficult and accommodating those contraction stresses harder.

- **Oil.** Absorbed into the material's micropores and held on graphite in its structure, oil vaporizes under welding heat to leave weakening porosity in the joint.

Just to muddy the waters a bit more there are several sorts of cast iron, some of which can be welded and some that can't. To sort out which is which, see Box 'What have you got?' and use the tests suggested. Older castings in particular often have high levels of sulphur and phosphorus, neither of which help when it comes to welding. Later ones are at least better in this respect.

Assuming the defunct chunk turns out to be grey cast and thus

6.1. With the right technique and consumables, welding cast iron need not be (too) scary.

potentially weldable, there are two ways to go about it. Or four, though option 3 (fusion welding with oxyacetylene) involves thick filler rods and very big flames, and option 4 (GMAW) falls more in specialist territory. On most farms the likely options are bronze welding with a gas flame and filler rod, or stick welding with the arc set.

Clean up first

Cast iron repair is not necessarily cost-effective, as the box 'Is welding worth it?' shows. But where the sums do add

up or repair turns out to be the only option, the first thing is to minimize the chance of the job cracking. Take a close look. Are there existing cracks? These are very likely to spread through cast iron's coarse grain structure as the joint cools and pulls, so stop any you find by drilling both ends to full depth (6.2).

Next comes **cleaning,** which is definitely something not to be skimped on. As with any weld, start by grinding away dirt and paint. Clear an area of about 1" (25mm) on either side of the joint, going down through any hard outer skin.

Gearbox casings or similar are likely to be steeped in oil, which over time worms its way deep through the metal's tiny interconnecting pores, or latches

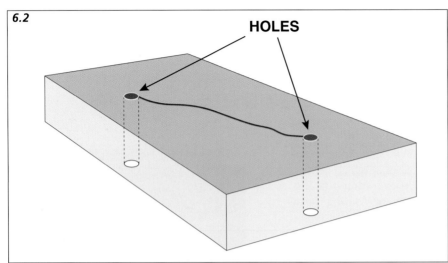

HOLES

6.2. Cracks spread easily through cast iron's coarse structure. Look very hard to find the exact ends of a crack, then drill ⅛" (3mm) holes to full depth to stop it.

on to its graphite flakes. While the ideal solution is to hold the whole thing at 752-932°F (400-500°C) for several hours to burn oil out, your oven probably doesn't go beyond 482°F (250°C).

The best plan is let nature take its course. If possible, first steam clean or hit the parts with strong solvent, wearing appropriate personal protection

as required. Weld, then grind out the porous layer and repeat the process until weld metal is solid. Each time you grind back, leave a thin 'buttering' layer of new metal on the parent plates. If you're fusion welding, cast iron's high carbon content is thus progressively diluted into the weld so the joint ends up stronger.

Joint preparation is a little different to normal. As always the idea is to open up the area to allow full-depth penetration, leaving a small step at the root so broken parts can fit

accurately back together. But grind to produce a U-groove rather than a Vee, sloping the sides to about 30° and rounding off sharp edges to minimize heat concentration (6.3). If you have them, gouging electrodes are good at producing the right shape and the arc heat helps clear contamination. If the joint faces show dirt-holding blowholes, drill these clean.

Get hot under the collar

With the job prepared, think about pre-heating. You may get away with welding the job at room temperature, or not; it's unpredictable. Warming the work first always helps. But how hot is hot, and do you need to heat the whole thing?

Like most humans, cast iron hates nasty shocks. So heating and cooling both need to be slow, and the slower the better. Ideally, all but ductile castings are best brought evenly up to 932°F (500°C) and then cooled very gradually so stresses can release. That's fine in industry but not on the farm, where the aim must be more modest.

Preheating is achievable with a gas torch and will help all weldable castings. After cleaning and U-preparing, lay the work on a hearth built from old firebricks, walling it in as much as possible. Then – keeping the

6.3

30°

A

80° - 90°

6.3. Grinding or gouging a U-groove is the best way to prepare cast iron, though a wider-than-usual Vee is OK. Leave a small step (max ⅛" [3mm] deep) so the jigsaw can fit back together accurately. Rounding off all sharp edges prevents local hot-spots which would otherwise overheat bronze filler metal.

6.4. A Tempilstik melts at a defined temperature, showing when a casting is up to pre-heat. For castings 482°F (250°C) is a good target, easily achievable over a substantial area with a neutral gas flame.

torch on the move – use a cutting nozzle to heat the whole job if it's small enough, or as much of it as you can manage. At the very least, heat enough to evaporate all surface water. Otherwise bring the job to 250ºC (low black heat), and if possible up to black red heat (about 480ºC, visible only in low light). To make the process more certain invest in a pair of Tempilstiks (6.4), waxy crayons which melt at an exact temperature when rubbed or pre-marked on a hot surface: welding suppliers have them. Once the job is up to heat, weld immediately.

Gas welding grey cast

The less heat that goes into the weld zone, the less likely is cracking. So bronze welding – a relatively cool process – is a good technique to use. (6.5 – 6.7) The joint faces must be COMPLETELY clean or the bronze can't 'wet' them, so thorough grinding is vital. Round off sharp edges which will otherwise overheat and oxidize, stopping the bronze from keying.

Rather than welding the joint in one go, butter one joint half at a time. That is, lay down a thin coat of bronze on each. Use the normal bronze welding technique (pages 73 – 74). Settle on a nozzle which brings the work quickly to red heat but allows control over the flow of filler. To weld, use plenty of cast-compatible flux (check the packaging), a slightly oxidizing flame and a manganese bronze filler rod. Be sure to use **manganese** filler – this has a higher bond strength than the more common silicon bronze, so produces a stronger joint. It also wets cast iron better.

Flow filler metal over one face (6.5). Work as fast as possible to minimize heat build up, but slow enough to be certain that wetting is complete.

What if bronze won't wet an area? Grind it clean, reflux and try again until the buttering layer is finished. To finish the job bring both halves together and weld, re-melting the buttering layers as you go and adding more flux as required. Multiple runs will fill a deep joint, but keep heating to a minimum.

Tips for Success

- Weld cracks in the middle of items from the center outwards. If a crack runs to an edge, weld from the fixed end to the edge.

- Leave a small (⅛" [3mm] max) step on each broken face to allow parts to be fitted back together before welding. Thick sections can be ground out from both sides to produce a double-U preparation.

- If you can't pre-heat, weld in short sections using a backstep technique (page 71). Let each weld cool to touchable temperature before starting the next.

- Think about cutting out a cracked area and replacing it with a mild steel plate. This often works with thin castings. SMAW or bronze welding will handle dissimilar metals, but check the rod specification first. A steel plate about half the thickness of the casting it replaces is usually plenty strong enough.

- Where the repair is highly stressed, it may be worth bolting a mild steel brace over the area to spread the load. Things always break at the point that stress concentrates!

- With thin sections, minimize weld metal deposit (and thus contraction stress) by welding in the vertical down position where possible. Check the electrode for suitability first, though, and try it on a bit of scrap to decide current and technique.

Arc welding grey cast

Rod choice is critical. All makers produce specific high-nickel SMAW electrodes, with ESAB's OK 92.58 good. This iron-nickel mix handles various cast irons, can be used in all positions including vertical down, and its low OCV requirement (50V) suits it to any good AC set. DC set owners might try running the electrode DC positive: the arc will have more force and the electrode will perform a little better. If the rods are

6.5. A silicon bronze filler rod wouldn't wet this ¹⁵⁄₃₂" (12mm) grey cast plate (right), even with generous fluxing. But the preferred manganese bronze rod would (left). After grinding off excess, buttered plate could be laid alongside another and the joint made. Re-melting both buttering layers while building up the Vee with bronze.

6.6. On your marks. The starting positions for nozzle and filler rod: travel will be from left to right. Note that nozzle angle is steeper than for normal bronze welding. Dipping the heated rod into general-purpose flux produces a generous coating. Wiping flux into the joint helps too.

6.7. Bronze welding technique. With the nozzle angled steeply into the work, the filler rod is dipped into the molten pool of bronze and withdrawn.

6.8. When arc welding cast iron, break a long run into short sections. Weld one, let it cool, weld the next. Backstep in thick sections and to minimize heat input, don't weave a root run.

damp, dry them at 392°F (200°C) for 2 hours, oven permitting.

As with gas welding, minimum heat input is the game. Use the smallest diameter rod and lowest current you can get away with. Don't let the electrode's typical soft, fluffy arc tempt you into turning up the wick – stick to recommended settings.

Clamp the joint halves as loosely as possible, then weld. In thick sections or on cold joints, keep heat input local by breaking the first run into 2" (50mm) sections and not weaving. On long joints space these first welds well apart, then backstep between them to fill in the gaps. On heavy sections needing multiple passes it's a good ruse to butter the joint faces first. Not only does the buttering layer reduce dilution from below, but it absorbs contraction stresses from subsequent runs.

After welding

With cast irons, what happens after welding is just as important as what went before. Two things minimize the chance of cracking; very slow cooling, and for arc welds, hammer peening.

6.9. Peening the hot weld with a blunt chipping hammer does wonders for stress in the weld (and in the welder).

Peening releases stress in the weld zone and should be done **straight after each run, while the weld is hot.** Tap the surface all over with a blunt chipping hammer, keeping it at an angle to avoid generating cracks (6.9).

Slow cooling is vital no matter how the joint was welded. Think of the host casting as an old lady with piles; keep it away from cold surfaces and draughts, and don't even think about plunging it in cold water. The best plan is to leave the repair among the firebricks of your temporary hearth, cover it with dry sand or a fire blanket, and don't go near it for a couple of hours. At least that way you won't hear it crack.

What Have You Got?

The following recaps information on pages 9–10. Castings are given away by their complex shape, rough surface finish and any raised lettering. To tell cast iron from cast steel, grind a sample. If the sparks are yellow and bushy, it's a steel. If sparks are dull orange and short, it's cast iron (6.10 and 6.11).

Separate the different irons by application. Anything used in a high-abrasion situation is probably white or chilled cast iron. This is very brittle, with freshly broken faces showing silvery white with very coarse grains. White cast iron is not weldable.

The most common stuff is grey cast iron, which turns up as about 70% of castings and holds its 2-5% carbon content as graphite flakes. These bring some lubricating properties (so grey cast is used in machine beds, pistons and such) and give a fractured face its color, but they make excellent planes of weakness. Grey cast iron is weldable with the right electrode or filler rod and careful post-weld cooling. Typical applications are belt pulleys, bearing housings, electric motor mountings, machine tool beds and exhaust manifolds.

6.10 Cast steel produces plenty of bushy yellow sparks under the grinder...

6.11 ...while with cast iron it's more a question of spot the sparks, which will be fewer, shorter and redder.

Where a cast part needs to be straightenable or has to handle high shock loads, it's likely to be malleable cast iron. Produced by heat treating white cast so its graphite flakes turn into less fracture-assisting aggregates, malleable cast is weldable but may lose resilience if heated too much or cooled too quickly. Uses are gearbox housings, bench vises, cutter bar fingers and so on.

2. Pipe Welding

Next to vertical work, joining pipes or other circular things is the job most likely to give welders the willies. The problem is truly three dimensional: the target area curves, making it tricky to hold a reasonably constant angle between the electrode/torch and weld pool. Keeping the angles right is hard enough when you're joining a vertical pipe to a flat plate; harder still when welding round a horizontal pipe, where the working position must slide seamlessly from vertical to downhand, back to vertical and then to overhead. Doing it with a cow nibbling your overalls is downright improbable.

In production work the pipe is often rotated slowly past the operator in a bringing-the-mountain-to-Mohammed exercise. But in the middle of a windy stockyard, Mohammed has to get himself to the mountain. The easiest way is to divide the joint into segments, then weld each separately (6.12).

Two joints – a butt and a fillet – show how to crack the main problems. In each case the basic strategy is the same:

divide and rule. The solutions work for both SMAW and MIG, though MIG's lack of slag and good angle-tolerance make it that much easier.

First steps

The pre-welding sequence is the same as for any job. Prepare the joint, choose the rod or wire, set the plant, and tack.

Preparation. As always, what you put in determines what you get out. At the very least the joint area has to be ground free of rust and rubbish. In non-critical applications, pipes can be just butted together and welded. Strength will then be confined to the bridging weld, but for gates and such this is enough.

Where strength matters more, Vee-grind the joint faces (6.13). For the best chance of controllable full-depth penetration and maximum strength, leave a ⅛" (3mm) vertical root face at the pipe end(s). Strip the flux from a ⅛" (3.25mm) rod, snip off a section, bend into a U-shape and slip it between the

joint halves as a spacer which can be pulled clear after tacking (6.14).

Electrode/filler wire choice. Any good quality, general purpose SMAW electrode or wire is fine where vertical segments will be welded upwards. Check that information on the electrode pack confirms rod suitability for vertical up and overhead work. ESAB AWS-E7018 is a reasonable

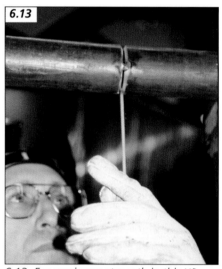
6.13. For maximum strength in this ¼" (6mm) wall pipe, preparation included Veeing the ends and leaving a ⅛" (3mm) penetration gap.

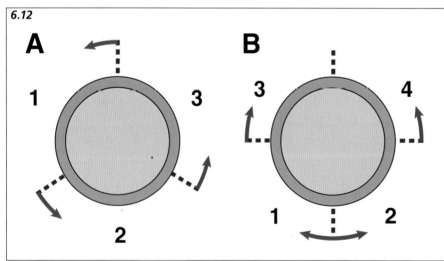
6.12. Divide and rule. Split pipe joints into segments, each small enough to weld in a continuous pass. Seen from above, a fillet joint (as in pipe to plate) is welded sequentially, here in three segments (A). Seen end-on, a butt joint between horizontal pipes (B) is usually split into four segments: welding usually starts from the bottom (runs 1 and 2) and finishes at the top (runs 3 and 4). The actual order and direction of welding depends on access and electrode. Start and stop each segment away from tacks.

6.14. SMAW core wire, bent into a U-shape, makes a quick gapping tool.

choice, along with equivalents in other brands.

If you have trouble welding vertically up, work down. In material over ⅛" (3mm) thick there are two choices. Either leave a good penetration gap (vital, particularly for MIG) and make multiple runs, or pick a specific pipe electrode. Penetration is potentially poor coming vertically down with a general-purpose SMAW rod, but pipe welding versions like Arcos Lincoln's E6010 are designed specifically for the job. Check the set's available open circuit voltage (OCV) against the rod's requirement before buying to, as they say, avoid disappointment.

For MIG work up or down, grade ER70S-6 wire is fine. Ideally team it with Argon/20% CO_2 shield gas for maximum penetration in thicker material.

Plant setting depends on the joint. For butt welds in pipe using SMAW and welding vertical segments upwards, set current toward the bottom end of the rod pack's recommendation to give maximum control of the weld pool. Try a run on scrap; if sticking or slag traps are a problem, increase current a little. If welding vertical segments down, set higher current for best penetration and slag control. For fillets welded on the flat around a vertical pipe, use current

toward the top of the recommended range to help penetration and minimize traps.

The same principles go for MIG. On vertical work, set welding conditions (voltage/wire speed) which give a steady arc at slightly less current than you would use on the flat. Where weld metal build-up is a problem, cut back on wire speed and travel faster – but do neither to the point where arc stability and penetration take a hit. On fillets, use higher voltages. The aim is always good edge fusion and a flat or slightly convex bead.

Tacks. These need to be fused into the work, which suggests using current on the high side of normal (6.15). Where joint integrity will really matter, grind off the leading and tailing edges of tacks to give a tapered ramp; this allows better fusion with the main weld metal. Start and stop away from tacks, welding over them as you go.

A few other thoughts. Comfort is the first: try to support your own weight (and the mass of the electrode holder or torch) by draping everything over any handy support. Keep your arms free to move. Use a welding helmet, rather than a hand mask, to leave digits available for steadying a GMAW torch or guiding an electrode. Before you start, make a dummy run to decide how far round the joint you can comfortably reach and see. During the actual run, stop as soon as control gets difficult, when you can't see the weld area, or if you simply fall over through holding your breath too long.

Divide and rule

With the work prepared and tacked, lay out your strategy. Mentally split any circular joint into three or more segments, with number decided by access and joint diameter (6.12).

Four divisions are normal on larger items. Butt welds in horizontal pipe are generally split into four quadrants, each starting and finishing on a main compass point, i.e. north, south, east and west. If it helps, chalk start and stop

points on the work.

Where the job can be welded in the flat (downhand) position and turned between welds, do it that way. If it's fixed, tackle each segment in turn and reposition yourself between runs.

When producing fillet welds (like joining a pipe to a plate, or pipes at 90° to each other), consider fillet thickness. For maximum strength, fillet depth should equal the thinnest joint component. As a rule of thumb, the following electrodes produce the following fillets from a single pass:

³⁄₃₂" (2.5mm) rod leaves a ⅛" (3mm) fillet

⅛" (3.25mm) rod leaves a ⁵⁄₃₂-0.2" (4-5mm) fillet

⁵⁄₃₂" (4.0mm) rod leaves a ¼" (6mm) fillet.

Where single-pass welding is not possible (either through lack of the right rod or enough current to run it) use multi-runs to build the necessary fillet depth. Multi-runs are also useful where a fillet joint has been Vee-prepared, as a big-diameter rod is unlikely to reach right down into the Vee. In such a case, fire in the first run with a ³⁄₃₂" (2.5mm) electrode, then build up fillet depth with bigger items.

The sequence and direction of welding is up to the operator, within the limits set by access, electrode type and individual ability. If you're using MIG it's worth setting the nozzle back from the contact tip so you can monitor stick-out and get the torch close into the joint. Too much stick-out lowers welding current; ⅜" (10mm) is maximum. On vertical segments current needs to be low anyway for best weld pool control, so watch stickout doesn't grow or fusion will suffer.

Butt joint, pipe laid horizontal

After dividing the job into four segments, start at the very bottom – six o'clock (6.16). From here weld upwards to nine o'clock on one side, then up to three o'clock on the other. For these first two runs, keep the electrode as near 90° to the work as

6.15. Small tacks are OK if fusion is complete – leaves less to weld over.

possible, hold a short arc (SMAW) and don't weave. If a penetration gap has been left, maintain an 'onion' shape above the weld pool and listen for the hollow crackle which confirms full penetration. If burn-through starts, weave a little to re-direct heat into the pipe walls. Steady the rod or torch with your free hand, as every little bit of control helps.

With the first two runs in place, the next two meet at the top. During these passes you'll find it hard to rotate your arm fast enough to keep ahead of the rod tip. Depending on how tolerant the electrode is of odd angles, it may be OK to finish with the tip actually trailing the weld pool – but don't make slag traps. If you don't like welding upwards it's OK to start at the top and weld down to meet the first runs, but only

if material thickness and preparation allow full penetration.

With all four runs in place, grind out any lumpy starts or humps where tacks have been welded over. To fill a Vee repeat the sequence, only this time weaving gently and pausing at the edges to melt them in. Finally seal it with a capping run, sticking to a diagonal weave to keep things simple. Otherwise it'll be like trying to ride a bike while juggling eggs.

Fillet joint to horizontal plate, pipe vertical

Joining pipe to a flat plate is a little easier. Either butt the joint components together, or for more strength, taper-grind the pipe end and tack to leave a penetration gap. Set SMAW current toward the top of recommended range to minimize the chance of slag traps. A little undercut on the pipe is OK if it will be filled by following runs.

Be sure you can see around all the intended segment before starting, and that your welding arm and the cable or torch are free to move. Start each segment forward of any existing weld, then fill the existing run's finish crater before moving off.

For strength, fillet depth should equal the thinnest joint component. So when joining ¼" (6mm) wall pipe to ½" (12mm) plate, look to end up with a ¼" (6mm) fillet. A ⅛" (3.25mm) rod leaves a ⁵⁄₃₂"-0.2" (4-5mm) fillet, so a capping run will make up the shortfall. If you're weaving this, use a simple diagonal pattern, pausing at each edge to allow full fusion. Three unweaved overlapping runs with a ³⁄₃₂" (2.5mm) rod will produce the same result and be marginally stronger, but will take longer: It's up to you. Either way, the final joint should be fused completely to full depth and leak proof. 6.17 shows a finished butt weld in ¼" (6mm) wall pipe.

6.16. Start at the bottom. Weld upwards to nine o'clock on one side, then the other.

6.17. The finished job: neat, strong, no leaks.

3. Hardfacing and Gouging

Hardfacing is something of a mystery. It's like driving round the farm on a foggy morning – all the familiar landmarks are there but somehow different, and you're not necessarily sure that you're looking at a profitable operation.

Still, this much is clear. Hardfacing is the business of laying down abrasion- and (maybe) impact-resistant metal on new or worn mechanical or soil-engaging parts, with the aim of extending service life.

Which welding process?

The speed and ease of MIG welding suggests that's the way to go. But hardfacing with MIG means using cored wires, and to get the required burn-off and fusion with these needs more current than single-phase sets can deliver. So for many farms, the weapon of necessity is a manual metal arc (SMAW) stick set. Depending on the rods you choose even that may not be up to scratch, as **Get set and go** explains.

Matching electrode and job takes us back into the fog. Most repair and fabrication involves mild or low-alloy steels, so you can jog along quite happily with general-purpose hardfacing rods; their forgiving composition handles surface contamination and minor variations in metal make-up.

But wear-resistant parts are made of sterner stuff. In the workshop it's impossible to fathom their composition, so the repairer can't properly match electrode and material in the way that industry can. The wrong rod and/or technique can see the expensive hard covering flaking off, and perhaps even the whole part cracking through – although with a little care neither should happen. To make sure it doesn't, here's the low-down on electrode selection and care, plant setting, pre- and post-heat treatment and welding technique.

6.18. ESAB's hardfacing consumables come vacuum-packed. Plant setting and re-drying requirements are on the pack.

First though, please take two cautions to heart – see **Alerts: manganese and fume.**

Rod selection and care

Hardfacing rods can be formed as a tube packed with flux and powdered metal, or as a conventional coated stick. ESAB offers the latter (6.18 and 6.19).

Four ESAB electrodes cover farming's needs:

- **OK 83.28** is a low-alloy rod designed for building up parts in metal-to-metal contact: gears, sprockets, dog clutches and so on. Hardness is 30 HRC, machinability is good. Min OCV 70V, AC or DC+ operation.

6.19. The rod's thick coat contains metal powder, so hardfacing consumables lay down more material than core wire diameter alone suggests. In other words, the recovery rate is more than 100%.

- **OK 83.50** is a low alloy, high carbon electrode for repair and build-up of worn parts. Runs from small sets with low open circuit voltage. Resistant to abrasion and impact. Hardness is 50-60 HRC and, it can only be ground, not machined. Min OCV 45V, AC or DC+ operation.

- **OK 84.78** contains chromium carbides and is for surfacing only. Ideal for very abrasive soils or corrosive conditions. High recovery rate – that is, it puts down a lot of metal for a given rod diameter. Hardness 59-63 HRC so can only be ground. Min OCV 50V, AC or DC+ operation.

• **OK 84.84** is a very expensive, complex carbide-containing rod for surfacing only, suited to extremely abrasive soils where pressure on the part is high. Good for edges and unusual in giving high hardness from a single layer. Hardness is 62 HRC, can only be ground. Min OCV 45V, AC or DC+ operation. Keep rod vertical to work while welding.

Note: Equivalent rods are available in other brands.

The electrodes above come vacuum-packed to keep them dry. Once opened and stored, all four types should be oven-baked before use, or water in the coating is likely to produce hydrogen cracking in the weld. Re-drying instructions are on the packet, along with info on welding current range, OCV requirement and so on (6.18).

To buffer or not?

The harder the deposit, the less flexible and more brittle it is. If very hard material is laid directly over substantially softer metal, the top layer may crack on cooling and can flake (spall) off altogether, and the expensive hard metal is diluted by mixing with the softer stuff.

One way around cracking and spalling is to use a buffer or buttering layer between soft and hard metal, like the jam in a sandwich. ESAB's OK 67.45 lays down the required tough, stress-absorbing buffer, while dilution can be kept down by welding relatively quickly, and by using minimum current and minimum weave to restrict melt and mix.

How do you know when to butter? This is formally defined according to parent material and impact level in service, but lacking accurate information on the former you'll have to suck it and see. The simple way is to hardface a few trial parts without buttering, and if the top coat stays put in the work you'll have the answer. The more complicated – but much better – approach is to badger the maker of the part to be surfaced for

info on its composition, then to ask an electrode supplier about the best technique and rods for the job.

Importantly and irrespective of buttering, at least two hardfacing layers are usually needed for the top one to show maximum hardness.

Preheating and post-weld cooling

While not all hardfacing rods require it, pre-heating and slow cooling of the work make good insurance against cracking. Usually pre-heat is to a specific temperature, but in the rough-and-ready workshop it's enough to warm the part evenly and thoroughly with a gas torch (6.20). The aim is just to drive off any water, so don't overdo it. After welding, let the work cool slowly in air. Quenching is a sure way to

6.20. When preheating, keep the torch up from the work and on the move to spread heat evenly. Cool slowly in air.

6.21. Use conventional arc length, travel speed and rod angles when hardfacing. For overlapping passes, angles are roughly 60° from vertical, 45° from parent plate.

produce cracks or worse.

Technique

Nothing out of the ordinary here in rod angles, speed of travel, arc length and plant setting – just keep within the requirements laid out on the packet and weld as you would with a general-purpose rod (6.21). Expect a fluffy arc punctuated by quiet spittings (much like cast iron or special-steel rods) with a lacy slag covering to follow. Watch your eyes with this, as bits can ping off spontaneously as the weld cools.

Hardfacing electrodes are designed to give a quick-freezing deposit which helps when working along edges, but paradoxically the weld pool tends to be wide. This makes working away from the flat rather tricky; use the shortest arc, lowest current and fastest travel consistent with good fusion to control the pool. Overhead work is best avoided or left to owners of a thoroughly fireproof hat.

Weaving

There is only one rule concerning hardfacing weave patterns, and it's that there are no rules. How (and when) you do it depends on the wear that you're trying to repair or to stave off, and how much money you like to spend on electrodes.

Having said that, the more and wider you weave the more heat goes into the work, the more diluted the expensive hardfacing metal becomes and the more likely you are to end up with slag trapped in the deposit.

Mega heat input is never a good thing when welding, producing extra distortion and often a greater chance of weld failure through cracking, particularly in the heat affected zone alongside the bead(s). And high heat input from over-enthusiastic weaving is also very bad news when hardfacing high manganese steels or brittle cast iron.

Control your weaving to make best use of hardfacing rods.

Some surfacing metal dilution is inevitable, and can even work in your favor when laying softer material on high-alloy steels. But normally the hardfacing layer is thinned by the softer base metal that you're trying to protect, so in general you'll need to put down two or even three layers of hardfacing to end up with the material's full benefit. Either way, proper current selection and minimum weave is a priority.

The rule of thumb when weaving is simple: go no wider than 3x the electrode's core wire diameter. That'd be ⅜" (10mm) tops for a ⅛" (3.2mm) rod, and so on. In fact, thanks to hardfacing rods' high recovery rate you can cover a lot of ground with a relatively narrow weave pattern, so the restriction isn't so bad.

Take your pick

Although there are as many patterns as people laying them down, a few principles will see you right. Clearly it makes sense to fully protect the leading edge of a soil-engaging part, usually with overlapping runs (6.22).

Side faces of thick items are often best tackled by laying down parallel beads, one along each edge, then filling the gap between them with a simple side-side weave (6.23). Depending on rod diameter, sides can also be covered by a side-side weave alone (6.24); in both cases the rod's fast-freezing deposit helps preserve the shape of the edge.

During the weave, pause briefly at the end of each sideways movement to let the crater fill. If the build-up in the center of the weave is too heavy, either travel faster across that section or move a little further forward each time.

Away from tips and sides, exactly where you put the hardfacing is set by the likely wear pattern. A worn part is the best guide here, showing the areas where pressure from soil or metal-to-metal engagement scallops away the steel. When facing new parts, it's not always necessary to deposit great swathes of hardfacing. Instead, a criss-cross pattern (or even many large dots) creates a grid which fills with soil (6.25). Earth then flows over this so can't reach the soft base metal below. Bucket vertical sides and chisel plough points are good recipients of criss-cross weaving.

GOUGING

How do you cut grooves or holes, Vee-prepare joints or slice away old metal and rusted parts without a grinder or gas cutter? With a gouging/piercing electrode.

ESAB lists only one – OK 21.03 – so rod choice is as simple as the technique. As the rod's coating burns it develops a very strong gas jet, and this blows away metal melted by arc heat. OK 21.03 works with steel, stainless steel, cast iron and most other metals apart from pure copper, and is particularly good for weld preparation in cast iron; arc heat dries out and burns off graphite and contaminants which would otherwise increase cracking risk. It's also handy for opening a groove on the reverse side of a welded joint, prior to laying in a sealing run.

There are a couple of mini-snags. OK 21.03 needs 70 OCV minimum, so can't be used with most small air-cooled sets. When cutting and piercing it prefers to be run DC+ (that is, with the electrode holder plugged in to the positive line); so if the farm only has an AC set you won't get the best from it. The grooves and holes you make won't be millimeter-precise, and by its very nature, a gouging electrode can never be used to join material.

6.22. This slab of 1" (25mm) plate shows how hardfacing can be used. If it were a soil engaging part the leading edge (arrow) would take most wear, so is faced with overlapping runs. A second layer would counter dilution.

6.23. The long edges could be faced by two parallel runs (long arrows) filled by a compact weave...

6.24. ...or, depending on electrode diameter and part thickness, by a single weave.

6.26. Strike a gouging rod vertically, then quickly lay it at a 5-10° angle. As soon as the gas jet starts to dig, work the rod forwards and back like a saw.

6.25. Away from maximum pressure points, a criss-cross weave holds soil to protect the underlying soft metal.

6.27. The rod pack suggests current setting and gives OCV requirement. When both are right there will be a little slag (A), which chips off easily to leave a clean, ripple-bottomed channel (B).

Technique

A gouging rod is used like a saw. To open a groove, strike the arc with the rod vertical to the work then quickly lay it down, ending up almost parallel to the surface – an angle of 5-10° is good (6.26). As the jet starts to open a trough, work it forwards and back as if you were cutting with a hacksaw.

The gouged channel will show a series of ripples corresponding to your sawing, like sand on a beach when the tide has gone out (6.27). To cut a deep groove make one run, clear any slag, then repeat as necessary.

Stick to rod pack suggestions for current. When this is right the gouged channel will be largely clean and any slag will chip away easily. If the cut won't clear and fills up with foamy clinging slag, try more amps. If it's blasted into a wide channel and fills with tenacious slag, reduce current. Figure 6.28 has unpleasant examples.

Gouging can be done on the flat, vertically (start at the top and work down) or horizontally. Overhead work is advisable only for a paid-up masochist.

6.28. Too little current limits gas jet size, so it can't clear tenacious slag (A). Too much current sees the gas jet overwhelmed by slag from the wide channel cut by arc heat (B). Either way it's a mess.

Piercing and cutting

Quick'n'dirty holes can be chopped out or made bigger with a gouging rod. Though crude, the technique throws a lifeline to workshops without gas cutting facilities.

Strike the arc with the rod vertical, then once the gas jet is established, saw the rod down through the plate (6.29). As with gas cutting, the first stage until breakthrough is the hardest bit.

Once the arc is bellowing through the bottom of the plate, work round the edges to enlarge the embryo hole. Arc-pierced holes aren't likely to win many beauty prizes, but the technique is a good way to make big openings in heavy sections when more sophisticated, neater methods aren't around. It's also handy for rough-cutting away broken parts or seized fixings.

6.29

6.29. To pierce or enlarge a hole, strike the arc with the rod vertical. Saw it down through the plate (arrow) then round the edges.

Get set and go

A voltage – the open circuit voltage or OCV – must exist between the electrode and work before the arc can strike. Simple stick units have one output terminal and generally offer 50V OCV. Others provide a second line at up to 90V.

Stick welding electrodes always have a specific OCV requirement. General-purpose rods are usually happy to strike and run at 50V, but specialist rods – including some hardfacing varieties – need higher voltage to strike cleanly and run with a stable arc. So before buying consumables, ask the supplier for their OCV requirement and check that your set can deliver the goods. If it can't the results will be poor.

Alerts 1: manganese

Don't hardface 12-14% manganese steel. Often used for bucket teeth and other bits which have to put up with high impact, this material is very tough but quickly turns brittle when reheated and slow-cooled – so the heat from hardfacing is very likely to crack it. If you must hardface or repair it, weld very short lengths and keep the temperature below 392°F (200°C). Use minimum welding current, lay down a little material, let the area cool until you can touch it, then repeat. Work with several components at a time if you can, switching to another while one cools. Note: Structural steels with lower manganese content are fine.

High manganese steels are typically used in crushing and milling applications and crucially, aren't magnetic. Otherwise they're light grey in color and are usually castings, designed to be bolted on to avoid welding. Sometimes they come with a warning label, and may have the letters 'MN' cast into them.

Alerts 2: fume

Gouging rods produce mighty clouds of fume. Hardfacing electrodes carry a lot of metallic elements in their flux coating – which is how even a small diameter rod manages to lay down a very substantial bead. Consequently, hardfacing fume contains much human-damaging heavy metal vapor, which won't do you any good at all. Ideally use forced fume extraction.

If that's not possible, wear a specific welding respirator marked EN149: 2001 (3M's disposable 06920 mask is an example). Work in moving air and stay out of the main fume column. Shield passers-by and livestock from eye-damaging arc light.

Health hazard. Gouging rods are best used with forced extraction.

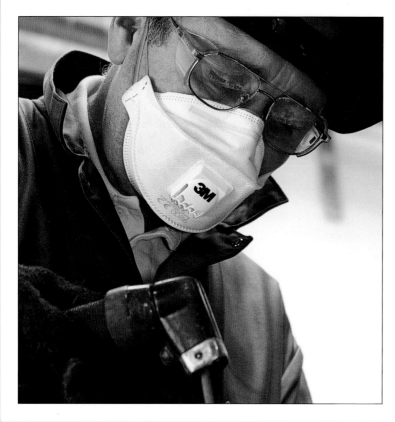

Hardfacing releases more hazardous metal vapor than general repair work. If fume extraction is not possible, wear a purpose-designed welding respirator and stay out of the main fume column. Nuisance dust respirators will not protect you!

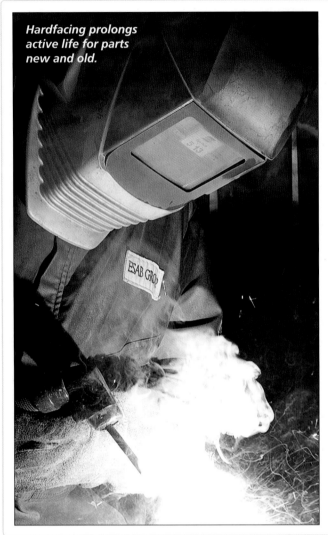

Hardfacing prolongs active life for parts new and old.

Economics

Should you hardface or buy new? Or to put it another way, how long is a piece of string? It clearly depends on a three-part equation – your soil's abrasiveness, the cost of genuine or pattern bits, and the cost of the hardfacing consumables plus the labour to use them.

Naturally the equation balances differently for every farm. To help find where it settles for you, here are prices of the ESAB products discussed above. We've quoted 2007 UK costs on a kg basis, to get round any difference in rods per packet between different brands. Costs are recommended retail; your mileage will vary depending on distributor.

Electrode	Diameter	Cost (£/kg)	Cost ($/lb)
OK 83.28 Hardmat	(3.2mm) ⅛"	10.31	36.31
	(4.0mm) ⁵⁄₃₂"	9.21	32.45
OK 83.50	(3.2mm) ⅛"	16.46	57.98
	(4.0mm) ⁵⁄₃₂"	14.98	52.77
	(5.0mm) ³⁄₁₆"	13.25	46.67
OK 84.78	(3.2mm) ⅛"	16.57	58.37
	(4.0mm) ⁵⁄₃₂"	16.08	56.65
OK 84.84	(4.0mm) ⁵⁄₃₂"	48.74	171.74
OK 67.45	(3.2mm) ⅛" (others available)	20.95	73.81

Section 7

Soldering

Soldering is a lower-temperature version of bronze brazing, using filler alloys that are less physically strong and melt at lower temperatures. As with bronze work, the bond between metals is not made by fusion. Instead it's formed partly by the filler hooking into the tiny hills and valleys of the joint metal surfaces, but mainly from the solder dissolving (not melting) into a very shallow surface layer of the joint. So for soldering to work, it must have free access to ultra-clean parent metals. For this reason flux is always used as a chemical backup to mechanical surface cleaning.

Silver soldering suits dissimilar metals and is generally used with capillary joints, leaving little or no external build-up of filler. The filler itself is a fairly expensive mix of copper, zinc and silver which, being tougher than soft solder yet still electrically conductive, is useful where a joint must stand moderate heat and vibration. Electrical heating elements are often silver-soldered. The temperatures needed for silver soldering can only be achieved by a flame (or arc), not an iron. If the work is not too big it can be laid on a firebrick hearth and heated with a small butane torch.

The steps necessary for a sound job are the same as for brazing (page 75). Buy the flux when you buy the silver solder. Take great care over preparation. Pre-flux the joint, then dip the rod in flux. Work quickly so the flame does not tarnish the cleaned surfaces. Let the silver solder melt with the heat of the joint metal, not directly by the flame. After soldering the flux residue can be washed off with hot water.

Soft soldering is the much more common form, used on heat-sensitive items or on joints that don't need much mechanical strength. Filler metal melts at 482°F (250°C) or below, so the necessary heat can be transferred from an iron. The alloy is a lead-tin mix, often spiced with antimony. Soft-soldered joints are everywhere – in vehicle wiring, radiator header tanks, plumbing joints in copper pipe. Different metals can be joined too, like copper to steel.

Three things are necessary for soldering success:

- Clean parent metal
- The right temperature
- The right flux.

So, effectively it's brazing all over again. Cleaning is, as ever, a matter of elbow grease. Soft solder is even less tolerant of dirt than bronze, so it's essential to be thorough. Grind surfaces where possible then bring them to a bright finish with emery cloth. Dubious-looking or corroded surfaces must be scoured clean.

Flux protects the metal from oxidation; breaks down the liquid solder's surface tension to let it flow; boosts wetting on the metals to be joined and brings some limited cleaning action. **Paste** fluxes generally have a resin base and are relatively non-corrosive. They're used primarily for electrical work and come in a tin or as a core in the solder itself. **Acid** fluxes come in liquid or paste form, have a more vigorous cleaning action and are generally used on plumbing or sheet metal work. Being corrosive, they're not for delicate electrical stuff and should be washed from both the joint and your hands afterwards.

Iron options

Heat for soft soldering comes from an iron. Why it's called an iron when the business end is made from copper isn't clear, but there it is. The bigger the copper end (or bit), the greater is its heat reservoir, so the bigger the job that can be tackled.

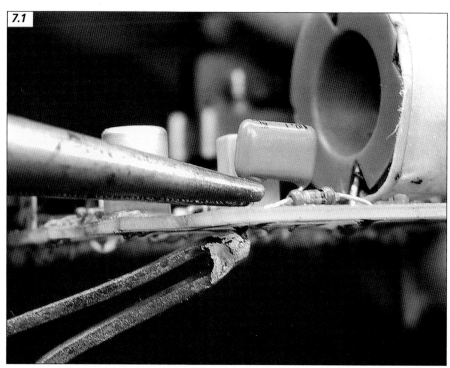

7.1. Whenever an electronic component looks as if it might be cooked, grab its leads with pliers to siphon off soldering heat.

7.2. *Traditional soldering irons hold the bit in a steel shaft. Heat comes from a separate flame.*

7.3. *No matter how the bit is heated, it must be kept clean. The dirty-looking, oxide-covered specimen (a) won't transfer heat properly and brings contamination to the joint. File it or wire brush it, then keep it wholesome during work by wiping it on a damp cloth. Any bit must be tinned before use: fluxed, covered with a thin coat of fresh solder and refluxed to leave it shining silver (b).*

The key thing is to *match the iron to the job.* If the iron is too small it won't put enough heat into the work and the solder won't flow. If it's too big, access may be difficult and solder will flow all over the shop. And while we're on the subject, electronic bits and bobs can be terminally damaged by heat – so whenever there's a risk of cooking a component, say on an alternator diode pack, use long-nosed pliers to divert the threatening therms (7.1).

The traditional soldering iron holds its copper bit in a steel/wood handle (7.2). The bit is generally heated by blowlamp or propane torch. If you're pushed a neutral oxyacetylene flame will do, but this must be used with great care if the bit isn't to be overheated and covered in oxide scale (7.3a).

How do you know when a traditional iron is hot enough? Settle the flame over the bit's thickest section. Eventually the metal will flicker clear copper-colored and a green flame will ghost round it, and then you're ready to boogie.

7.4. *Three types of electrically heated soldering iron. The 20W miniature variety (right) is, naturally, for small jobs. The much bigger version (center) has a jumbo-sized tip, giving a good heat reservoir for big work. The 100W instant heat gun (left) is a good all-round tool, coming quickly to temperature and usually taking interchangeable tips.*

7.5

7.5. *Modern self-contained gas irons are ideal for jobs in the cab. A good brand like this Antex generates plenty of heat. Kit's attachments extend usefulness into jobs like cutting/sealing polyprop rope. Liquid butane is held in the handle/reservoir.*

Irons heated by electricity or integral gas container have all but displaced the old sort. Small versions are perfect for wiring and electronic work (7.4). Bigger ones can be backed by fast-acting heater coils, making an 'instant heat' gun. At the top of the scale are jumbo electric irons, which take an age to get to full working temperature but supply plenty of heat for larger jobs. Self-contained irons heated by butane gas from a canister let you solder anywhere (7.5). Ah, the freedom.

Traditional or modern, any iron has to be cleaned and 'tinned' – given a fresh coat of solder – before work. A tatty burnt tip won't transfer heat quickly and imports oxides to the joint. Titivate a dirty bit by wire-brushing or gently filing it back to bright copper metal while it's hot. Then tin the tip by sizzling it in flux and flowing on a little solder to form a bright silver jacket (7.3, b). When you need to clean a hot tip during a job, wipe it on a damp cotton cloth.

Making the connection

Whatever the work, it's worth remembering that like all glues, a soldered joint is at its strongest where the bond layer is kept thin. If not, joint strength drops to that of the solder itself. Joint design is critical too – soldering works best where the joint has a large surface area, and where it's loaded in shear rather than peel. Pic 7.6 explains more.

We'll follow in pictures, two jobs which show soldering's usefulness. First comes joining electrical wires and then fitting a cable nipple; then a quick look at soldering copper plumbing fittings.

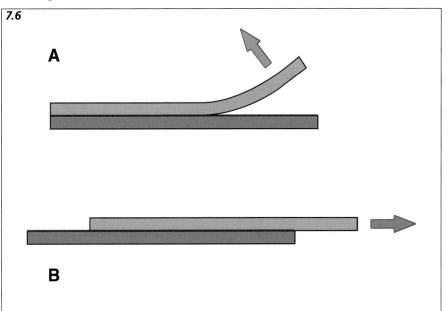

7.6

A

B

7.6. *Soldering uses soft metal alloy as a glue. Glued joints are weak when peeled (A); think of pulling off a sticking plaster. Joints loaded in shear are much stronger (B). So a lasting soldered joint is one with a big surface area which will only have to cope with straight pulling loads.*

Soldering Copper Wire

7.7

7.7. Peripherals for soldering. Resin flux and cored solder (center) are primarily for electrical work. Acid flux (left) scours surfaces and will corrode if not washed off: it's generally used with plain solder (right and front) on plumbing and sheet work. The gas blowtorch (top) has replaced the blowlamp for heating traditional irons.

Wire soldering can be anything from joining an electric fence's leads to replacing a tractor battery cable terminal; the principles are the same. Every time you tin the parts first, then join them by heating, adding more solder if needed.

Electrical work needs a non-corrosive flux. Use flux-cored solder and back it up with a separate supply, like a tin of Fry's 'Fluxite' (7.7). Proceed as follows.

Wire is only clean enough to solder if it's bright and shiny. Where there's any sign of corrosion – as there will be in old trailer light cable or anything that's seen much service and been exposed to the elements – tease out the strands and rub them between folded emery cloth until they shine. Clean your fingers, twizzle the strands back into shape and dip them in the flux pot.

Bring the iron up to temperature, which means a green flame around a traditional copper bit or a good smoking heat for electrical irons. Clean and tin the iron tip, then sizzle it in flux (a, opposite).

Tin the first wire's end. Lay one face of the iron – not the point — on the cable so maximum heat flows from that wire to the other (b). The flux will melt first. Leave the iron in place and touch the solder on the wire, not the iron. When the work is hot enough, solder will melt into it.

Don't transfer liquid solder to the cable with the iron, as the solder will pick up oxides.

If the solder won't melt reasonably quickly, just hold the iron where it is. Reaching melt temperature may take a while, particularly when the iron is only just big enough for the job.

Tin the second wire's end in the same way.

Then lay the two tinned wire ends alongside each other. Don't twist them together as the two will unwind under load – a pull concentrates shearing force in a small area, destroying the bond.

Bring a hot, flux-dipped iron down on the joint, holding it until all the solder turns liquid silver and runs in both halves. If necessary (and if you've got three hands) add more solder to the joint to fill gaps (c).

Take off the heat and hold the wires still until the solder freezes, turning from bright silver to dull grey. Any movement during this step will give a crystalline 'dry' joint with little strength and poor conductivity. Clean off flux residue.

The end result takes a fair pull (d). Twisted wires would unwind under this load.

To insulate the joint, slide on some heat-shrink tubing before soldering (e). Buy it from auto factors and electronics shops. Gentle heating will shrink the wrap down over the bare wire, giving a finish much tidier and longer-lasting than insulating tape. If waterproofing is required, clean the area then wrap it in self-annealing tape. Available from electronics shops, this bonds with itself to form a waterproof coat.

Adding a Cable Nipple

Soldering a nipple on to a Bowden cable is useful for a quick repair or when making controls for a one-off machine. This technique also covers attaching 'bullet' wiring connectors, but for those leave out the last two steps. Use non-corrosive resin-based flux and flux-cored solder, as acid flux will attack and rot the cable strands.

Cut the cable end cleanly. An efficient (if rather unkind) way of doing this is to hold the cable between the cutting jaws of pliers or nippers, lay the pliers on a vise and give the jaws a sharp whack with a copper-faced hammer. Watch out for flying bits – wear goggles.

Clean and tin ¼"-⅜" (6-10mm) of the cable end (a). Old cable will be oil-soaked, so degrease and abrade-clean it first or the solder won't wet.

Slide the nipple down the cable until ⅛"-⁵⁄₃₂" (3-4mm) is left sticking out. Gently gripping the cable at the right height in a vise makes

this easy. Hold a hot, fluxed iron on the nipple and cable until both are smoking, at which point add solder: this should flow down between them (b). If it won't, carry on heating or re-clean. Add solder until it pops out at the nipple base and the nipple's hollow head is part-filled. Let the solder solidify.

Working with a knife blade on the protruding cable, separate individual wire strands and bend them back to form something that looks like a chimney brush (c). *This step is vital for strength:* once buried in solder, the splayed ends won't pull out under load.

Now bury the strands. Turn the cable over and reheat it so the nipple slides upwards, settling the splayed wire ends into the nipple cup (d).

Turn the cable right way up and add more solder until the nipple cup is filled and all splayed strands are buried (e). Take off the heat and hold everything steady until the solder sets.

Finish off by grinding back any projecting strand ends. If you've forgotten to slide the cable into its outer sheath or have cut it to the wrong length, kick yourself and start again.

What's going wrong? Common soldering problems

Soldering snags always come down to a lack of heat, contamination or a shortage of flux.
Or some combination of these. So problems aren't hard to fix.

Solder won't melt on to the joint or melting stays local, next to the iron. Solder flows sluggishly or not at all.

Cause: Insufficient heat.

Remedy: Check tip is clean, tinned and not covered in heat-transfer reducing oxides. Use flat face of iron for maximum contact area. Don't be impatient; heat transfer takes time. If none of the above work, the iron is either not hot enough or is too small for the job.

The joint is up to temperature but solder won't flow, maybe spreading in some areas but refusing to wet others.

Cause: Surface contamination or inadequate fluxing.

Remedy: Stop trying. Clean the target until it shines. Coat it with flux and try again with a clean, hot, fluxed iron. The problem can also be in the solder itself – dull grey, oxide covered stuff won't flow easily. Shine it's surface with emery cloth and try again.

Section 8

Welding Plastics

What happens to damaged plastics on the farm – the split mudguards on tractors and materials handlers, the torn waterproof covers on the drill or spreader hoppers, the leaking tank where someone got a little out of shape with the muck fork? Chances are the damage is either left, bodged up with glue, or patched with a bit of sheet and rivets.

But there's a much better way. For a modest investment in kit you can make permanent repairs that are pretty much as strong as the original. And the very good news is that if you know how to weld steel the technique's easy to pick up…and it's not much harder even if you don't.

The Swiss make the best kit in the shape of Leister equipment, so unusually we'll specify by model. While some Leister machines work their magic by ultrasound or laser, most heat the work with nothing more than a directed blast of hot air, much in the way of politicians.

For farm work we're interested in hand-held models. Designed originally for the manual repair of vehicle bumpers and other high-cost bits, these come in two forms. Both are like rather clever hair driers – see (8.1) – with accurately variable output temperature and interchangeable nozzles. For farm work

Can I Join It?

Only **thermoforms** can be welded. Thermoforms soften on heating then harden as they cool, and will put up with many heat/form/cool cycles.

The other main group – **thermosetting** plastics – can be melted only once and harden as heat is added, generally in a mold. Thermosetting plastics crack if reheated. Though not weldable, they can often be repaired with the right adhesive and joint design.

Luckily, most of the moldings found on farms and in vehicles are thermoforms. To weld these successfully you must have a matching filler material, and use a temperature which allows fusion but stops short of burning. That's where a purpose-made welding gun comes in – a soldering iron or the wife's hair drier just won't do.

Choices

If you're fired with a desire to join plastic you must have the right equipment. All the following are made by Leister. The Triac 1G3 gun (8.1) is industrial tackle at a premium price – a complete kit includes four nozzles, a rotary burr, case, stand and a selection of filler rods. If you prefer a pistol-grip model, the Ghibli gives a similar performance at the same price.

If that sort of money is too steep, consider the EcoTool Weldy, a pistol-style hobbyist version that handles the same range of work as the Triac but delivers roughly half the welding speed. Preset temperatures and airflows for different materials are called up on a neat LCD display, making life simple. It'll also solder, shrink-wrap, weld bitumen roofing felt, strip paint and heat seized parts. A Weldy kit includes 3/16" (5mm) pendulum welding and tacker nozzles. Extra nozzles, a silicon roller and a bundle of mixed filler rods may also be added.

Weldy programs temperature and airflow automatically to the material, with manual setting also possible. It's cost-effective for on-farm repairs, though workrate is halved compared to more expensive Triac. Green plastic roll at rear acts as stand.

Ghibli pulls all Triac features into a pistol-grip gun, and as a bonus, can take a de-horning nozzle (above).

the Triac S 1G3 is ideal.

Welding plastic is a fusion process, like stick or MIG in steel. The joint is heated to melting point, then if necessary a filler rod is fused into the parent material to fill and reinforce it. Unlike in an arc method, though, the filler does not need to be completely melted; fusion happens only where the rod and parent plastic meet.

We'll look first at the techniques. As with steel it's vital to pick a filler rod which matches the material to be welded: for more on that, see **Sherlock time.**

Heat for the job

Welding plastics is no different in principle to welding steel. The same four things must be right: the filler rod,

8.1

8.1. To weld plastics you'll need a welding gun (1) with adjustable heat setting (2) and heat outlet (3). Nozzle (4) slips over the outlet and is used for local heating and pendulum welding. Separate smaller nozzles push-fit over it. Part 5 is for tacking, (6) and (7) are for speed welding. A rotary burr for Vee-preparing joints (8) completes the outfit.

Don't know what material you have? Make short test welds with different fillers. The rod that won't pull off when cool is the one to use.

Three different filler rods will cover most farm jobs: mixed packs are ideal. Store them so the labels stay readable.

Sherlock Time

It's crucial (but not hard) to identify the material you're dealing with. Thermoforms fall into three broad groups – the polyethylenes, the polypropylenes and the polyvinyl chlorides or PVCs. If the part up for repair carries no identifying code (see below), see what happens when you try to bend it:

PVCs are rigid and won't bend easily

- **Polypropylenes are flexible and show stress marks at the point of bend**

- **Polyethylenes are flexible and show no stress marks when bent**

That'll get you into the ballpark. For confirmation make a short test weld somewhere out of sight, not behind the barn but on the inside of the thing you're repairing. Run a series of short pendulum welds using different-material rods, leaving a stub on each. When cool give each a hard tug. Only the compatible filler(s) will have fused; the others will just lift away.

A reliable identifier may be on the part itself. All modern vehicle bits (and many

other things) carry an ID card, primarily to help in recycling. Typically it's a group of letters, with perhaps a date stamp. Sample codes are in the table below. There's no absolute guarantee that you'll be able to weld an item once you've pinned down what it is – allegedly some car makers use additives to counter fusion repair, presumably to sell more spares. It's a wicked world.

Table 8.1: **Plastic Codes**	
Code	**Material**
ABS	Acryonitrile Butadiene Styrene*
ABS/PC	Polycarbonate alloy of ABS
PA	Polyamide (Nylon)
PBT	Polybutylene Terephthalate
PC	Polycarbonate
PE	Polyethylene
PP	Polypropylene
PP/EPDM	Polypropylene/Ethylenediene rubber
PUR	Polyurethane**
PVC	Polyvinyl Chloride
GRP/SMC	Glass fibre reinforced plastics***

Notes:

*ABS is very commonly used for vehicle moldings

the rod angle, the speed of travel and the temperature. If the work isn't hot enough then there's little or no fusion; if it's too hot, the plastic distorts or burns. In most cases, smoke coming off the weld says things are definitely too hot.

So what's right? Most plastics are welded between 518 and 752°F (270 and 400°C). You must have a proper heat source: a paint stripping gun simply hasn't the required temperature control and can't deliver enough hot air to weld. Leister's Triac 1G3 (used to make all the welds shown here) allows precise temperature setting, then maintains outlet air at the specified heat. Table 8.2 lists the requirements of different materials.

Table 8.2: **Welding Temperatures**

Code	Temp (°C)	Temp (°F)
ABS	350	662
ABS/PC	350	662
PA	400	752
PBT	350	662
PC	350	662
PE hard (HDPE)	300	572
PE soft (LDPE)	270	518
PP	300	572
PP/EPDM	300	572
PUR	300/350	572/662
PVC hard	300	572
PVC soft	350	662
Xenoy (PC alloy)	350	662

Ways to go

Three techniques – tack welding, pendulum welding and speed welding – cover the majority of work. Different nozzles are used for each.

Unlike arc or gas processes, welding plastic is a very physical job. You must put steady pressure on the filler rod (and sometimes the welding nozzle) to push it into the joint, where it fuses with the hot plastic below. You'll quickly get a feel for how much pressure to use with

different fillers and different techniques, and then it's a very satisfying thing to do. And as there's no arc to transfer metal across and no molten weld pool for gravity to pull on, the technique is the same for butt joints and T-fillets, for repairing cracks and working vertically or overhead.

There's one other big difference. Apart from when welding PVC sheet – the stuff used to make hopper covers, truck curtain sides and the like – there should be no fume. If a joint smokes, it's too hot.

Preparation

Fusion just ain't gonna happen where there's glue, paint or dirt. So get rid of them: work very gently with a 120-grit disc or flap wheel to clear an area around the joint.

Plastic welding doesn't have the penetration of an arc process, so repairs in all but the thinnest sheet must be opened out to create a bed for the filler rod to lie in. If you're fixing a crack, first drill the end(s) to stop it spreading (a ⅛" [3mm] hole is good) and carry on Vee-preparation beyond the end of the fault line.

Leister kits comes with a rotary burr for crack preparation, or you can buy

one from a model shop. Mount the burr in a Dremel tool or similar, and spin it fast so it won't snag. Open a Vee-shaped groove along the repair line to about half of the material's depth. Wear eye protection – plastic swarf is as nasty as metal.

Tack welding

An effective tack in plastic fuses the bottom of the joint, seals it against leaks and holds the parts in accurate alignment. Tacking is always full-length along the joint, rather than in short stitches, and filler rod isn't used.

A tacking nozzle has a thin tip, backed by an exit slot for hot air (item 5 in picture 8.1). Once up to temperature for the specific plastic to be welded (opposite) the tip is drawn fairly briskly along the bottom of the joint, using very light downward pressure (8.2). Angle the gun so only the tip's forward segment makes contact (concentrating heat where it's wanted) and position it so joint halves get an equal melt. Although it's important to align parts accurately before tacking, hot plastic's malleability often allows for limited re-jigging before the weld knits.

8.2. Tacking is always full-length. The heated nozzle is angled so only its tip touches, then is simply drawn along the joint with very light downward pressure. Hot air from a slot before the tip preheats the work.

8.3. Support for joint's edges comes from a fusion weld, stitched at one or more points on the reverse of the work.

8.4. For pendulum welding, the gun stays at a low angle while the filler rod is almost vertical.

If the joint needs bracing up after tacking, turn it over and run one or more short welds across the main line (8.3). See next for technique.

Fillers

Plastic welding suppliers offer rods in various materials and sections, either separately or as a mixed bundle. Round filler can be used in any joint; ⅛" (3mm) diameter covers most work. Triangular section fillers are ideal for either Vee–prepared, T-fillet or butt joints, the latter where a penetration gap has been left. The ⁷⁄₃₂" (5.7mm) variety leaves a smart profiled bead (8.6) and is best used through a speed welding nozzle.

8.5. During pendulum welding, constantly swing the nozzle in a slow arc (arrow). Let some hot air wash the lower part of the rod, but concentrate mainly on preheating the weld zone.

Pendulum welding

The most flexible of the three techniques and the one best able to get into tight corners, pendulum welding gets its odd name from the grandfather-clock swing of the nozzle during work.

Prepare and tack the joint as above. Choose a filler of the right material and with the best profile for the joint, then snip the business end to a tapered point: the taper lets it melt progressively into the start. Hover the rod at 176-194°F (80-90°C) over the surface (8.4), then hold the nozzle's air-slot over the end of the joint until the surface just starts to sweat or slightly changes texture. To begin the weld, push the filler firmly into the joint. Use enough pressure to bow the rod in the direction of travel

8.6. A good T-fillet weld made with a profiled filler. During work, adjust travel speed and downward pressure on the rod until molten ridges (A) are squeezed out where rod and joint meet. These ridges confirm good fusion and should appear in every weld. Excess rod was snipped off once it cooled (B).

(8.5). If you're not sure how much force to use, try pressing on the bathroom scales until they register about 2.2lbs (1kg). Where the heat is right, you'll see a ridge of shiny molten plastic squeezing up on both sides of the filler (8.6).

Move off down the joint. As you go, swing the nozzle slowly backward and forwards along the repair line, preheating mainly the unwelded area but also washing the rod tip with hot air on every swing (8.7). Steadily push filler into the joint and hold travel speed steady.

If you run out of filler before the finish, stop before you burn your fingers. Snip off the stub as close as possible to the joint. Clip the end of a fresh rod, preheat the restart area and off you go. Fuse the

very end of the joint properly, take off the heat and leave the rod attached to the work until it cools enough for a clean snip.

What happens where there's a hole to fill? It may be possible to heat a damaged, folded-down section of the part and tease it back into place before welding. Where a hole still has to be patched and you've identified the material needed, your local plastic supplier (see Yellow Pages) should be able to set you up with sheet stock. Alternatively, rob a bit from a broken piece of the same material.

Although pendulum welding lets you operate in tight corners and gives the most flexibility over working

angle, it isn't particularly fast. Where large repairs have to be made in rigid material, speed welding may be better.

More haste, more speed

Speed welding is the easiest, fastest but least flexible of the three welding techniques. The big difference is the use of a boot-shaped nozzle, slipped over the small tube nozzle used for pendulum work (8.8). The forward part of the boot is an open tube which takes the filler rod, while the rear opens into a slot which ducts hot air to preheat the weld zone. Different nozzles accept round-section or profiled (triangular-section) rods.

Speed welding technique is much the same as for crack repair, butt welds or T-fillets. Prepare the joint properly or the weld will fail – abrade away any paint, grease or dirt, then Vee-out a crack to half-depth using a small, high-speed rotary burr.

Then tack the joint on both sides down its full-length to fuse and seal the bottom edges. Don't skimp this step; sealing is vital when repairing tanks and suchlike.

8.7. No fancy protective equipment is needed to weld plastic – just the right tools and a modest helping of skill.

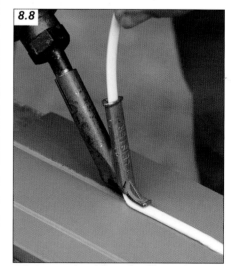

8.8. In speed welding, the filler rod (here white) is fed under firm downward pressure through a boot-shaped nozzle. The weld is carried right through the end of the joint so fusion is complete. The nozzle is slid up and off the filler, then excess rod is simply snipped off.

After tacking you'll need to wait a couple of minutes for the speed-welding nozzle to come up to full heat. Meanwhile, snip the filler rod at an angle to produce a tapered, quick-melting tip. When the nozzle is ready, hover its air outlet over the start of the joint, angled so the bottom of the boot is parallel with the work. Position the gun so that both joint halves receive equal heat.

As soon as the plastic starts to change texture or sweat slightly, feed the filler into the nozzle. Don't do this too soon or it'll melt and stick in the tube. If that happens, stop. Clean out the goo while it's still warm and start again.

Push the filler rod firmly into the hot joint. As you do so, lift the nozzle a little so it rides over the just-fused rod. Draw the nozzle along the joint, keeping a steady, firm downward pressure on the filler.

It may help to put a little light pressure on the nozzle too – experiment to see what gives the best fusion. As with pendulum welding you're looking for a quick, even melt of filler, shown by molten ridges squeezing out on either side of the just-fused rod – check (8.6).

Draw the nozzle along the joint in the way you'd weld with a stick electrode, i.e. trailing operation. That's from left to right for a righthander, or right to left for a lefthander. Either way, a blast of hot air from the slot pre-heats the joint plastic for welding.

Weld right past the finish of the joint to make sure the area is completely fused. Then slide the nozzle off the remaining rod and, once it's cooled, snip the surplus flush. Any remainder can be sanded off when cold.

Stops and starts

What's the deal when you run out of filler rod part-way down a joint? The principle's simple; slice out a notch in the warm, just-finished weld, then snip a matching point on the new length of filler. Preheat the restart area and fuse the new rod into the notch before continuing down the joint. Figures 8.9–8.11 show how it's done.

Flexible sheet repair

So far we've looked at ways to join or repair rigid- or semi-rigid plastics. Also very handy on farms is the ability to fix holes and rips in flexible stuff like hopper covers, trailer sheet and truck curtain sides.

These are usually made from PVC. Filler rod isn't used: instead the clean sheet and patch are heated until they melt, then the joint is made by quickly applying pressure to fuse them together.

You'll need a 1½" (40mm) wide slot nozzle, a silicon roller (able to stand 572-662°F [300–350°C] without wilting) and either a good flat bench or a stiff backing board, the latter used for jobs away from the workshop. Cut and clean a patch from similar material, sizing it to allow at least 2" (50mm) overlap round the repair site. Clean the parent sheet and position the patch over it.

8.9. First step in making a restart is to notch out the warm, just-laid down bead into a shallow Vee, paring away the stub of old rod. A hobby knife is ideal.

8.10. Here's the Veed-out bead (A), with the trimmed end of a new filler rod poised over it (B). See how the trim angles match.

8.11. For the restart, the notched-out section of bead is heated then the new rod is fused into it. Any lumpiness can be smoothed away by reheating the join and running a finger over the area, or by sanding when the joint is cold.

8.12. When repairing vinyl sheet, cut a patch with a generous overlap. Use a 25/32 or 1½" (20 or 40mm) slot nozzle and keep it moving. Heat equally between the patch and torn material until smoke just starts to billow out, showing that the joint halves are melting. Pressure the patch into place by a hard rub with a silicon roller. Fusion should show all round the patch edges. If not, reheat the area from above and roll again.

Starting at one corner, slip the nozzle between patch and sheet (8.12). Keeping it moving from side to side, heat a small area until blue-white smoke just starts to blow from between the sheets – this is the one and only time that smoke is a good sign. Pull out the nozzle then quickly and firmly roll the patch down. A thin line of molten plastic should appear at the joint edge. If it doesn't, heat the area and roll again. It's vital to keep the nozzle on the move to avoid overheating. When the first area is done, work across the patch until the repair is finished.

Problem solving

Plastic welding suffers from the ills of all fusion processes – poor preparation, not enough heat or too much of it. Fig 8.13 shows a good weld; 8.14 a couple of common faults.

8.13. A good weld shows a start properly fused into a Vee-prepared plate (A) and equal fusion ridges along the bead (B). Temperature, pressure on the rod and speed of travel were right.

8.14

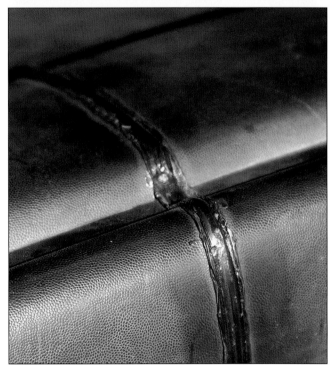

8.14. Too much heat produces scorching and/or bubbling along the bead flanks (A). Air coming from the gun is too hot for the material. In (B) the temperature is fine but excessive downward pressure has forced the filler to sink, leaving a recessed, weakened bead.

This is a car bumper repair, but it could equally be a tractor mudguard or water tank. The bead can be sanded flat when cool.

Section 9
WORKSHOP TECHNIQUES

1. Taps and Dies

A good set of taps and dies tucked away in the workshop will definitely save on heartache. Their uses go way beyond the obvious one of cutting your own threads – for example, crossed-up nuts and bolts can be saved, holes can be revitalized after broken studs are extracted, threads can be extended beyond a worn section, a damaged bolt can be drilled out and a new, oversize thread made; the possibilities are many.

Cutting a good thread isn't rocket science. Follow a few rules, work carefully and the job will be good, but rush at it and you'll probably make out-of-true, poorly-cut and perhaps shallow threads that won't have much strength. And if you accidentally break a tap in something that matters, extracting it can bring drama. So here's a few tips, starting with the oily stuff.

Lubricants

Lubricating a tap or die in work cuts wear and greatly reduces the chance of it jamming or producing torn threads. All common metals except cast iron and brass benefit, as will your biceps and temper. Purpose-made liquids, soluble cutting fluid or greases are the best bet (9.1) but in a pinch you can use ordinary oil. Greases help by collecting some swarf. Cast iron and brass can be threaded dry, aluminum prefers kerosene to prevent tearing.

TAPPING

Whether you drill a fresh hole before tapping or use an existing one, its size is critical. Too big and the threads will be shallow and weak, too small and the tap will jam.

Identity Crisis

Before you can tap or repair a thread you'll need to decide which it is. The informal way is to offer up various taps to a pattern bolt until you find the one which meshes exactly with the bolt threads; measure the bolt diameter to check the required size and off you go. If it's info on a nut or hole you need, find a bolt which screws into it and measure that.

A more formal method is to use a thread gauge. These often come with a tap and die set, or can be bought separately. Like a feeler gauge the thread version has fold-out fingers, only each is cut with a named thread profile. Find the one which interlocks snugly with your sample bolt (top).

The third option needs an accurate ruler, good eyesight and a little patience. If you suspect the thread is Imperial (maybe from the age of the machine or bolt diameter), count the number of thread crests in one inch to find the tpi (bottom). If you suspect it's Metric, measure the distance between two crests to find the pitch. Check the bolt's diameter on an unthreaded section, look this up in a data table, then run through the thread forms until you find the one whose tpi or pitch corresponds to your sample.

Thread gauges have different profiles. The one which exactly matches the unknown thread identifies it.

An engineer's steel rule is best for counting threads per inch or measuring pitch – the distance between two adjacent crests.

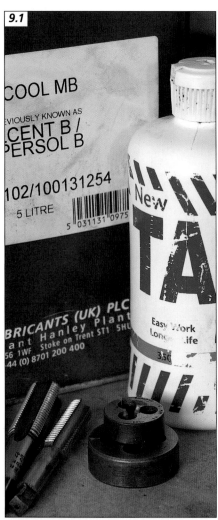

9.1

The Naming of Parts

- **Taps** cut internal threads in holes.

- **Dies** cut external threads on round stock.

- Taps are held in a twin-handled **wrench**, dies in a **stock**.

- A **die nut** – a die with hexagonal spanner flats – is ideal for quickly clearing clogged or damaged threads.

- The **pitch** of a thread is the distance between adjacent peaks (or crests) and shows how far the fastener advances in one full turn. It's used to identify Metric threads.

- The number of **threads per inch** (tpi) is used to identify Imperial threads.

- A **pitch gauge** identifies unknown thread forms.

- **Data tables** are used to identify threads and find tapping hole diameters. Good engineering suppliers have them.

- A **tapping drill** bores a hole of the right size to accept a thread.

9.1. Ideally, use a specific tapping lubricant (right) or undiluted cutting fluid (left). But ordinary oil or grease will do at a pinch.

So how do you find the tapping hole to match a given tap? For Metric threads it's simple: just subtract the pitch from the bolt diameter. So for a 10mm bolt with 1.5mm pitch, the ideal tapping drill size is 10mm-1.5mm = 8.5mm. Pitch will be marked on the tap, usually next to the item's size in mm.

Tapping drill sizes for Imperial threads are best looked up in a data table (9.2).

Whether you use the recommended drill or one a touch larger depends on the circumstances and material. A sharp bit in a drill press will cut to the expected diameter. A blunter one used manually is more likely to leave an oversized hole. Usually a slightly oversize tapping hole helps, particularly in hard materials. The thread won't be made to full depth but strength isn't compromised much, and cutting will be easier. The deeper the hole and the longer the bolt, the more

9.2

I.S.O. METRIC COARSE THREAD FORM
r = Basic Radius = ·1443 p
hn = Basic Height of Internal Thread & Depth of Thread Engagement = ·54127 p
hs = Basic Height of External Thread = .61344 P
p = Pitch

nom. dia.	pitch	basic major diameter	basic effective diameter	basic minor diameter of external threads	basic minor diameter of internal threads	recom- mended tapping drill size	clearance drill size
mm	mm	mm	mm	mm	mm	mm	mm
1	0.25	1.000	0.838	0.693	0.729	0.75	1.05
1.1	0.25	1.100	0.938	0.793	0.829	0.85	1.15
1.2	0.25	1.200	1.038	0.893	0.929	0.95	1.25
1.4	0.30	1.400	1.205	1.032	1.075	1.10	1.45
1.6	0.35	1.600	1.373	1.170	1.221	1.25	1.65
1.8	0.35	1.800	1.573	1.370	1.421	1.45	1.85
2	0.40	2.000	1.740	1.509	1.567	1.60	2.05
2.2	0.45	2.200	1.908	1.648	1.713	1.75	2.25
2.5	0.45	2.500	2.208	1.948	2.013	2.05	2.60
3	0.50	3.000	2.675	2.387	2.459	2.50	3.10
3.5	0.60	3.500	3.110	2.764	2.850	2.90	3.60
4	0.70	4.000	3.545	3.141	3.242	3.30	4.10
4.5	0.75	4.500	4.013	3.580	3.688	3.70	4.60
5	0.80	5.000	4.480	4.019	4.134	4.20	5.10
6	1.00	6.000	5.350	4.773	4.917	5.00	6.10

ZEUS PRECISION

DATA CHARTS AND REFERENCE TABLES FOR DRAWING OFFICE TOOLROOM & WORKSHOP

METRIC REVISION

9.2. Once you know the thread's size and form (yellow, left) look up the required tapping hole diameter (red, right). Data tables come from engineering suppliers. (Table © Dormer Tools).

9.3. *A taper tap (1) has many chamfered threads for a progressive start. A second (3) has fewer, while a plug tap (3) has one or two. If you have only types (2) or (3), you'll need to countersink the hole and take particular care to start the thread square.*

threads there are to share the load so the shallower they can be. Suck it and see, cautiously re-drilling the tapping hole larger if a sharp, well-lubricated tap won't cut freely.

The luxury of choice

Taps come in many forms. For hand work we're concerned with only three – the number 1 or taper, the second and the bottoming (or plug) tap (9.3). Only the best combination sets have all three.

They should be used in order, first to start a thread, then bring it to final size. The harder the material, the more important a stepwise approach is, or the risk of breaking a tap goes up. But many sets only have a second and plug (the latter is vital to tap to the bottom of a blind hole), while still cheaper versions compromise with just a second. If you're stuck with only one form of a carbon steel tap, bore the tapping hole a little oversize and countersink it to help the tap start square, then proceed with caution.

Breakage? Don't panic

Taps usually break in direct response to gorilla tactics. These may be prompted by misalignment, tap bluntness, lack of lubricant or reaching the bottom of a blind hole. When the worst happens

there are still a few options: assuming there's no stub to unscrew, try tapping the tap's flutes round with a pointed drift. If that won't work it may be possible to break up the brittle tap where it sits, though at the risk of damaging the surrounding item. If you go for that option it's essential to wear eye protection.

A third possibility is to heat the tap to soften it, then drill it out. Again, that depends on the situation. Or use a specialist tap extractor (which slides prongs down between the flutes to allow unscrewing), though these can only operate where there is clearance. The best route of all is not to break the tap. How to use taps is covered in pictures 9.4-9.6.

DIES

Now for the other half of the story – cutting external threads with a die. First though, a word on choosing and buying sets: see Pick Wisely (page 138).

Identification of unknown thread forms is the same for taps and dies. Here's a quick recap – pitch gauges are the quickest and most certain way to put a name to what you have, followed by counting the number of threads per inch of fastener and looking up the result in an engineer's data table. Clues can come from the machine's age and origin; older equipment from the UK or USA will probably use Imperial fasteners (Whitworth, UNF, UNC or BSF; BA for small items, BSP for pipe), while

9.4. *Use plenty of lubricant on the tap and in the hole. Hold the wrench lightly and steer, not force, it around while keeping it level. If the tap is sharp and the hole size is right, it'll bite quickly.*

9.5. Once the cut is established, take off the wrench and check the tap for squareness in two planes. If it isn't running true, gently center it when you restart. Check at every turn and correct as you go until it's cutting straight. Don't leave an error too long.

modern kit or older stuff from Europe will probably use Metric coarse or fine thread forms.

As with taps, lubrication is a vital part of using dies. A good helping of the slippery stuff minimizes wear on the die and reduces thread-tearing. Guidelines are unchanged – purpose-made fluids or greases are ideal for steels (though ordinary oil is better than nothing); aluminum is partial to a drop of kerosene, and brass and cast iron can be threaded dry.

Pictures 9.7-9.12 detail the way to cut an external thread on round bar or pipe. Keeping the die square with the work is harder than with a tap, as less of the die is chamfered; but it's no less vital. Skill and care are needed to produce a good result.

9.6. Good technique keeps the tap cutting freely. Make no more than half a turn clockwise at a time (step 1, above) then reverse direction until you feel the new-cut chips break (step 2 above). Don't force the tap: if resistance grows, back off and try small cuts. Clear chips from the bottom of a blind hole or the tap will jam. Once the tap exits or reaches the bottom of a hole, back it right off. Re-lubricate, run it in and out a couple of times and you're done. Finally, clean the tap ready for next time.

9.7. The die must go into the holder (or stock) the right way round, or starting the cut will be difficult. The stock is partly closed at the top and open at the bottom. One side of the die has its first few threads chamfered to help it start cutting; this chamfer is usually on the side with lettering (1). Clean any swarf from the stock and die so they come together squarely, then fit the die chamfer-side toward the work with its split lined up with the stock's center screw (2).

9.8. Three screws locate the die and vary its diameter, opening it to ease the first cut, then closing it to bring the new thread to size. For the first cut, tighten the center screw to widen the die and just settle the outer screws into contact.

9.9. Starting the cut will be much easier if the bar is chamfered generously, as here. The die and the bar/pipe to be threaded must have the same nominal diameter. That is, a ⅜" (10mm) die will only cut easily and produce full-depth threads on ⅜" (10mm) rod, and so on. Clean off any black mill scale.

9.10. Lubricate the target – here neat cutting fluid is used.

9.11. To start cutting put light downward pressure on the stock and steer it around, keeping even pressure on the handles. It will bite quickly only if it's sharp and fitted the right way up in the stock, and if the bar or pipe has been chamfered evenly. It's crucial to check that the stock stays at right angles to the target, both initially and all though the cut. If it tips, the thread will be skewed. Check for squareness every half-turn, correcting as you go. Once the thread is running true don't push down on the stock; let it find its own way.

1: Half-turn (180°) clockwise

2: Turn back 90° to break chip

9.12. Cutting action is the same as with taps. For right-hand threads make half a turn clockwise, then a quarter-turn back to break the swarf chips. Keep the die and rod lubricated. Once the first cut is done, unwind the stock. Back off the center screw and wind in the outer screws evenly to close the die a little. Re-lubricate and re-cut. Depending on die sharpness and material toughness, two or three cut/adjust cycles may be needed to form the final thread. Clean out the die, and job done.

Cheat a Little

A lathe can help cut a parallel thread. Chamfer the item to be threaded and center it in the chuck. Position the die stock over the target, then extend the lathe's tailstock mandrel until it gently holds the stock square to the work. Turn the chuck by hand to start the thread, then keep the mandrel in very light contact with the stock as the cut progresses. The same technique can be used with a good drill press.

Oddments

Round split dies are fine for diameters up to 1/2" (12mm). Bigger threads are best formed with two-piece dies held in a rectangular, adjustable stock; this gives more scope for progressively bringing the thread to size.

Cutting fine threads needs particular care. If you have many to do it's worth investing in a stock that takes replaceable guide bushes in its lower face: the bush fits over the item to be threaded, holding the two square and preventing crooked threads.

Die nuts (picture) have hex faces to take a spanner and are not split. Use them only for cleaning up existing cruddy or damaged threads.

Die nuts give fast thread clean-up.

Recycle or Throw Away?

A tap or die blunts when its first few cutting edges chip or round off. You'll know when it's on the way out as starting a thread is harder, the thing takes more effort to turn and will be more likely to tear new-formed threads.

Trying to re-sharpen blunt taps manually will only make things worse. The best bet is to throw smaller ones away, but send bigger, expensive ones off to a specialist for re-grinding.

Pick Wisely

Taps and dies come in different qualities. The key choice is between carbon steel and high speed steel. High speed steel (HSS) is the engineer's favorite; items made from this very durable material are usually ground to size, so can cut an accurate thread and will hold a keen edge.

Taps and dies made in high carbon steel (HCS) cost substantially less, produce a less accurate result and lose their edge faster. But don't dismiss them – away from a production environment, carbon steel items are fine when used properly. If you aspire to a HSS set but can't afford one, a good compromise is to buy a big-name carbon steel set and replace individuals with HSS versions as the originals blunt.

Your set should cover today's common thread forms, i.e. Metric coarse/fine and UNC/UNF. A set handling older forms like BSF and Whitworth will be useful if you have dated machinery or are into vintage kit. Individual taps or dies can be bought for one-off jobs, including cutting left-hand threads. When choosing dies go for split versions rather than solid ones; the latter are best used for cleaning and re-cutting threads rather than forming them from scratch.

And sizes? Farming's needs are pretty much covered by Imperial sizes ¼" to ¾" and Metric sizes 6 to 24mm. Not many suppliers offer this range in one box, whereas sets covering Imperial ¼"-½" and Metric 6-12mm are very common. So an option is to start with one of these, then add bigger individual taps or dies as needed.

For last-a-lifetime quality, shop at an engineering tool supplier handling premium brands like Hanson or Irwin and have items reground as they lose their edge. Expect to pay upwards of $1,100 for a big set, or about $130 for a single threadform in limited sizes. Modest pockets are better served by mass-market suppliers such as Vermont American and Sears, who offer coverage in the $130-190 bracket. Either way avoid cheap bargains; they are unlikely to be cheap in the long run.

2. Drill Sharpening

Trying to make a hole with a blunt drill is a mug's game. At best, progress is slow and the blessed thing runs off-center. At worst your eyes bulge, the muscles knot, the drill squeals then either breaks or expires in a wisp of smoke. Compare that to the bliss of using a new one ... the way those twin spirals of swarf wriggle upward, the soft hiss as hardened steel pares away metal, the satisfying speed of cut, the simple smoothness and truth of the finished hole ... whoops, better stop before someone gets arrested.

What does it take to get from a blunt drill to a sharp one? Not a lot – a bench grinder with the right wheel(s), and some practice. Various jigs and rigs can be bought to make the job largely foolproof, but knowing how to sharpen freehand is very useful. So that's what we're looking at here.

Half the battle is knowing what you're trying to achieve, then fixing that picture in the mind's eye and matching your handiwork to it (9.18). But first the grinding tackle must be put into shape.

Good and true

Which grinding wheel should you use? Good quality twist drills are made from high speed steel (HSS) and are best sharpened on a 60-grit aluminum oxide wheel. If you're looking to buy one of these, a typical type designation is A60-L5-V30 and engineering suppliers are the best source.

The wheel MUST be in good physical shape, both to do the required job and to keep the user in one piece. An exploding grinding wheel takes no prisoners, so a whole slew of regulations govern wheel mounting and use. Sensible preliminaries before dressing (re-facing) a wheel include testing it for cracks (9.14) and making sure that cushioning paper washers sit between the wheel and clamps. For proper procedures, see OSHA 1910.215A, "Safety in

9.13 A fresh edge on a blunt drill speeds up work.

Grinding Wheels."

The grinding surface must be flat to generate straight cutting edges on the drill. It follows that a wheel face resembling a map of the Norwegian fjords is not much use, so you'll need a dressing stone or a star wheel to level the surface and get rid of dulled abrasive grains (9.15, 9.16). These are not expensive and again come from engineering suppliers.

Once the wheel is dressed, adjust the grinder's tool rest so the stone has minimal free running clearance (9.17). Keep the gap small to lower the chance of the drill being pulled into the space between stone and rest – something which will likely damage it, you, and the wheel. With the bench unit's own eye shield in place or safety specs/goggles installed on the user, sharpening can begin.

9.14. To check a grinding wheel for cracks, support it on an edge and tap gently with something metallic. If it rings it's OK. A dull clunk suggests trouble.

9.15. Two options for wheel dressing. The Huntingdon or star wheel (left) is best used with a tool rest. ...

The cutting edge

How does a drill cut? By its two lips peeling chips from the material, much as a wood plane or chisel produces shavings. Although a small army of things influence how well any drill does this, three factors stand out: the clearance behind each lip, the total point angle, and the balance of lip length and individual point angles. A fourth factor (web thickness) starts to play a part as the drill is ground down.

The best way to see how each of the key areas should look is to eye up a new drill, using 9.18 and 9.19 as guides. The bigger sample drill you use, the easier the detail is to see. With an automatic drill sharpener the right angles are relatively easy to achieve. Handwork is more hit-and-miss (particularly with drills under ⅛" [3mm]), so here's some suggestions to help.

Clearance. Any cutting edge needs a clearance behind it, otherwise it just rubs over the surface rather than slicing in. For the purpose of hand sharpening, a twist drill's clearance is the gentle fall away from the cutting edge and back across the flank (9.18). If this clearance angle is too small the drill just skates. If it's too large, the cutting lip has little support and will chip or break. For general work in mild steel, aim for a 10-12° slope.

Point angle. Looked at from the side, the cutting lips steeple upward into a roof (9.19). If the angle they make is too steep, the lip edges turn concave when seen from above and won't cut efficiently. If the point angle is too shallow the edges go convex, so cutting efficiency again takes a hit and the outer lip corners are weakened. For drilling mild steel the ideal angle is 118°, though this is not a fixed quantity. Shallowing it helps produce clean holes in thin sheet and will ease the drill through hard stuff.

Three DIY gadgets help get point angle right, though you'll soon do it by eye. Number one is a small template, easily knocked up and used to check individual angles during grinding (9.20). Number

9.16. To true-up the wheel face, work the dressing stone gently across it.

9.17. After dressing, adjust the tool rest to give minimum running clearance. This lowers the chance of an accident through work being trapped between the wheel and rest.

9.18. Each cutting lip (A) must have a clearance behind it. This is the gentle slope backward from the lip edge – (arrow) The right manual grinding technique automatically produces this clearance. Aim for a 10-12° slope.

9.19. The tip angle under the roof (A) has to be right if the drill is to cut efficiently, though it can float a little around the 118° ideal and still give good results. When freehand sharpening it's very easy to get individual lip angles (B) or lip lengths (C) wrong. Then the drill will vibrate, run off-center and bore a more-or-less oval hole.

two is much the same, only made by soldering a pair of big nuts together and using the 120° angle between the flats as the guide. Number three is a 60° line scribed on the grinder's tool rest, along which you lay the drill while grinding.

Lip length and individual angle. Do your holes run off-center and end up oversize? Does most of the swarf come from one drill flute? If so, one cutting lip is longer than the other, one lip angle is steeper than the other, or both. Either way, one cutting edge (the one with the shallowest angle) is doing most of the

work. For the lips to cut equally, they must be physical twins. Angles can be checked with a template as above and the lip lengths with a steel rule or calipers (9.21). Unsurprisingly the smaller the drill, the harder this is to do.

The not-so-long grind

Take a close look at the drill to be sharpened, using a new one for comparison. All damage to cutting lips and their corners must be ground away. If this will take a lot of work (as it will if a drill has sheared off) rough-grind it first then fine-tune.

The grinding operation is in two parts:

• Offering up the drill at the proper angle

• Making the grinding stroke.

If the stroke happens as it should, good clearance is produced automatically.

Angle first. Support the drill with one hand, hold the shank end with the other. Plonk the support hand on the grinder's tool rest, angling the drill so it sits just above horizontal with one cutting lip parallel to the wheel face (9.22). If you've scribed a guide line on the tool rest, use it now.

The **grinding stroke** is marginally harder to describe than to do. Pictures

9.20. Made and used with care, a simple guide gives a quick, accurate check on individual cutting lip angles.

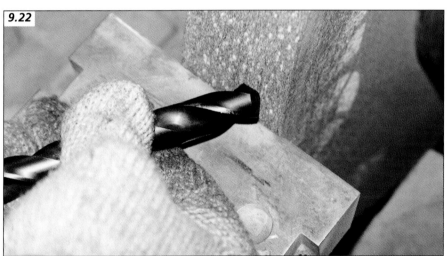

9.22. The grinding sequence starts by positioning the drill so one cutting lip is parallel with the wheel face. A 60° line scribed on the tool rest will show the right approach angle – particularly useful if a drill has been mis-ground or broken.

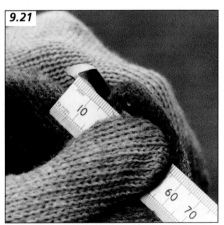

9.21. Use a steel rule or callipers to monitor lip length during grinding. (Fashion note: cotton gloves protect against sharp edges).

9.23. The right hand steadies the tip, the left guides the shank. Starting with the shank slightly below horizontal, begin a smooth, continuous scoop movement. Lift the tip and feed the cutting lip gently into the wheel.

9.23, 9.24 and 9.25 break it into stages, though the reality is a smooth single stroke. Bring the cutting lip into light contact with the wheel (9.23) Then, while keeping stone and lip in contact, lift the drill tip and lower the shank. This scooping action moves the tip forward and upwards in an arc (9.24 and 9.25). Think of someone standing inside a huge pipe, brushing upwards from waist height with a broom; scale the vision down so the broom is drill-sized and you've got it. During the stroke, keep the approach angle constant and don't rotate the shank.

Make several light cuts on each lip, checking angles and lip lengths as you go. Go easy on the pressure – the cutting edge must not get too hot. If it blushes blue, hardness has been lost and the edge won't last.

Which brings us to cooling. Some say that drills should either be ground dry or under a torrent of coolant, but never anything in between. Others reckon it's perfectly OK to take out tip heat in a pot of water as long as an overheated drill isn't quenched. Little and often is the watchword for the second route. If the drill gets too hot before each dip, the softened cutting edge will turn brittle and crack or flake in work.

Thin that web

It's easy to forget the drill's central strengthening core or web, which gets thicker from tip to shank. As the drill shortens from repeated sharpening, web thickness at the tip grows. Why should you worry? The web is a dead, non-cutting area which has to be forced though the work, so the thicker it gets, the harder the drill needs to be pushed. Where a drill is only to be used for enlarging holes then there's no problem; the web plays no part. But where you're boring to size in one operation, web thickness does matter.

Thinning is usually needed after drill length has fallen by about one-third. The job needs a shaped grinding wheel, which can be produced by careful work with the dressing block.

9.24. Here we're halfway through the stroke, with the tip scooping upwards across the grinding wheel face. The left hand maintains the original approach angle and does not twist the shank.

9.25. End of the grinding stroke, with the cutting lip just clearing the wheel. Follow the arc of drill tip movement through the last three pictures – it's the key. Now switch between lips, grinding lightly until all damage is taken out. Quench often to avoid tip overheat.

9.26. Web thinning calls for a wheel dressed to an angle of about 45°, with a radius on the high shoulder. Relieve the web equally on either side of the central chisel edge, grinding out a shallow arc.

To slim a web, hold the drill vertical and just knick in along both sides of the point (9.26). Aim to produce a shallow arc, taking equal volumes from each side of the tip and ending up with a central chisel point measuring about one-ninth of the drill diameter.

Knowing what you're looking for when sharpening drills is the key, practice is the lock in which it fits. With the right grinding wheel and a little patience, the days of blunt-drill irritation will be gone.

Section 10

Basic Blacksmithing

Not so long ago the blacksmith kept a farm going. His farrier's skills kept horses at work, his forging ability shaped and repaired iron. All manner of things passed across the smith's anvil – chains, tools, bits of implements, household stuff, ironwork of all sorts. Bigger farms had their own smith, smaller outfits employed the village man.

Time passed, tires replaced hooves. Mass-production methods priced out handwork. The electric arc set gave every farmer the option to weld if he wanted, so gradually the forges grew cold. A lot of the contents went for scrap, or into pubs and gardens for decoration; but luckily many anvils ended up in farm workshops. That's excellent news for today's users, not least because the sound of a few blows (repeated at strategic intervals) has always been a good way of convincing a passing boss that great works are underway.

Village forges have largely gone but the practical skills live. Our tutor here is the late Frank Dean, a blacksmith with sons working in the Sussex smithy established by their grandfather at the turn of the century. While the written word always comes a poor second to direct tuition from a skilled man, the pictures here will help. Try the techniques, using the pictures as a target.

Equipment and basics

If you're lucky enough to have a forge, then you'll appreciate how quickly and easily stuff can be brought to red heat in it. If not, all of the jobs shown here can be managed with the gas torch and a modicum of patience. It'll just take longer and cost a bit more in fuel. Or you can make a simple forge from a big truck brake drum, a length of through-bored bar for the tue, a 12V car heater blower and an old steel drum to house the blower and other bits.

If you're using gas, choose a cutting or (preferably) a heating nozzle that puts heat quickly into the job. A hearth made up from old firebricks helps to hold warmth round the work.

Getting comfortable is just as important as it is in welding. Arrange the anvil so its table is directly under your working hand. The pointed bick is then to the left of a right-handed man or vise versa. Strike blows from the elbow, rather than the wrist. Along with a proper grip this helps control the hammer head. Work in a steady rhythm – frantic activity will only leave you knackered – and don't let the work get too far out of shape. Bring it back to close to what you're aiming for at the end of each heat.

Light taps on the anvil between strings of blows can keep a rhythm going. But when driving a punch, don't make a preliminary 'sizing up' tap as this often jogs the point off-target.

Finally, keep the anvil clean and free from scale and the floor clear of tools and scrap. Tripping up with hot metal is, at the very least, painful.

Taking heats

When is steel at a good, easy-working temperature? The best way to find out is by experiment. Try working a piece of bar and see how its plasticity increases as surface color changes. Dull red is hard work, blood red is better, and cherry red easier still. By yellow (about 1300°C) the steel works very freely. But go one step too far and it becomes incandescent, with sparks flying off in all directions. A few degrees more (or seconds in the fire) and the metal will crumble away.

Make a plan

Decide what you're going to do before heating. Think which part of the job needs to be tackled first, as it's often difficult or impossible to do one thing after something else. For instance, you can't forge a bar into an eye or hook and then taper the tip: things have to happen the other way round. Also work out which part of the anvil you'll use, and which way to hold and present the work. Puzzling this out on the spot loses valuable working heat.

10.1. Air blast for the fire comes from the central tuyère or tue. To light the forge, first rake out any old fused clinker. Then excavate a pit to below tue depth. Check that the tue's exit hole is clear, and set a gentle draught on the blower to keep it that way.
Paper and dry kindling starts the fire. Fuel is ideally smithy 'breeze', but if your coal merchant has never heard of that or can't get it, Sunbright singles will do. Pile fuel into a banked mound. Lay extra around the edges for raking-in later. During work don't let the fire burn hollow: keep it banked up on three sides, leaving clear space on the working side. If the fire spreads out too far during work, damp down the edges.

10.2. The tue in a big forge is usually water-cooled, circulating coolant by thermal action. Check that the reservoir is topped up. You can make a portable forge from a truck brake drum and angle iron frame: the tue can be an uncooled 2" (50mm) bar with a ½" (12mm) hole bored through it for air passage. Draught can come from an old 12V motor with a simple butterfly valve to control blast.

10.3. This 2½cwt London-pattern anvil sits on an elm post, and there's as much of that under the floor as above it. Working from right to left, the anvil has a tapered bick (or beak, or beck: depends where you hail from - A). Then comes the step (B). This is left soft during manufacture to provide an area where a cut-off chisel can be used without damaging itself or the anvil. The table (C) is the main flat working surface. It has two hardie holes: the round one primarily a clearway for punching operations, the square one to locate anvil tools securely. A farrier's anvil has no step.

10.4. Commonly used tools for the hardie hole. A chisel-faced hardie (right) is used under hot metal when cutting, so that metal is sliced between it and the hammer face. The anvil stake (left) provides a small-scale bick for finer work. Or a twin-prong 'horn' tool (not shown) can be used for bending material.

10.5. Tongs are tools you can't manage without. They must match the metal they hold or it'll slip about, which is irritating and potentially dangerous. From left to right: bolt tongs with a flared section for the bolt head or any shouldered work; goose-billed tongs for holding flat rings and the like; small close-bit tongs for horseshoes or jobs where there's no great length of material to catch hold of; grooved hollow-bit tongs for round bar; and hollow bit tongs with a three-sided jaw for square material. Tongs can be suited to different-sized material by heating and bending their reins (handles). Secondhand tongs still turn up at farm sales or can be bought new, while experienced smiths make their own. In work, keep tongs cool.

10.6. Getting a grip. Frank Dean's hammer is balanced in his hand. His thumb is on the top side of the shaft, pointing toward the head, allowing good control and rapid rotation when the pein end is needed. "Holding the hammer too close to its head robs you of control", he says, "But holding it at the far end of the shaft is just as bad. Choose a shaft that's nicely oval, and lies comfortably in your hand. If the hammer is balanced there's no need to grip it tightly." Most hammering action must come from the elbow, not the wrist.

Pictures 10.1–10.6 run through the basics on the forge, anvil and tools. Then separate panels detail different jobs, starting with **drawing down** a round bar into a point. This basic exercise is useful in its own right and a jumping-off point for all sorts of other operations.

General pointers cover all the work:

- Start with straight metal so you can concentrate on the task, not problems in the steel that were there before you began. True the steel first. If things get well out of shape during work, stop and put them right.

- Think about exactly where your blows should land. If the plan is to stretch the steel, make a sandwich of it between the hammer and anvil to squeeze metal and change its section. But if the plan is to bend something, then place it and hit it so each blow has a bending (rather than flattening) effect. Hit 'off' the anvil – pics 10.11 and 10.12 make this clear.

- Two tips on marking out. To know how much metal is needed to make a ring of a given size, multiply its planned internal diameter by 3.14 and add the thickness of the material. If you're aiming for a given external size, subtract the material thickness from it and then multiply by 3.14. Where precision is not vital the anvil table can be used as a rough length guide. It's generally 5" (125mm) across.

- Often you'll need to mark metal to show where an operation (say, bending) has to begin. Center-punch the inside of the bend. That way, the mark closes up as the metal goes over. If you punch-dot the outside, the dot elongates into a nasty knick. Just right as a start-point for failure.

Drawing down a point

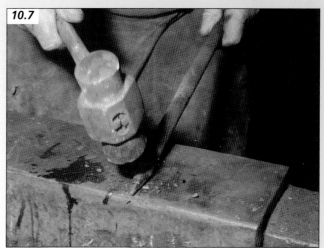

10.7. Tapered points or chisel ends are easily made by drawing-down, which is the old way to give new life to harrow tines. The metal is brought to heat and held at an angle to the anvil. The steeper the angle, the steeper the point will be. See how the metal is held near the edge of the table, and the hammer face is angled to form the taper? This shapes the steel on two sides simultaneously. Between blows the work is constantly turned, always in the same direction (like a lathe) to draw the metal down evenly. Heavy stuff is worked first into a square, then an octagon, then a cylinder. Smaller metal can be tapered directly. For a long, gentle taper, first form the tip and then use the bick for the long work; its rounded profile draws down metal much more quickly than the table. "Worth a second hammer", Frank Dean says. If the tip splits, take a very good heat and draw it back together with light blows. With practice, multi-sided material can be reshaped to round or vice versa, using just a hammer and anvil.

10.8. The finished article. A coarse wire brush on the hot work shifts scale to leave a good finish.

Now for some specifics, starting with **edge bends.** Persuading a flat strip to bend against its width is not so hard (10.16–10.21) The method here produces a bend with a rounded outer corner. If you need a square corner, first thicken the metal locally at the bend point by 'upsetting' or 'jumping-up'. Page 153 lays out how.

Before twist drills arrived, the blacksmith punched holes with a steel drift and muscle power (10.22–10.33). It's still a useful way to make square holes, rectangular holes, round holes… or big holes bigger. The old way may be slower than a drill but it's more flexible. Neither is it wasteful; a surprisingly small chip of steel pops out as a hole forms. Instead metal is displaced by the punch, leaving a void the shape and size of the thing that produced it.

Punches are easy to make. Shank length is a compromise – too long and the punch will bend, too short and you'll singe your hand. Slot punches are used first, do the hardest work and so need to be made from the best material; something combining strength with resilience. Frank Dean suggests an old file makes a good starting point. "Take out brittleness by bringing it up to a uniform blood-red heat, forge out serrations, and then cool it very slowly under a bed of ashes or lime to prevent

Making Eyes

10.9. Step one in forming an eye is to true-up the metal, in this case ½" (12.5mm) bar. Notice how Frank Dean uses the hardie hole as a focus for straightening, lifting his left (or back) hand a little to give more clearance. Both give the metal somewhere to go. "It's hard to straighten something on a flat surface", he says. "Hitting down on the anvil's table will only achieve anything if it's worn into a saddle shape."

10.11. Take a fresh heat and move up to the bick. Here Frank is putting shape into the eye. See how his blow is directed to the side of the bick? This bends, rather than crushes the metal.

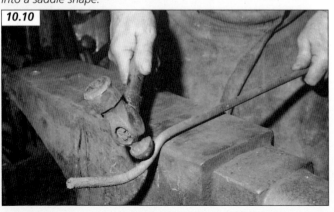

10.10. Unlike rings, eyes seldom need to be made to specific dimensions. Just make them so the eye looks right in proportion to the bar's thickness and length. Estimate the internal diameter, then work out how much metal you'll need from the formula on page 145. Then shaping begins. The first 5" (125mm) of the table after the step generally has rounded shoulders, so use this area to avoid putting a nick in the underside of the bar. With the metal at bright cherry red, strike the first blows as shown with the hammer pein. Hit just off the table's edge so the bar's free end kicks upward and the bend starts to form automatically. Don't hit too far off the table or a straight portion will be left just beyond the start point. Aim to make a gentle 'S'-shape.

air-hardening", he suggests. "You can then forge or grind the tip to size."

Don't let the punch get too hot in work, he stresses. "Dip it in water every few blows, but don't quench it right back to cold or it'll turn brittle again."

A punch likes to stick in thicker material. A pinch of coke dust in the embryo hole helps it let go, and the black dust makes a visible marker through thin, hot metal when the work is turned over to finish operations. If it's round

holes you need, one or more mandrels (or drifts) will follow the slot punch. These enlarge rather than pierce, so can be made from mild steel. First to be used is a flat-ended mandrel, which takes the slot gently to a circle. Further enlargement is by tapered drift.

By swelling steel rather than chopping it away, **punching** allows much bigger holes to be made than with a drill. As with all forge work, thinking ahead pays off. If it looks as though punching will

leave too little metal round the hole, steel thickness can be increased locally by **upsetting or jumping-up**.

10.34 and 10.35 show how to do this. Upsetting is a powerful weapon in the smith's armory which finds plenty of uses. It's often the first job in a sequence, done to build a reservoir of metal for following operations. Where you can do it, upsetting can be a much better way to thicken a section than laying down weld metal.

10.12. Now roll over the bar's tip. This is forethought in action, as it's impossible to do the job once the eye closes down. Again, the hammer strikes off the bick, rather than straight down on it. Frank's back hand is tipping the bar to provide clearance.

10.13. With the tip turned it's time to close the eye. Start by bringing it round the bick.

10.14. Then roll it shut by gentle blows to the top (a) and front (b), supporting the work on the table edge or bick as necessary to preserve the initial bend.

10.15. The finished article is a pleasure to look at. And beauty is more than skin deep. Centering the eye over the shank lets load fall in direct line with the shank: an off-center eye is more likely to pull open. The same goes for hooks.

Edge Bends

10.16. Bring the bend area to heat, localizing this by either pushing the work through the fire or quenching the end before work starts. Put in a set as shown. If the work bows sideways, bring it back to flat with gentle taps.

10.17. Form a rough bend over the bick. Again, see how Frank's hammer will fall on the free end: the bick is just a pivot point.

10.18. It's tempting to form the corner over the table, as here. But don't: blows will only draw the metal thinner, necking it down. You want it to bend, not stretch.

10.19. The rough-formed bend has a large radius. To make it tighter (that is, move toward a squarer shoulder) you must push metal toward the corner. Imagine a diagonal line through the required bend. Then, resting the work on the table, strike just off that line. Blows tighten the bend by pushing the top leg down.

10.20. Work alternately on the legs, driving them together and so pushing the joint closer to a right angle. Too much effort will pucker the inside radius, so work gently from both sides. The bend will want to bow sideways so straighten before it goes too far.

10.21. Out comes the try-square (a). The initial bend was too tight, so a couple of light taps brought it back to true (b). See how the anvil is again used as a fixed rest while the hammer does the work? Knowing where to position the work and strike the blow is down to practice. An experienced smith makes it look so easy. It's a bit like the man who charged $160 for five minutes' work in knocking out a dent in a boiler. "$8 pays for my time," he explained. "The rest is for knowing where to hit it."

Punching Holes

10.22. A selection of punches, used in order of appearance. Right to left: slot punch; flat-ended mandrel or drift; two different-sized round mandrels. All these are easily made to suit different jobs.

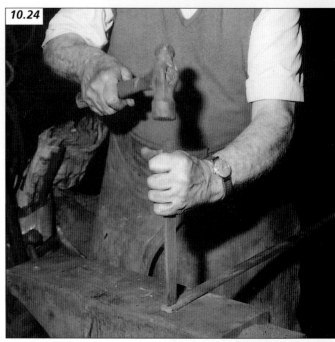

10.24. With the corners rounded and someone holding the work, punching begins. Frank uses the anvil table, striking hard to drive the slot punch quickly. After three or four blows, the punch is cooled.
The punch must be centered if metal is to be pushed equally to either side; don't give it a pre-tap before striking in case it moves.

10.23. Frank Dean demonstrates punching technique by putting an eye in the end of flat stock. The same method is used for slots and round holes along the length of a job. For these mark the target area by a row of punch marks, which will remain visible when the work is up to heat. The first operation with an end-eye is to round-up the corners, working the metal between hammer and anvil as shown.

10.25. In goes a pinch of coke dust from a pile on the anvil step. See how much heat is in the work? It's just short of sparkling white. Ease of punching goes up with temperature. On thick work, the punch must be cooled every few blows.

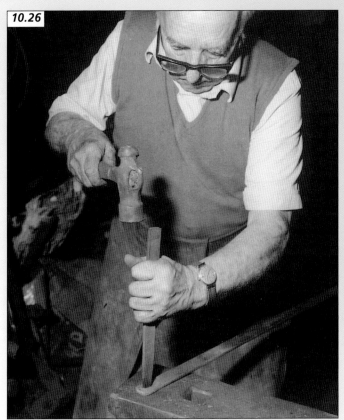

10.26. Frank drives on until feedback through the hammer tells him that the table is nigh. Then he turns the steel and, using the coke dust mark as a guide, drives the slot punch through again. Working over the table hole gives the punch somewhere to go.

10.27. This tiny sliver of metal is all that's lost from the slot. Most has been pushed sideways.

10.28. Now follows the flat-to-round mandrel, again used over the anvil hole. This tool gently takes the oblong to a circle. Bigger, tapered mandrels then follow until the hole is up to size. Very accurate fits can be achieved this way.

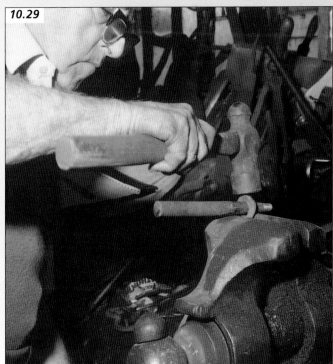

10.29. The ring's outer edge is brought true by light blows, using the mandrel and vise as support.

Punching Holes *(continued)*

10.30. There's a twist to this ending. With the eye completed, Frank is ready to put a 120° set below it.

10.31. Heat must be localized for the steel to bend only where required. The whole end is brought to heat in the forge, then the target area is isolated by ladling cold water to either side. Gas users can just heat the local area.

10.32. Into the vise, where a quick twist with the tongs puts a right-angle in the shank …

10.33. … leaving a neat and tidy ring.

Upsetting

10.34. *Upsetting redistributes metal for later operations. Frank brought the bottom few inches (centimeters) of the bar to a good heat and is now using vertical blows from a big hammer to push the steel up into a bulge. Short work like this can be managed on a normal-height anvil, though the Dean forge has another set flush with the floor for longer stuff. A solid, non-bouncy surface is needed – a concrete floor isn't good enough. The process is repeated, taking fresh heats and re-truing on the way.*

10.35. *The end result is plenty of local thickness for subsequent forging operations. Using selective cooling (10.31) the upset area could have been made partway along the bar instead of at the end – an ideal way of concentrating extra metal before punching a large hole.*

Tired of all that welding?

Every repair job involves making decisions. Not the least of these is allocating blame afterwards or – more importantly – absolving yourself from it. This is often the fitter's most basic and pressing dilemma. The handy cut-out flowchart which follows covers most eventualities. Keep it out of sight as a solution to any given situation. Tested thoroughly in farming, it hasn't failed yet. *(Chart courtesy of the Institute of Diagnostic Engineers.)*

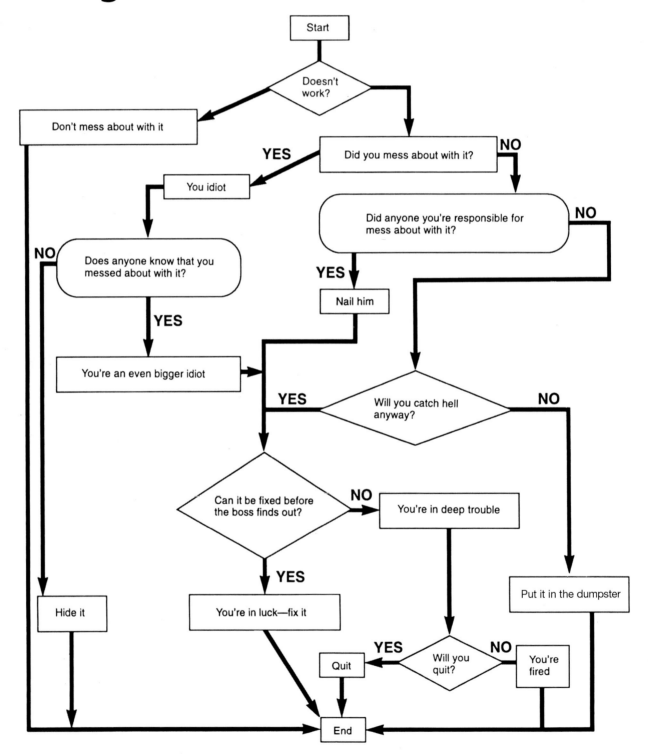

Appendix 1

What's in a name?

Process Terminology

All technologies have their formal and informal sides. Welding's no exception – depending on who you are and where you are, the same thing goes by different names.

As the formal tags can be hard to get your tongue around, this book generally sticks with common terms. For reference and to help when reading more learned tomes, here's a round-up of the alternatives.

Common name	Formal name
Stick welding, SMAW	Shielded metal arc welding
MIG (metal inert gas welding), GMAW	Gas metal arc welding
Cored wire MIG, FCAW	Flux-cored arc welding
TIG (tungsten inert gas welding), GTAW	Gas tungsten arc welding
Gas or oxyacetylene welding	Oxyfuel welding
Plasma cutting, PAC	Plasma arc cutting

Appendix 2

Heat Colors

Color	Temp °F	Temp °C	Use for
Black red (visible only in dull light)	797-824	425-440	Pre-heat before welding, toughening carbon steel after quenching
Very dark red	1094-1202	590-650	Hardening and annealing carbon tool steel
Dark red	1292-1400	700-760	
Cherry red	1499-1697	815-925	Hardening alloy tool steel
Orange red	1796-1895	980-1035	
Yellow	2003-2192	1095-1200	
Yellow white	2300-2399	1260-1315	Hardening high-speed steel
White	2498	1370	Forge Welding

Note: Temperatures are approximate.

Appendix 3

Useful Conversions

Electrodes and cored wire

Need to find the American equivalent of a 2.5mm electrode, or the metric equivalent of 0.045in welding wire? You've come to the right place.

Notes
Common sizes are shown in bold text. These tables take millimeters as the base unit. The nearest commonly-used imperial equivalents are shown: these may not be an exact conversion.

If you need to make specific conversions, check the internet for an online calculator.

American welding wires are usually specified according to US Steel Wire Gauge. A wire of a given US gauge is generally slightly larger than its equivalent number in British Standard wire gauge (SWG).

SMAW ELECTRODE DIAMETERS

MM	Inch	Wire gauge (SWG)
1.60	1/16	16
2.00	0.08	14
2.50	3/32	12
3.25	1/8	19
4.00	5/32	8
5.00	3/16	6
6.00	1/4	4
8.00	5/16	n/a

Note: With SMAW consumables, 2.4mm electrode is rounded up to 2.5mm

SMAW ELECTRODE LENGTHS

MM	Inch
250	10
300	12
350	14
400	16
450	18
600	24
700	28

TIG ELECTRODES, TIG/GAS FILLER ROD DIAMETERS

With nearest common American inch and wire gauge equivalents

MM	Inch	Decimal inch
0.5		0.020
1.0		0.040
1.6	1/16	0.062
2.4	3/32	0.093
3.2	1/8	0.125
4.0	5/32	0.156
5.0	3/16	0.187

MIG/CORED WIRE DIAMETERS

With nearest common American inch and wire gauge equivalents

MM	Inch	Wire gauge (SWG) [U.K. only]	Decimal inch
0.6			
0.8			
0.9			0.035
1.0			
1.1			0.045
1.2			
1.3			0.052
1.6	1/16	16	
1.7			0.068
2.0	0.08	14	
2.4	3/32	12	

Index

Note: page numbers in italics refer to illustrations

More Great Books from Fox Chapel Publishing

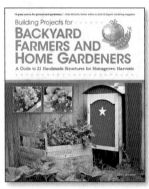

Building Projects for Backyard Farmers and Home Gardeners
ISBN: 978-1-56523-543-4 **$19.95**

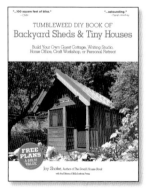

Milling for Home Machinists
ISBN: 978-1-56523-694-3 **$12.95**

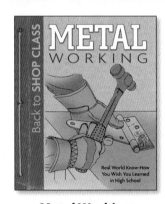

Metal Working (Back to Shop Class)
ISBN: 978-1-56523-540-3 **$19.95**

Metal Lathe for Home Machinists
ISBN: 978-1-56523-693-6 **$12.95**

Tumbleweed DIY Book of Backyard Sheds & Tiny Houses
ISBN: 978-1-56523-704-9 **$19.95**

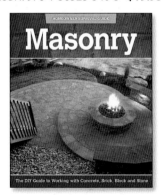

Masonry
ISBN: 978-1-56523-698-1 **$24.95**